INTRODUCTION TO U.S. LEGAL SKILLS FOR INTERNATIONAL LAW STUDENTS

DAVID LEE MUNDY

Issachar Academic Press
Pohang, Republic Of Korea

For permission requests, write to the author at:
mundy@handong.edu.

Issachar Academic Press
An imprint of Bezzle Books

Pohang, Republic of Korea

U.S. Legal Skills for International Law Students / David Lee Mundy
—Version A
ISBN 978-0-578-45063-6

Contents

[1] Introduction to Law School 1

[2] Introduction to Law Practice 11

[3] Introduction to the American Legal System: Part 1 21

[4] Introduction to the American Legal System: Part 2 33

[5] Understanding Common Law 45

[6] Reading and Briefing Cases: An Introduction 53

[7] Reading and Briefing Cases: An Example 67

[8] Reading and Briefing Cases: An Exercise 71

[9] Introduction to Legal Reasoning 77

[10] Legal Reasoning: An Exercise 87

[11] Researching Secondary Sources 95

[12] Secondary Sources: Research & Writing Exercise 109

[13] Secondary Source: Electronic Research Exercise 121

[14] Reading Rules of Law 133

[15] Researching Statutes 149

[16] Statutes: Research & Writing Exercise 157

[17] Statutes: Electronic Research Exercise 177

[18] Case Analogies: An Introduction 187

[19] Legislative History Research & Exercise 197

[20] Researching Cases 209

[21] Researching Cases: Research & Writing Exercise 219

[22] Researching Cases: Electronic Research Exercise 22

[23] Case Analogies: A Single Analogous Case 243
[24] Case Analogies: Multiple Analogous Cases 259
[25] Case Analogies: Writing Exercise 5 [W5] 299
[26] Researching with Citators 325
[27] Administrative Law Research 333
[28] Research Plan: An Introduction 341
[29] Research Plan Exercise 349
Appendix A: McBoyle Case Brief 353
Appendix B: "A Message To Garcia" 355
Appendix C: Research Plan Example 361

[1]

Introduction to Law School

"WHAT DO FEAR, frustration, anger, and a sense of isolation have to do with the study of law?"[1]

Fear, anger, frustration, and isolation are common to all law students.

Incoming law students sometimes feel these emotions. As one first year student said, "Professor, I am barely keeping my head above water. I feel like I am in the middle of the ocean, treading water, with sharks all around me."

I smiled and said, "Welcome to the law."

Top Ten Myths: Busted!

Law school is hard. The practice of law is even harder. Yet both the study and the practice of law can be enjoyable—especially if you have realistic expectations. Maybe we can help manage your expectations of law school by busting these "top ten" myths:

MYTH 1: You are in law school to memorize rules.

To paraphrase a famous jurist: Any fool with a laptop can find the law.

---

[1] Thus begins a famous introductory textbook to law school. Eva A. Hank et al., *Elements of Law* at xxxv (1994).

What, then, distinguishes an average lawyer from a good lawyer? For that matter, what distinguishes a good legal education from a poor one?

Before coming to graduate law school, you may have studied law in undergrad. In Asia, that often means memorizing and regurgitating rules. That is not what we do in an American, common law education.

You might get frustrated in class. You may want the professor to tell you what the "black-letter" law is. Meanwhile, the professor uses the Socratic Method—asking you questions instead of "teaching" you. The professor makes you read cases instead of making you memorize rules. Why?

MYTH 2: Learning law by reading appellate court decisions is anachronistic and stupid.

Certainly, the "case method" system is not an efficient way to memorize the black-letter law. Your professors know this. Yet we persist. Are we sadistic?

In the alternative, is it possible there are other reasons we use the "case method" system?

Yes.

First, learning to read cases is a critical skill. It is a skill that takes a lifetime to develop.

Once, I walked into Dean Enlow's office prior to his Torts class. He apologized, saying he didn't have time to meet because he was preparing for class.

I was a young and naïve professor back then. I remarked that preparation couldn't be too difficult; after all, he must have taught the same case a dozen times!

I will never forget his response.

"Yes," Dean Enlow said, "but I read each case before every class, and every time I learn something new."

Those who have ears to hear, let them hear (Matthew 11:15).

Second, from a practical perspective, by reading cases you learn how legal experts write and how they analyze the law. It is like sitting at the elbow of a famous jurist, learning from the best decisions and from the worst decisions.

Knowing the "black-letter" law isn't enough. You must also know how to apply the law.

MYTH 3: The Socratic Method is pure evil.

"Socratic Method" describes the way law school classes are conducted. Professors call on students. The professor asks a series of difficult questions about the case readings for the day.

Being "put on the spot" in class can be frightening—especially if English is not your native language. Many students worry that their English is not as good as their fellow students. They might feel embarrassed.

The best advice is not to worry: just go for it!

In fact, many ESL (English as Second Language) students tell us that at the start of the semester, they understand less than 50% of what their professors say in class. By mid-semester, they are usually up to at least 75%.

Don't get discouraged. Your language skills will increase with practice and use. So, please follow the law school's English Only Policy.

The Socratic Method is not used for "hazing" new students. In fact, the first year of law school is not meant to be a stressful, boot camp experience.

Rather, questions are asked in class to help you think and to help you examine a case from many different angles.

A professor might begin by asking basic questions like: what are the facts of the case, what is the rule that is being applied, or how did the court apply the rule to the facts. The professor might ask whether you agree with the court's reasoning.

The professor might go on to probe your understanding of the case by asking a "hypothetical question." A hypothetical question usually involves changing a few key facts and asking whether those changes might affect the outcome of the case.

Hypotheticals are crucial to developing legal reasoning skills. By handling hypothetical questions, students learn to distinguish relevant facts from irrelevant facts. Students learn to apply rules to the relevant facts. They learn to predict what a court is likely to do in a given situation. Students learn that small changes in fact or policy can create big changes in the outcome of a case!

MYTH 4: I can study in law school like I studied in college

Reading for law school is not like reading a college textbook. If you read a science textbook in college, you might start with the assumption that the information contained in that textbook is true.

Law students do not assume everything in their casebooks is true. Legal readers are critical readers.

When we read a case, we interact with it. We ask whether the reasoning is sound: whether each step of logic, each inference, has been explained and supported.

You might be surprised when your professor disagrees with a case in the casebook. You might ask, *why did he make us read that case? Why not choose a better casebook if he disagrees with every case?*

You'd be missing the point.

Law students must learn to read critically and comprehensively.

Likewise, when we do legal research, we don't ask how many sources we have to read in order to write a memorandum of law to our supervisor. That's a wrong way of thinking.

A lawyer must become a subject matter expert on each problem he researches. Every case must be read and synthesized—that is—compared to every previous and future case. Every rule must be understood as well as the reason behind the rule.

In fact, legal research and writing is a lot like an iceberg. You only get to show the reader a small part of your underlying research and hard work.

MYTH 5: The best law professor is the one who communicates information in an entertaining way.

If you want to download data into your brain, read a book.

Frankly, many of you are smart enough that you could take a bar study course and pass the bar examination right now.

Why, then, do most state bar associations require a legal education before turning you loose on an unsuspecting public?

You are entering into a profession. A juris doctor degree is a professional degree. You need to learn what it means to be a professional. As much as we care about you as a student, we also care about your future clients.

Hence, law school is not only about the transmission of information. We want to transmit a profession.

As a Christian school, our goals are even more specific.

The best law professor is one who puts you in right relation to the practice of law in that area.

The best Christian law professor is one who relates all areas of life, including a particular legal practice, to the great salvific work God accomplished in Christ Jesus.

MYTH 6: I was the smartest in my class in college; I will be just fine. Alternatively, I couldn't hack it in medical school or the hard sciences, so why not go to law school?

Sherlock Holmes may be regarded as the most rational mind in literature. Yet, the greatest example of wisdom in the Bible is the Proverbs 31 woman. Those who have ears to hear, let them hear (Matthew 11:15).

Please remember: law school is hard. Professors grade tough. You may not make an A in every class. That is okay. Give yourself some grace.

The average grade in law school is a B minus. But, hey, if you make Cs and pass the bar, you're still a lawyer!

As for those with "emotional intelligence" who dropped out of pre-med, welcome!

You should know, however, that law school is for people who want to practice law. Law practice isn't as exciting as it might seem on TV. There are precious few jobs out there for "helping poor children." Most of our graduates work in an office pushing paper.

It's a job.

For those who are called to the profession, it can be rewarding and enjoyable work. Most days, it feels like being in an air-conditioned coal mine. Occasionally you get to work on an intellectually stimulating case.

For those who choose not to practice law, that's okay too. Some of our favorite graduates never took or passed the bar.

Many people can benefit from a legal education and the discipline it provides. Not everyone is called to be a lawyer. Many CEOs and U.S. presidents studied law. Most even passed the bar exam—though some were later disbarred or surrendered their license rather than face disciplinary charges.

Some famous theologians studied law: John Calvin, for instance. Martin Luther avoided the study of law through divine intervention!

During difficult times at law school, try to remind yourself why you came. Remember why God called you to law school.

MYTH 7: Working in law firms in my home country or watching a lot of TV dramas from America has prepared me for U.S. law school.

After one year of law school, you will openly mock most legal dramas. Professor Collier's stories aside, practicing law is not so entertaining.

In addition, legal practice in America differs from that of other countries. For instance, although our system partakes of the common law, we don't divide lawyers into solicitors and barristers like in the UK.

Although we partake of the civil law, our judges are passive and do not take an investigative role in court proceedings like in Korea.

In many states, juries—not judges—apply law to facts to decide cases.

Moreover, the analytical patterns (used to reach a decision) employed by the American system may differ from that of other countries or cultures. Many of these analytical patterns have ancient roots in Greek rhetoric. These include analogous, deductive, and inductive reasoning patterns.

Other reasoning patterns, not based on logic but on shared cultural values have developed over time: public policy arguments, for example, or arguments about what the law should aspire to be—critical race theory, for instance.

In addition to using particular analytical patterns, American lawyers also use certain genres to communicate.

You are entering a professional discourse community. We talk. We discuss the law in legal briefs, in law journal papers, in client letters. The cases we work on today become the legal precedent of tomorrow.

Some of these genres, like contracts, are different in America than they are in other parts of the world.

For example, many contracts in Asia are formalized when they are stamped with a seal. If it has a seal, it's a contract. Whereas, in America, contracts require "consideration"—a change in legal status by both parties—before a contract will be enforceable.

Other legal communications include internal office memorandum, wills, client letters, as well as motions and legal briefs to the court. You will learn each of these genres in your legal skills courses.

Finally, American lawyers also use a particular set of legal terms. In the same way Korean legal documents use Chinese characters, American Legal English contains terms of art, some of which are written in a foreign language like Latin.

These "terms of art" or legal register have developed deep meaning over time. For example, you might find yourself struggling to understand what a court means by the term "reasonable person."

A term of art can also mean different things in different areas of law. For example, the term "consent" has a different legal meaning in personal injury law than it does in criminal law.

MYTH 8: I speak English and studied in an English speaking college. Alternatively, I don't speak English well, but I can learn English during law school.

In law school, we use Legal English. It's like learning a new language. Learning the "legal register"—the terms of art that are used in legal practice—will take some time.

For example, the Korean dialect in the small town of Pohang is different than the dialect in Seoul. Same thing with English and Legal English.

The practice of law has its own culture and language. You are here for three years to steep yourself in that culture and language.

If you don't speak English well, law school isn't the best place to learn it. Even the best English speakers struggle. Students read more than fifty pages of technical material every night. No pictures.

Moreover, by the end of the year, you will be expected to write long, complex legal documents.

Students who struggle with English or who struggle academically often turn from academic pursuits and immerse themselves in other activities like joining the praise team or prayer team. Maybe they think serving God in this way will result in God's favor on the bar exam. Who knows; anything is possible.

We believe studying the law is, itself, an act of worship.

If you are struggling with English, we encourage you to immerse yourself enthusiastically in our English Only Policy. We encourage you to speak up in class at every opportunity. Join the student newspaper. Keep a journal in English every day. Start a blog about law school.

What you are doing is incredibly hard and brave. Your professors have profound respect for students who operate at a deep, technical level in more than one language, while most of your professors can't even order pizza delivery from the local Dominos!

Finally, some of our students graduated from a four-year university in America. Yet their English is not very good. Or they struggle with technical logic and legal analysis. As with any U.S. law school operating in America, not every undergraduate is a good fit for law school. Fortunately, or not, we don't require students to take the LSAT, which is a good indicator of law school performance and bar passage. Just be aware that, even if you studied in America, or at an English speaking institution, since middle school or high school, you might struggle with law school.

MYTH 9: After law school, my life will be like the music video "Gangnam Style!"

Maybe.

You'd need to work hard in school and have excellent networking skills to get a job at a major law firm in Seoul. Some of our graduates work at top firms in Korea. They work very, very hard.

Most of our graduates work as in-house counsels for Korean corporations. They are part of a legal team for the corporation doing things like drafting and reviewing contracts, auditing corporate compliance with best operating practices, supervising outside law firms, and translating technical legal documents.

A few graduates practice in America. Fewer still see the inside of a courtroom.

Some of our favorite students never passed the bar. Some never took the bar. Some went on to become professors. Others went to NGOs. Some are in the mission field. Others are raising a family.

That said, finding a job is like a job in and of itself. We encourage you to take advantage of our career services office. Plan your internships carefully. Identify lawyers who are doing what you want to do and interview them. Begin networking—perhaps by joining a legal society.

Don't wait till you take the bar exam to begin looking for a job!

We support you in fulfilling God's calling for your life. We encourage you to seek God's guidance. After all, God says He already prepared good work for you to do in advance (Ephesians 2:10).

MYTH 10: Law school is the hardest thing on earth.

Law practice is harder. Enjoy your time in law school.

Conclusion

Think about your expectations from law school. Are they realistic? Which of the top ten myths was most surprising?

Law school offers training to become a professional.

You are here to learn a profession. You might learn as much about the practice of law by joining a moot court team or by taking a trip to Cambodia as you do from your substantive law classes.

Your professors care about you. It's called "tough love." We want to model—to the best of our ability—a professional spirit. We seek to communicate that spirit to you, and not just the spirit of secular law. Though we see secular law as part of God's providence here on earth, there is also the temptation to make it into an idol.

We want to communicate the Spirit of Christ. Without God's Spirit guiding us, we might become emotionally-driven Ninth Circuit judges or grouchy rationalists like Ebenezer Scrooge. We want to model what it means to be a Christian lawyer.

Facts are complex. The law is complex. As Christian lawyers, we bring that complexity to the court, without bias, and ask the court to decide.

To be Christian lawyers, we need the Holy Spirit's help and instruction (Romans 8:14). We want you to be even wiser than your teachers through the power of the Holy Spirit (Psalm 119:99). The Holy Spirit can enliven and enlighten your understanding through the God-breathed revelation in the Bible (Ephesians 1:18-21). We want you to take the motto to heart: "do justice, love mercy, and walk humbly" with God (Micah 6:8).

We want you to relate everything you do in life and in the law to the great salvific work God accomplished on the cross in Christ Jesus.

[2]

Introduction to Law Practice

LAWYERS MAY BE viewed differently in America than they are in Asia.

In Asia, experts are respected for their knowledge, training, and dedication. In America, experts may not have the same social status.

Hence, some doctors in Asia may become frustrated by Western clients. American clients ask a lot of questions. Doctors may feel these clients do not trust their expertise or might view questions as a challenge to the doctor's social status.

Similarly, legal clients in America may ask a lot of questions. Clients may not be satisfied with simple assurances as to the probable success of a case. Instead, clients expect to be fully informed about the law, so that the client is able to make the best decision.

Roles Lawyers Take

In Western legal practice, a lawyer, while expected to be an expert on the law, is a servant to the client. As such, the lawyer has three basic roles:

(1) Investigator

(2) Advisor, and

(3) Advocate

In order to help their clients, lawyers must investigate. Lawyers investigate both the law and the facts of a client's case. Sometimes this involves "hitting the books" in order to research the law. Sometimes this involves "hitting the streets" in order to conduct an investigation of the facts.

A lawyer also serves as an advisor. Attorneys are sometimes referred to as "counselors." Lawyers serve as a confidant and guide. Not only concerning legal matters, Lawyers can help their clients resolve personal disputes as well.

As we will see below, lawyers also have a duty to advise their clients as to the morality of legal options. This means Christian lawyers can use their biblical worldview to inform clients.

Lawyers also advocate on behalf of their clients. You represent, fight for, protect, and promote the best interests of your clients. We serve in an "adversarial" legal system. There will be confrontation. But, that confrontation does not have to be unethical or vitriolic. Like disciplined athletes, we can compete in a respectful manner.

These three roles have one thing in common: lawyers serve clients. This underlines a basic point in American law: The client is in charge. The lawyer provides a service to that client.

In contrast, in many countries in Asia, lawyers occupy a high position in society. Clients may be seen as supplicants. This is especially true in countries where people become lawyers by virtue of passing a difficult civil service examination.

Rather, in the Western mentality, a lawyer occupies a position in the service industry, albeit, a highly specialized part of the service industry requiring a good deal of professional training.

In fact, the American system is a bit strange because, whereas the lawyer serves the client, the lawyer is also an officer of the court. Lawyers are sworn to carry out certain obligations both to the court and to the client.

Thus, being a lawyer is a noble profession. We must act in a professional manner.

PROFESSIONAL LEGAL ETHICS

Because an American lawyer is an officer of the court, we must fulfill certain ethical requirements. Otherwise, the court might suspend or cancel one's law license.

We have certain duties toward the legal system and toward our clients. These rules have been summed up in the *Model Rules of Professional Conduct*. American lawyers must pass an exam based on these rules in order to enter the profession. You will learn more about these rules in a class called Professional Responsibility. A few of these rules are summarized below including the:

1. Duty to Keep the Client Informed
2. Duty to Explain the Law in Plain English
3. Duty to Discuss All Relevant Considerations
4. Duty of Candor; and
5. Duty to Preserve Client Confidences

1. Duty to Keep the Client Informed

Lawyers must keep a client reasonably informed both as to the client's case and as to the law. For example, Rule 1.4(a) of the *Model Rules of Professional Conduct* says: "A lawyer shall keep a client reasonably informed about the status of a matter and promptly comply with reasonable requests for information."

Hence, lawyers must inform clients about changes in the status of their cases and also give them periodic progress reports. Dissatisfied clients can report a lawyer to the bar association.

In fact, most complaints against lawyers arise from failures to communicate with clients. Lawyers may face disciplinary action if they fail to return phone calls and e-mails or if they fail to inform clients about the disposition of a case.

2. Duty to Explain the Law in Plain English

Lawyers also have a duty to explain the law to clients in plain English so that the client can choose how to proceed in a case. While lawyers are responsible for tactics and procedure, it is the client's responsibility to define the object of the representation.

Therefore, lawyers must explain the law and must consult the client as to the means by which a client's goals are pursued.

First, lawyers have a legal obligation (an ethical duty under Model Rule 1.4) to inform a client about the law "to the extent reasonably necessary to permit the client to make an informed decision regarding the representation."

Explaining the law to a client does not mean you can counsel a client on how to break the law or how to violate the rights of others. However, a lawyer may, under Rule 1.2(d) of the *Model Rules of Professional Conduct*, "may discuss the legal consequences of any proposed course of conduct with a client and may counsel or assist a client to make a good faith effort to determine the validity, scope, meaning or application of the law."

In addition, the language of Model Rule 1.2 reads as follows: "[A] lawyer shall abide by a client's decisions concerning the objectives of representation and, as required by Rule 1.4, shall consult with the client as to the means by which they are to be pursued."

This rule might sound crazy from a non-Western perspective. But we need to remember that, in American law, the lawyer serves the interest of the client. Therefore, as lawyers, (1) we must clearly explain the law in plain English to our clients. (2) The client sets the objective. Then, as lawyers, (3) we choose the best means to obtain that objective in consultation with the client.

Consider the lawyer Mr. Jaggers, introduced in Chapter 18 of the classic novel *Great Expectations* by Charles Dickens. When Mr. Jaggers first meets the lead character, Pip, he introduces himself as follows:

> *"My name," he said, "is Jaggers, and I am a lawyer in London. I am pretty well known. I have unusual business to transact with you, and I commence by explaining that it is not of my originating. If my advice had been asked, I should not have been here. It was not asked, and you see me here. What I have to do as the confidential agent of another, I do. No less, no more."*

The lawyer, Mr. Jaggers is a servant fulfilling the will of a client quite apart from his own will.

Consider the following exchange between the lawyer and young Pip. The lawyer tells Pip that Pip is to inherit a great deal of money and that Pip must try to become a gentleman by hiring a private tutor:

> *"There is a certain tutor, of whom I have some knowledge, who I think might suit the purpose," said Mr. Jaggers. "I don't recommend him, observe; because I never recommend anybody. The gentleman I speak of is one Mr. Matthew Pocket."*
>
> *Ah! I caught at the name directly. Miss Havisham's relation. The Matthew whom Mr. and Mrs. Camilla had spoken of. The Matthew whose place was to be at Miss Havisham's head, when she lay dead, in her bride's dress on the bride's table.*
>
> *"You know the name?" said Mr. Jaggers, looking shrewdly at me, and then shutting up his eyes while he waited for my answer.*
>
> *My answer was, that I had heard of the name.*
>
> *"Oh!" said he. "You have heard of the name. But the question is, what do you say of it?"*
>
> *I said, or tried to say, that I was much obliged to him for his recommendation—*
>
> *"No, my young friend!" he interrupted, shaking his great head very slowly. "Recollect yourself!"*
>
> *Not recollecting myself, I began again that I was much obliged to him for his recommendation—*
>
> *"No, my young friend," he interrupted, shaking his head and frowning and smiling both at once,—"no, no, no; it's very well done, but it won't*

> *do; you are too young to fix me with it. Recommendation is not the word, Mr. Pip. Try another."*
>
> *Correcting myself, I said that I was much obliged to him for his mention of Mr. Matthew Pocket—*
>
> *"That's more like it!" cried Mr. Jaggers.—And (I added), I would gladly try that gentleman.*
>
> *"Good. You had better try him in his own house. The way shall be prepared for you, and you can see his son first, who is in London. When will you come to London?"*
>
> *I said (glancing at Joe, who stood looking on, motionless), that I supposed I could come directly.*

What do you think of Mr. Dickens' characterization of Attorney Jaggers? Does it surprise you that he refuses to personally recommend a tutor? Would a lawyer in your country or culture act in this way?

Mr. Jaggers seems to be following the Model Rules. The lawyer provides the client with necessary information. The client must choose the course of action.

Of course, lawyers who have been in practice may be familiar with the following conversation:

> *Client: What do I need to do to win my case?*
>
> *Lawyer: Why don't you tell me what you'd like to accomplish?*
>
> *Client: I want to win. Now, tell me what to say so that I can win.*

If a lawyer succumbs to the temptation to tell the client what they should do, is that lawyer behaving like a good lawyer?

In the Western model, a good lawyer is one who educates a client, allowing the client to make a reasonably informed decision about how to pursue their legal rights or responsibilities.

3. Duty to Discuss All Relevant Considerations

A lawyer may counsel a client as to the morality both of the means and of the ends.

According to Rule 2.1, when a lawyer counsels a client, "a lawyer may refer not only to law but to other considerations such as moral, economic, social and political factors that may be relevant to the client's situation."

For example, it is ethical for a lawyer to counsel a client as to the morality or economic factors of divorce. The lawyer might note the impact divorce will have on the client's financial prospects. The lawyer may also point out the way divorce might affect the client's family and children. The lawyer can appeal to the client's personal morality and ethics.

The lawyer's advice can be based on normative morals and ethics (or even based on that lawyer's personal moral convictions). For example, a lawyer might have a duty to inform a client who had manufactured a harmful product to recall that product regardless of potential legal liability.

People turn to lawyers for advice to real world problems. Rule 2.1 assures that, unlike Mr. Jaggers, lawyers do not have to jettison their common sense or sense of morality when giving legal advice.

4. Duty of Candor

You must be scrupulously honest. A good reputation once lost is impossible to reclaim.

We owe a duty of candor not only to our clients, but also, as member of the court, we must be candid with the legal system as well. For example, in America, we may have a duty to inform the court and opposing counsel about contrary legal authority. Moreover, if a client lies to the court, we may have a duty to inform the court.

A lawyer must also inform clients about good news and bad news.

Lawyers must be objective. We should not paint an overly rosy picture or deliver an optimistic opinion in order to preserve a good relationship with the client.

This duty of candor can sometimes be frustrating to our clients. For instance, if a lawyer is not certain about the outcome of a case, the lawyer will not guarantee a result. The lawyer will speak in terms of probabilities rather than giving a definite yes or no.

This often makes it sound like the lawyer is using "weasel-words" or that she is being intentionally vague. (Maybe she is!)

In a non-Western context, the concept of speaking candidly to a client or of delivering bad news, especially when that news might cause the lawyer or the client to lose face, is almost unthinkable.

Frankly, nothing drives an American lawyer or businessman crazier than not receiving a straight answer to a question, even if that answer is "no."

The Western penchant for receiving a direct or straight answer comes from the prioritization of information over relationship. In an Asian context, for instance, one should be sensitive to the relationship and should operate within the boundaries of obligations that such a relationship creates.

On the other hand, Westerners, and especially lawyers, want to define the business relationship strictly in writing, usually as a contract.

For Westerners, the written contract defines the relationship. It is not seen as a starting point for the development of a business arrangement that evolves over time as the relationship evolves.

Westerners may become upset if a portion of the written contract is later ignored based on what may seem like perfectly reasonable circumstances within the context of the relationship of the parties.

Rather, Westerners tend to see the writing as creating rights or obligations that they will expect to be fulfilled or will otherwise feel that they have had their "rights" violated. There is no use trying to talk sense with them on this point.

It may feel strange and constricting, having your relationship with a client defined entirely by a piece of writing. You might feel terrible if you are forced to write a negative opinion or to give a negative answer to a client. Yet, Western clients will expect you to be completely straightforward and direct in your response.

Westerners are often tone-deaf to innuendo and do not have the cultural training necessary to correctly use intuition to reach a conclusion or understanding.

Americans have no concept of the Korean term "nunchi."

Westerners expect to have everything spelled out for them very clearly. To the extent that you do this, they will be happy and may feel that, in you, they have found someone who truly understands them.

5. Duty to Preserve Client Confidences

You may have received an e-mail from an American lawyer with the following confidentiality clause attached to it:

> *This electronic message is confidential and is intended only for the use of the individual to whom it is addressed. The information may also be legally privileged. This transmission is sent in trust, for the sole purpose of delivery to the intended recipient. If you have received this transmission in error, you are hereby notified that any use, dissemination, distribution or reproduction of this transmission is strictly prohibited. If you are not the intended recipient, please immediately notify the sender and delete the message from your system.*

These clauses are meant to preserve a client's confidential information (or, more likely, to insulate the lawyer from a lawsuit should he accidentally hit the "reply-all" button).

A lawyer who is in possession of confidential client information must take reasonable steps to preserve that information in the way it is stored, accessed, and communicated.

Confidential information is defined as information "other than information that is generally known."

Lawyers are expected to keep secrets and to be discreet.

Despite what you might think, there are only a few times a lawyer should break secrecy—and only when the lawyer personally knows the client is doing something wrong like lying on the witness stand or committing certain crimes. You will study these situations in your Professional Responsibility class.

Conclusion

As a lawyer, you will spend your career in service to clients.

Being a servant is a humbling experience. Yet, Jesus tells us that the first shall be last and that the greatest in the kingdom of God is the servant of everyone else (Mark 9:35).

We know that Jesus was humble (Philippians 2:6) and that he is serving as our advocate in heaven (1 John 2:1).

Moreover, we want to encourage you to think of God as your first client. Whatever we do, we do with all our heart, soul, mind and strength and do it as unto the Lord (1 Corinthians 10:31).

Whenever we are serving others, we acknowledge that it's not us, rather "it is God who works in you to will and to act in order to fulfill his good purpose" (Philippians 2:13).

We pray you will have a fulfilling career in your chosen profession.

[3]

Introduction to the American Legal System: Part 1

THE AMERICAN LEGAL system can be confusing. First, it's huge. It includes international, national, state, and local legal authorities.

The American legal system is also comprehensive. It governs everything from family relations to nuclear energy policy to the height of the grass on your lawn.

No wonder there are so many lawyers in America!

The American legal system is also confusing because it is a hybrid system. It is part common law and part civil law. It is part national law and part state law.

America has statutes like a civil law system. It also has case precedent like a common law system.

Under the common law system, case precedent can be as authoritative as a statute. For example, many areas of state law, like contracts and personal property, are governed by common law—that is, judge-made law.

The trend is to codify everything. Statutes have superseded many areas once under the common law. Even so, case precedents may be used to interpret statutes.

For example, a court will look to case precedent—judicial decisions that have interpreted a statute—to determine how that statute should be applied.

In this way, judicial decisions *about* a statute can become binding. For example, a court might interpret a particular word or phrase in a statute. Lawyers must be aware not only of the statute but of the court decisions that have interpreted the statute.

In addition, a court might apply a statute to a particular set of facts. That decision would become binding on non-parties whose cases present similar facts.

We call this the principle of *stare decisis*: similar cases should be decided in a similar way.

Stare decisis is justified as a way of preserving fundamental fairness, as a means of preserving the rule of law, or as a way to provide predictability as well as economic and social stability.

To understand America's hybrid legal system, it may help to review a brief history of the development of the American legal system and the sources of American law.

Legal History

America came into being in reaction to certain aspects of the British monarchy. Hence, America started with a strong distrust of centralized authority. The guiding principle of the American government wasn't economic efficiency but the preservation of hard-won rights. This sentiment arose from Anglo-Saxon tradition going back to and even beyond the Magna Carta.

After a Revolutionary War, America broke away from British rule. The original thirteen colonies set themselves up as independent nations. These "states" were loosely associated under an Articles of Confederation.

Think about the current European Union—individual nations have ceded various degrees of autonomy to the collective government in Brussels. America was originally like that.

When you think of American government nowadays, you likely think of the federal government in Washington D.C.

Originally, however, America consisted of 13 sovereign states united under the Articles of Confederation. Each state managed its own business, including controlling immigration and printing their own currency.

Arguments arose that the national government lacked the power to do its job. Delegates from the states headed to Philadelphia to reform the Articles of Confederation. They emerged instead with the Constitution.

The delegates then encouraged the states to ratify (agree to) the Constitution. It was a close thing.

Proponents argued, most famously in the *Federalist Papers*, that the new government wouldn't become too powerful. They said the language of the Constitution ensured it would be a government of "limited and enumerated powers." They said a Bill of Rights wasn't even necessary because all rights not expressly given to the federal government were reserved to the states and to the people.

Others weren't convinced.

A Bill of Rights was added, becoming the first ten amendments to the Constitution.

After the addition of the Bill of Rights, the states ratified the Constitution. A new form of governance was born.

The Constitution is a document wrought of negotiation and compromise, the result of disputes over many issues including slavery. You will learn more about the Constitution in your Constitutional Law classes.

Unfortunately, the authors of the Federalist Papers were wrong. The federal government became more and more powerful. Eventually, this led to a struggle between the American federal government and the states. As with the EU, there was a Southern "Brexit." Rather than allow the South to secede peacefully, the North invaded, resulting in a Civil War. The North won.

After the Civil War, some remnants of state sovereignty remain which will be discussed below. Practically speaking, however, after the Civil War, the states became more like Jeju Island in Korea—regions of limited autonomy overseen by the national government.

Nevertheless, the Constitution is a marvel of concise legal writing. It is only four pages long. You can see it in the National Archives in Washington D.C.

Wary of a centralized authority, the writers created three co-equal branches of government: the executive branch, the legislative branch, and the judicial branch.

The idea was not that these branches would cooperate in glorious harmony. The idea was that, jealous of each other, they would fight for power among themselves. For instance, the President and the Vice-president were originally elected separately and might be (and sometimes were) bitter political enemies. The idea was not to create economic prosperity by governmental policy but to safeguard personal liberties from government intrusion.

The Constitution created a federal republic, giving the federal government certain "limited and enumerated powers" and reserving all other power to the states and to the people (according to the Tenth Amendment).

This arrangement created some interesting paradoxes. For instance, immigration is not mentioned in the Constitution. For a long time, the states controlled their own borders.

Then, one day, the Supreme Court decided that the power of the federal government's power over immigration was "absolute." Where this power comes from, nobody knows.

Perhaps former president William Jefferson Clinton said it best, "The Constitution means whatever the Supreme Courts says it means."

For example, the Supreme Court claimed in an early decision named *Marbury v. Madison* that the Supreme Court is the final arbiter of the Constitution. An odd decision, considering there are three co-equal branches of government, but one that proponents say is practically necessary.

Regardless, the Constitution purported to create a federal republic. The phrase "federal republic" describes the sharing of power between the national government and the states. It also describes the balance of power between the branches of government—referred to as "checks and balances."

For example, the President can veto an act of Congress, but Congress can override the veto with a super-majority.

The Supreme Court can say that an act of Congress is unconstitutional, but Congress can amend the law or even limit the jurisdiction of the Supreme Court to hear certain types of cases.

One U.S. president even refused to enforce a Supreme Court decision. President Andrew Jackson allegedly said, "[Justice] John Marshall has made his decision; now let him enforce it!"

Each branch of government in our federal republic is also a source of law.

Sources of American Law

The sources of American law are as follows:

- Constitutions (state and federal)
- Statutes (legislature)
- Cases (judiciary)
- Administrative Regulations & Executive Orders(executive)

Statutes are written by the legislature. Case decisions are written by judges. Administrative regulations are made by administrative agencies under the executive branch.

We sometimes refer to these sources of law as primary sources of law—that is, the law itself. Primary sources are distinguished from secondary sources. Secondary sources are writings about the law. Secondary sources include legal encyclopedias, law journal articles, or even blog posts.

We further divide primary sources of law into two categories: (1) binding law and (2) persuasive law.

Binding law describes law that is controlling in a particular case. Simply speaking, if a case is brought in Tennessee, the court is bound by Tennessee statutes and case precedent. Those would be "binding law" (sometimes called "mandatory" law).

Persuasive law, on the other hand, is not controlling. It may be followed if it makes good common sense and doesn't contradict binding law. In a typical example, a court in New York might consider, but does not have to follow, a decision made by a court in nearby New Jersey.

When advising a client, our goal is to sort through the legal sources of authority. We are *looking for primary, binding legal authority.*

In order to decide whether a legal authority is binding, we follow three steps: (1) identify the locus of jurisdiction, (2) identify the level of the court, and (3) make a careful comparison between our case and the case precedent.

1. Jurisdiction

First, we need to determine who has jurisdiction. Because ours is a federal system, either the federal court or a state court might have power over a client. Sometimes both. (Consider the criminal whose act is considered both a federal crime and a state crime).

We have to ask the big question—who has jurisdiction?

Federal courts have jurisdiction over federal issues including federal statutes and U.S. Constitutional rights.

Federal courts also have jurisdiction over cases involving "diversity of citizenship" where the parties are from different states. The idea is that a federal court may be impartial, while local courts might favor their own citizens.

Federal law also "preempts" (take precedence over) state law in certain instances. Generally speaking, federal law preempts state law where (1) Congress has passed extensive legislation thereby "occupying the field" or (2) where a state statute or regulation conflicts with a federal statute or regulation or (3) frustrates its purpose.

Otherwise, it is perfectly acceptable for a state regulatory agency and a federal regulatory agency to make similar regulations. For instance, both state and federal agencies regulate things like food safety.

In addition, states will often grant more constitutional rights than the federal constitution. Many states recognized gay marriage prior to the *Obergefell* decision.

Questions of federal "preemption" and state sovereignty are complex ones that you will study later in law school.

You will also run into "Conflicts of Law" in your legal studies—that is, when two possible laws apply, how does a court choose which one to apply?

Consider a typical case where a driver from California gets involved in an automobile accident in Arizona. Where can the lawsuit be brought (who has jurisdiction) and which law applies? You will study questions like this in your Civil Procedure class this year and your Private International Law class next year.

Suffice it to say, states have jurisdiction over state issues and over people and businesses in their state. Hence, things like contracts, property, and inheritance are the exclusive domain of state law. In some states, some of these topics are governed by common law.

Therefore, when deciding whether a source of law is binding, we have to determine which jurisdiction applies. Once we make this determination, we know where to look for statutes, cases, or administrative regulations.

Jurisdiction determines *where* you search for binding law.

Meanwhile, the type of law: common law, statutes, or administrative regulations, determines *how* you search for binding law. For instance, do you begin your search in a code book or in a case reporter.

2. Level of the court

When it comes to statutory law, jurisdiction determines whether a statute is binding.

However, when it comes to case precedent, we have to take additional steps.

For example, we have to look at the level of the court making the decision to see whether that decision is binding. Decisions from higher courts are binding over lower courts.

In general, court systems in America have three levels of courts: trial courts, appellate courts, and a court of last instance like the U.S. Supreme Court.

Higher-level court decisions may be binding on lower courts. For instance, U.S. Supreme Court decisions are binding on all lower federal courts and all state courts.

Meanwhile, federal appellate court decisions are binding on the district courts directly beneath it.

There are 13 federal appellate courts including the Federal Circuit. Each appellate court governs a particular geographical region or "Circuit"—an anachronism from a time when judges used to ride the "circuit"—physically travelling by horse to different cities to hear cases.

Interestingly, appellate court decisions are not binding on other appellate courts! Moreover, appellate court decisions are only binding on their own district courts. They are not binding on district courts under another court of appeals.

For example, the Ninth Circuit includes California. Ninth Circuit decisions are binding on district courts in California. But Ninth Circuit decisions would not be binding on district courts in Georgia, which is under the Eleventh Circuit.

When circuit courts disagree, it is up to the U.S. Supreme Court to reconcile that disagreement. We refer to these disagreements as a circuit court "split."

Trial courts may also disagree with one another. Trial court decisions aren't binding on anyone, not even the same judge! However, a trial court must follow the Supreme Court and its appellate court.

Trial court decisions are not binding. However, it sometimes happens that a trial decision is so well reasoned that even the U.S. Supreme Court adopts it. For example, the *Daubert* rule for determining who can be presented to a jury as an "expert" witness comes from a trial court ruling.

The hierarchy between courts is also true for state court systems. For example, trial courts under the First District Court of Appeals in Florida may not be bound by decisions from the Second District Court of Appeals.

In some ways, this reflects a common law desire to keep decisions as local as possible. People want the law to reflect, and they want to be judged, under their local customs and traditions.

The hierarchy of courts seems clear. However, it gets fuzzy around the edges. For example, a federal district court sitting in a diversity case—with plaintiffs and defendants from two different states—has to apply state law. That federal district court is bound only by the decisions of the highest court of that state. Meanwhile, decisions issued by that federal court aren't binding on anyone. If the district court decision is appealed to the federal circuit court or all the way to the U.S. Supreme Court, the decisions of those federal courts aren't binding as to any state law issue!

If the preceding material is too difficult, don't worry. You will study it in detail in your first year law courses.

The main point is that we have to consider not only the jurisdiction, but the level of court as well in order to determine whether a case precedent is mandatory, binding authority.

3. Case comparison

The decisions of courts "up the chain" are binding on lower courts. That means if a higher court has interpreted a statute in a particular way, the lower court has to consider that ruling when applying the statute.

For example, the U.S. Supreme Court in *McBoyle v. United* States held that the word "vehicle" in the National Motor Vehicle Theft Act does not include "airplanes." Every lower court has to interpret the Act similarly.

Under the principle of *stare decisis*, a lower court is also bound when a higher court applies a rule to a factually similar case.

When a case precedent is factually similar, we call it an "analogous case." Analogies—or comparisons—are drawn between our own case and the relevant facts, the relevant policy considerations, and the rationales of the case precedent.

Sometimes the facts are so similar that a similar decision is virtually guaranteed to result. We call that a "case on point."

Other times the facts, policy considerations, or rationales might differ. Or there might be a compelling reason to ask a court to disregard a previous ruling.

Analogy—or comparison—is the weakest form of logic. When considering the same case precedent, one party can argue that although some facts are similar, the legally relevant facts are quite dissimilar.

Meanwhile, the opposing party will argue that although some facts are dissimilar, the relevant facts are actually quite similar!

Hence, analogous cases are only binding if you can convince a court to apply them in your case.

One time a student came to my office. She felt confused. As she said, "I feel like I can interpret a case to mean whatever I want it to mean."

I said, "Welcome to the law."

Lawyers use analogous cases to predict what a court is likely to do in a factually similar situation or to argue that a court should or shouldn't reach a similar conclusion based on the principle of *stare decisis*.

Hence, to determine whether a case precedent is mandatory, binding authority, we have to consider the jurisdiction. We have to consider the level of the court. And we have to consider whether our case is factually similar.

CONCLUSION

Having examined the sources of American law and the weight of authority, next we will return to our examination of the branches of government from whence these sources of law derive. Then we will look at a typical court case.

[4]

Introduction to the American Legal System: Part 2

Branches of Government

We next turn to the branches of government from which the sources of law arise. We will focus on the federal government. Most state governments are similar to the federal government.

By way of reminder, the three branches of government are the legislative branch, the executive branch, and the judicial branch.

The legislative branch is bi-cameral. It has two chambers including the House of Representatives and the Senate. The House of Representatives consists of representatives chosen by the people of a particular district. There are 435 representatives apportioned by population, by state. For instance, California has 55 representatives while nearby Nevada has only 5.

Representatives are elected every two years.

Each state has two Senators. Originally, Senators were chosen by the state government. This provision ensured the protection of state rights. However, the 17th Amendment to the Constitution changed this procedure. Now, Senators are elected directly by the people.

Senators have a six-year term of office. Elections are staggered to ensure stability.

The legislative branch writes bills. Those bills, if voted on and signed by the President, become law. Laws then make their way into the U.S. Code, which is arranged by subject matter. For instance, parts of a law that concern criminal matters would be put in a different volume than parts of the same law that deal with taxes.

The legislative process will be discussed in detail in a later chapter. This process is important not only for the legislative branch. The judicial branch sometimes looks to the legislative history to determine how to interpret an ambiguous statute. Legislative intent is the guiding principle of statutory interpretation.

However, Congress increasingly delegates its rule-making function to executive agencies. These agencies are part of the executive branch. Examples of administrative agencies include the Department of Homeland Security, the Federal Communication Commission, and the Environmental Protection Agency.

Executive agencies pass administrative regulations.

Some countries in Asia have had administrative bureaucracies for thousands of years. The existence of administrative agencies might not seem strange at all.

The following critical remarks are intended to provide context for readers coming from Asian countries with rich histories of administrative regulatory states. Without some knowledge of an Anglo-Saxon, historical preference for small, local governance, it might be difficult to understand why some Americans seem antagonistic or opposed to administrative agencies.

Recall, the Anglo-Saxon traditions of early America involved a distrust for centralized authority. Even though administrative, bureaucratic states were well known at the time, the framers did not choose to include such agencies as part of the Constitution.

The first administrative regulatory agency was not created till the turn of the nineteenth century (the Interstate Commerce Commission established in 1887)—one hundred years after the Constitution was ratified.

Recall, the Constitution created a government of "limited and enumerated powers." The federal government has only the powers expressly given it.

Executive agencies are not included in the Constitution.

Hence, the U.S. Supreme Court and Congress have struggled over time to "shoe-horn" administrative agencies into the American legal system of checks and balances.

It may seem strange for the executive branch to be (essentially) passing laws. It gets even stranger. These agencies not only pass regulations, they enforce the regulations and adjudicate them as well.

For example, the Patent and Trademark Office makes regulations about how people can apply for patents. It administers those regulations. Then, patent examiners and the Patent Court adjudicate disputes that arise. The PTO acts as legislator, judge, and executive.

That is just one example of the strangeness that results from "bootstrapping" an administrative bureaucracy to the U.S. Constitution. There are other examples.

For instance, the bureaucrats who make regulations are not elected by the people. To allay concerns about the lack of democratic process, administrative agencies follow a "Notice and Comment" procedure. This procedure ensures that the people are given "notice" of a proposed agency action and a chance to "comment."

In the battle over the repeal of Net Neutrality, for instance, hundreds of thousands of comments were received. These comments overwhelmingly opposed the Federal Communication Commission's proposal to repeal Net Neutrality. The Commission repealed it anyway.

Of course, Congress could choose to take responsibility and overturn the agency's action by passing a new law. Or the President could direct the agency to take a specific action. In the alternative, the judiciary could decide an agency had overstepped the authority given to it by Congress and overturn that agency action.

You can learn more about this fascinating area of law by taking Administrative Law. You might also take classes like Environmental Law, Immigration Law, or Tax Law, each of which concerns a small subset of federal administrative law.

As previously mentioned, the executive branch ostensibly controls the administrative agencies. The President can direct agencies to take certain action or to interpret a statute in a particular way. Presidential directives are called "Executive Orders."

The President can also veto a bill passed by Congress, though Congress can override the veto by a super-majority. Finally, the President appoints government leaders including federal court judges.

The system of "checks and balances" is complicated!

Turning to the judicial branch, Article III of the Constitution creates the federal judiciary.

The federal judiciary in Article III of the Constitution includes the U.S. Supreme Court and other courts that Congress might create.

The U.S. Supreme Court consists of nine judges, appointed by the President with "advice and consent" from the Senate. Federal judges are appointed for life. This was meant to insulate judges from the political process.

The Supreme Court has "original jurisdiction" over a small set of cases, such as disputes between the states themselves. Otherwise, the Supreme Court can pick and choose which cases it will hear. Cases come to the Supreme Court from the 13 circuit courts. Cases also come to the U.S. Supreme Court from the highest courts in the states, but only if there is a question of constitutional rights involved.

Aggrieved parties file a petition asking for a "Writ of Certiorari," urging the Supreme Court hear a case. The Supreme Court may decide either to grant or to deny that petition.

In addition to the U.S. Supreme Court, which was created by the Constitution, Congress created 13 appellate courts and as many as 94 district courts. In addition, Congress created a number of specialized courts like the Court of Federal Claims as well as Bankruptcy and Tax courts.

Because Congress creates the federal courts, it also controls the jurisdiction of those courts. For instance, Congress limited the ability of federal courts to hear certain immigration cases. Hence, refugees applying at the U.S. border cannot appeal to a federal court.

You will learn more about the structure and jurisdiction of federal courts in your Civil Procedure course this year. Civil Procedure class concerns the Federal Rules of Civil Procedure, which govern the legal process in federal district courts. (Appellate courts and the Supreme Court have their own rules of procedure.) The rules of procedure for state courts often match the federal rules.

Court Procedure and Legal Writing

Speaking of court procedure, let's examine a typical court case. We will focus on the trial court level.

Most of the cases you read in your casebooks come from appellate courts. Walking through a trial will help you understand the "procedural history" of a case—how that case got to the appellate court.

There are numerous points during trial at which a legal error might occur. These errors might be brought to a higher court on appeal.

There are also numerous types of legal writing utilized at each stage of the legal process.

1. Before filing

When a client first approaches a lawyer, the lawyer has to evaluate the client's factual circumstances and determine whether there is a legal remedy available.

For example, Ben might come to your office, claiming that he had been punched by Ashley in a bar fight. This sounds like an actionable personal injury or "tort."

By actionable claim, we mean: if you presented these facts to a court, the court may give Ben a legal remedy. In this case, Ben might receive money to compensate him for his injuries as well as for any pain and suffering.

Of course, you would also have to evaluate whether Ashley has any potential defenses. For instance, Ashley might have been acting in self-defense.

A lawyer might conduct an independent investigation to corroborate the client's facts (clients may lie to you or misremember) or to discover new facts. The lawyer might talk to witnesses or look at CCTV camera footage.

Maybe Ashley is also guilty of a crime.

Based on your investigation and analysis, you might advise your client to file a criminal report with the police. A criminal trial against Ashley would be initiated by a prosecutor. It is a completely separate process from a civil trial for damages. The plaintiff's lawyer has no control over that process.

In the American system, criminal courts don't award compensation to victims. If there is a criminal trial, you might have to wait till it finishes to bring an action for civil damages.

After you investigate Ben's case both factually and legally, a senior attorney might ask you to draft an internal office memorandum applying the law to Ben's facts. You would look for primary, binding authority (statutes or cases) in your jurisdiction. You might also consider persuasive authority—that is, similar statutes or cases from other jurisdictions. In the end, you would present your supervisor with a legal "memo." A memo is an objective, unbiased prediction of what a court is likely to do in Ben's case.

Your supervisor would advise the client based on your memo. You had better make the supervisor (1) look smart and (2) not be wrong. We will talk more about this next semester when you begin drafting memos.

Based on your legal analysis, you might be asked to draft a letter. You might write a letter to Ben explaining your analysis (a "client letter"). You might write a letter to Ashley demanding compensation (a "demand letter").

Lawyers often seek to settle a case rather than taking it to court. There may be some risk in going to court. We can't guarantee what a jury will do. Trials can also be long and costly. Hence, we may seek a settlement.

Even if a lawyer has a weak case, she might ask her opponent for a "litigative risk" settlement—to pay only as much money as it would cost to litigate the case.

Settlements are common. That doesn't mean you have to like them. I remember having dinner with a former student who works as an attorney in Seoul. This attorney seemed quite upset that his company settled a lawsuit. The company had been sued in America by a "patent troll"—a person who brought a specious challenge to one of the company's patents. The company decided that it could not risk losing the valuable patent and decided, against the attorney's recommendation, to settle the case.

Lawsuits get settled all the time, sometimes without a claim being filed in court. Experienced attorneys often have a general idea about whether a particular claim is likely to succeed and how much money a jury might award. This knowledge is used to negotiate an outcome that is acceptable to both sides.

2. After filing, pre-trial

If settlement negotiations are not successful, you might file a "complaint" on Ben's behalf at the courthouse.

A complaint sets forth a simple statement as to the basis for a legal claim. (You tell the court what happened factually and how those facts entitle your client to a remedy.)

A copy of the complaint must be given to the defendant (called "service of process").

The defendant, Ashley, may respond in several ways. She might make a motion to dismiss the complaint.

A motion to dismiss might claim that the complaint was brought in the wrong court, in the wrong manner, or not in a timely manner.

In the alternative, a motion to dismiss might argue even if every fact alleged in the complaint is true, those facts don't trigger any legal remedy. Put simply, those facts don't meet the legal elements of the claim. For instance, for most personal injuries, the plaintiff has to allege some actual harm. If the complaint fails to allege harm, such as a bruise or a bloody nose, then the court cannot grant monetary compensation.

Ashley also might make a motion to change courts. For instance, if Ben and Ashley were from different states and Ben filed the complaint in a state court, Ashley might ask for the case to be moved to a federal court.

Ashley might also simply choose to write an Answer to the Ben's Complaint. An Answer confirms or denies the facts alleged in the complaint.

At this point, other parties might be added to the lawsuit. Or Ashley might sue Ben, making a counter-claim. She might claim that Ben also did something wrong.

If Ben's complaint is not dismissed, and Ashley files an Answer, then the case moves into "discovery." Discovery describes the process of discovering evidence.

Despite what you might think from court dramas, trials in America are not conducted by surprise. The discovery process ensures that both parties have as much information as possible before going to trial.

Remember that lawyers are also officers of the court. They have a duty to tell the court and opposing counsel if they find any cases or authorities that directly contradict their claim. Lawyers may also have a duty to disclose things like the names of witnesses and other key evidence.

Parties can send questions to each other (called "Interrogatories"). Barring some objection, these questions must be answered. Parties can also ask each other for documents or for access to other evidence. If an opponent doesn't comply with a reasonable request, you can make a motion to compel them or a motion seeking monetary sanctions against them.

After evidence is "discovered," the parties will often ask the court to dismiss the case. This is called making a Motion for Summary Judgment. (A "motion to dismiss" happens immediately after a complaint is filed. A "motion for summary judgment" happens after discovery begins.)

Ashley might argue that there isn't enough evidence in discovery, even if it's all true, to show that she did anything wrong legally. On the other hand, Ben might argue that the evidence is so clear that there is only one possible outcome. Both parties are saying there's no need to get a jury involved in this dispute to find out what did or didn't happen, the judge can simply decide.

If the judge does not issue a summary judgment, then the case heads to trial.

Before trial, the parties might make certain motions. For example, Ashley might ask the judge to exclude certain evidence, claiming it might unfairly prejudice the jury against her. You will learn all about evidence disputes in your Evidence class next year.

3. At trial

The next step, if the parties don't reach an out-of-court settlement at this time (they often do), is to proceed to trial.

It might be a jury trial if the plaintiff has a right to one and exercises that right. Otherwise, it might be a "bench" trial, decided by a judge.

Trial begins with opening statements by both parties. Then the plaintiff presents his "case in chief." The plaintiff trots out all of his evidence and witnesses. The defendant might cross-examine witnesses.

After the plaintiff's case, the parties often renew their call for the judge to decide the case right away (called a "motion for a directed verdict"). The defendant, Ashley, may argue that even if the jury believed everything the plaintiff presented, she didn't do anything wrong legally. Ben would argue it is so clear from the incontrovertible evidence offered, that there is only one possible outcome.

Provided the judge doesn't direct a verdict, the defendant then presents her "case in chief."

Afterward, the parties make closing arguments.

At this time, if it is a jury trial, the parties may present the judge with "jury instructions." These instructions simplify the law for the jury. (Juries in America are often called on to reach a verdict—to apply to the law to the facts presented.) The judge selects jury instructions and gives them to the jury. Because jury instructions are summarized and simplified statements of law, they often become the subject of appeals for legal error.

4. Post-trial

After trial, the loser might ask the judge to reverse or reconsider the verdict. A losing defendant might ask the judge to reduce a jury award.

The loser might appeal to a higher court by filing an appeal, along with a written brief setting forth their allegations of error. The opponent would write a brief in response.

And so on, and so forth, through the court of highest appeal.

If Ben's complaint is heard in a state court and doesn't involve a U.S. Constitutional right (simple assault and battery usually doesn't), then the court of final appeal would be the highest court of that state.

Cases brought in federal courts, or cases brought in state courts that concern U.S. Constitution rights, may be appealed all the way to the U.S. Supreme Court.

CONCLUSION

The nuances of checks and balances are covered in your substantive law courses. We encourage you to work hard in those courses.

In legal research classes, students often complain that their research efforts are hindered because they cannot read cases quickly enough.

You learn to read cases in your substantive law classes. We will talk in subsequent chapters about how to read cases effectively.

Meanwhile, civil court procedure is covered in your mandatory legal skills classes as well as in a variety of elective courses. We encourage you to take these elective courses, like trial practice, to improve your legal skills.

NOTA BENE

Students often ask, *what is the best way to improve my Legal English?* The best way is to improve your legal writing is to write, to be receive feedback, and to re-write. The best way to improve spoken English is to be brave and to use it. The legal skills classes are designed to help you do just that.

You are competing for jobs with Korean graduates who went to prestigious law schools in America. To compete, you must have excellent knowledge of American law and a stunning command of Legal English. Often, your edge is that you may also have a better command of Korean language than those who studied in or who grew up in America.

You have three years of study to put yourself in the best position possible. Your professional career begins your first day in law school.

[5]

UNDERSTANDING COMMON LAW

FOR STUDENTS COMING FROM civil law backgrounds, the common law can seem quite confusing. Common law rules cannot be found in a statute or code.[1] They can only be known by reading court decisions.

Moreover, common law rules change over time. Each decision affects future decisions. Put another way, "appropriate references for justifying legal decisions are prior legal decisions of the same order, and . . . every decision serves as a reference for future decisions."[2]

The common law is unique to Anglo-Saxon American tradition, inherited from British law with all the benefits and baggage that pertain. It is gradually fading as cultural influences change. Yet remnants of the common law remain and must be understood.

For instance, students find it confusing when courts phrase the same rule in slightly different ways from case to case. Judges do this depending on the aspect of the rule they want to emphasize.[3]

---

[1] The common law is summarized in the Restatements of Law. These are secondary sources, but sometimes courts have even adopted a particular Restatement as primary, binding law.

[2] Arthur J. Jacobson, *Autopoietic Law: The New Science of Niklas Luhmann*, 87 Mich. L. Rev. 1647, 1677 (1989).

[3] Hence, the best statement of a rule from your client will usually come from a court decision where a judge reached an outcome similar to the one you want. We call this a "positive" analogous case.

For example, one court might say that a plaintiff must prove facts at trial "by a preponderance of the evidence" while another might say the plaintiff need only convince the court that a fact "more likely than not" occurred. These phrases, which define a plaintiff's "burden of proof," mean exactly the same thing.

Stated again: saying a plaintiff must prove her case by "a preponderance of the evidence" or "more likely than not" mean the exact same thing.

Welcome to the law.

This can be cause for consternation or celebration. As you enter into the legal discourse culture, your writings can also change the law.

You might write a persuasive law journal article that is cited by a court. You might make an argument that changes the interpretation of a statute.

The main vehicle for changing the law is case precedent.

When we talk about a "case," we mean a judicial decision that applies a rule to a particular set of facts to resolve a dispute between parties.

A lawyer also might use the word "case" to refer to a client's particular factual situation—as in, "You have a very strong case." The lawyer means the rule and case precedent indicate there is a legal remedy available.

Mainly, when we use the word "case," we usually mean a past judicial decision.

For example, consider the case *McBoyle v. United States*, 283 U.S. 25 (1931). We see that the U.S. Supreme Court resolved a legal dispute between two parties, McBoyle and the United States.

In that dispute, the court was called upon to determine the meaning of the term "vehicle" in the National Motor Vehicle Theft Act.

That case can be found in volume 283 of the United States reporter on page 25. You can walk into our law library and look it up. Or you can enter the legal citation, 283 U.S. 25, into an internet search to locate the case.

We will read *McBoyle v. United States* together, but before we do, it may help to remember the principles of *stare decisis.*

In *McBoyle*, the Supreme Court determined that an airplane is not a vehicle for the purposes of the National Motor Vehicle Theft Act. Therefore, all lower courts must apply that ruling when interpreting the National Motor Vehicle Theft Act, not only to cases involving airplanes but in cases that are factually similar to airplanes (like hovercrafts).

The Supreme Court also indicated in *McBoyle* that criminal statutes should be interpreted narrowly. This interpretation may be useful in *many* criminal cases, not just in cases involving the National Motor Vehicle Theft Act.

Criminal defendants in murder cases might point to the legal principle announced in *McBoyle*.

The McBoyle case pops up everywhere, even in places you wouldn't expect, like Immigration Law.[4] Case precedent, like *McBoyle*, affects future cases. But why?

Where does the idea of case precedent come from? Why should your client's case be determined by old, dead, probably white, probably men? Is it because legal "scientists" have created a taxonomy, a science of cases to determine what is or is not just?

Certainly, creating a taxonomy of cases is helpful—for example, dividing cases into tort or property. Yet, this approach breaks down at the edges.

Consider someone who is making a noise nuisance in an apartment that hurts the ears of other apartment dwellers. Is that a personal injury or a property issue?

Moreover, this taxonomy of law does not help us determine whether an outcome is just or righteous.

There were once great hopes that humans could develop a science of law. When that failed, law professors proposed other theories, claiming that the law is an irrational application of force by the

---

[4] McBoyle is used to argue that deportation statutes should be narrowly interpreted.

powerful on the weak. This Marxist philosophy underlies critical race theory and critical gender theory, for instance.

These legal theories attempt to describe the legal process, including common law case precedent, from a secular perspective, without reference to God.

Common law, however, derives from Anglo-Saxon culture and from Christian principles.

Hence, it is difficult to understand, to criticize, or to defend without reference to the Bible.

William Blackstone's famous commentaries on the law indicate that the common law system derives from Christian principles. (Not that it isn't possible to derive a civil law system from Christian principles as our brother Justinian famously did with Roman law.)

In considering the Christian roots of the common law system, we might consider some of the earliest case precedents. In fact, I am speaking of the decisions made by God through Moses. We find these cases in the Old Testament.

Once we realize that much of the Mosaic Law was the result of God's decision in individual cases, we begin to see how good God is. We can see God's loving and just personality reflected over and over again. We can read the Old Testament law not only to learn about law but also to meet God.

Let's read two cases. These cases involve the Daughters of Zelophehad.

Please read the cases and consider the questions that follow. These cases come from the King James Version of the Bible due to copyright considerations. Feel free to look these passages up in a version of the Bible that is easier for you to read.

Numbers 27

1 Then came the daughters of Zelophehad, the son of Hepher, the son of Gilead, the son of Machir, the son of Manasseh, of the families of Manasseh the son of Joseph: and these are the names of his daughters; Mahlah, Noah, and Hoglah, and Milcah, and Tirzah. 2 And they stood before Moses, and before Eleazar the priest, and before the princes and all the congregation, by the door of the tabernacle of the congregation, saying, 3 Our father died in the wilderness, and he was not in the company of them that gathered themselves together against the LORD in the company of Korah; but died in his own sin, and had no sons. 4 Why should the name of our father be done away from among his family, because he hath no son? Give unto us therefore a possession among the brethren of our father. 5 And Moses brought their cause before the LORD. 6 And the LORD spake unto Moses, saying, 7 The daughters of Zelophehad speak right: thou shalt surely give them a possession of an inheritance among their father's brethren; and thou shalt cause the inheritance of their father to pass unto them. 8 And thou shalt speak unto the children of Israel, saying, If a man die, and have no son, then ye shall cause his inheritance to pass unto his daughter. 9 And if he have no daughter, then ye shall give his inheritance unto his brethren. 10 And if he have no brethren, then ye shall give his inheritance unto his father's brethren. 11 And if his father have no brethren, then ye shall give his inheritance unto his kinsman that is next to him of his family, and he shall possess it: and it shall be unto the children of Israel a statute of judgment, as the LORD commanded Moses.

Numbers 36

1 And the chief fathers of the families of the children of Gilead, the son of Machir, the son of Manasseh, of the families of the sons of Joseph, came near , and spake before Moses, and before the princes, the chief fathers of the children of Israel: 2 And they said , The LORD commanded my lord to give the land for an inheritance by lot to the children of Israel: and my lord was commanded by the LORD to give the inheritance of Zelophehad our brother unto his daughters. 3 And if they be married to any of the sons of the other tribes of the children of Israel, then shall their inheritance be taken from the inheritance of our fathers, and shall be put to the inheritance of the tribe whereunto they are received: so shall it be taken from the lot of our inheritance. 4 And when the jubilee of the children of Israel shall be, then shall their inheritance be put unto the inheritance of the tribe whereunto they are received: so shall their inheritance be taken away from the inheritance of the tribe of our fathers. 5 And Moses commanded the children of Israel according to the word of the LORD, saying, The tribe of the sons of Joseph hath said well. 6 This is the thing which the LORD doth command concerning the daughters of Zelophehad, saying , Let them marry to whom they think best; only to the family of the tribe of their father shall they marry. 7 So shall not the inheritance of the children of Israel remove from tribe to tribe: for every one of the children of Israel shall keep himself to the inheritance of the tribe of his fathers. 8 And every daughter, that possesseth an inheritance in any tribe of the children of Israel, shall be wife unto one of the family of the tribe of her father, that the children of Israel may enjoy every man the inheritance of his fathers. 9 Neither shall the inheritance remove from one tribe to another tribe; but every one of the tribes of the children of Israel shall keep himself to his own inheritance. 10 Even as the LORD commanded Moses, so did the daughters of Zelophehad: 11 For Mahlah, Tirzah, and Hoglah, and Milcah, and Noah, the daughters of Zelophehad, were married unto their father's brothers' sons: 12 And they were married into the families of the sons of Manasseh the son of Joseph, and their inheritance remained in the tribe of the family of their father. 13 These are the commandments and the judgments, which the LORD commanded by the hand of Moses unto the children of Israel in the plains of Moab by Jordan near Jericho.

Questions

1. **Why didn't Moses declare the "rule" fully, right from the beginning? Why was there a need for two cases?**
2. **Put another way, did God not know the complications that would result?**
3. **Did Moses really get the decision from God, or did Moses do his best job as a man, which is why he had to "change it up" later? Did he actually "change it up"?**
4. **What do we learn from these rulings about common law "cases"?**
5. **Wait, I thought the Bible was sexist; what is this about daughters inheriting property?**

Conclusion

In this chapter, we considered God's decisions as given to Moses regarding the Daughters of Zelophehad. We could just as well have looked at Solomon's famous decision regarding the stolen baby; Mordecai's legal solution that saved the Jewish believers; Daniel's apocryphal cross-examination; or Jesus's alleged approach to the woman caught in adultery.

In each case, believers resolve a unique, incredibly difficult factual and legal situation as inspired by the Holy Spirit.

We should do the same.

The common law is one legal system among many. It is good for pushing law down to local levels; it's not so great for administering a multi-cultural empire. It's a great system if you trust judges, less so if you don't.

Then again, Moses wasn't told to pick judges for their intellect (Exodus 18:21) nor were deacons chosen that way (Acts 6:3). Paul essentially says that the dumbest Christian is better suited to judge a dispute than the smartest non-Christian (1 Corinthians 6:5).

I say this not to offend non-Christians, but to show how radically a Christian view of the gospel affects one's view of the law.

The Rawlsian idea of neutral, secular public discourse devoid of all religion seems bizarre (in practice devoid only of Christ while allowing every other form of specious logic and morality).

A Christian believer has the mind of Christ and a measure of the Holy Spirit. When faced with a difficult case, a Christian lawyer needs to be in the word of God, praying without ceasing, and guided by the Holy Spirit.

Learn to listen to God. He'll give you the answer. God will speak to you just as He spoke to Moses.

[6]

Reading and Briefing Cases: An Introduction

READING A CASEBOOK is not like reading an undergraduate textbook. When we read a case, we need to put on our "thinking caps." We need to read critically. We want to know what is the court doing, and we want to know why.

As questions come to mind while reading a case, we need to work actively to resolve those questions.

Do not make assumptions about what a court "likely" meant. Strive to understand why the court reached that ruling.

Often, the questions you have while reading are the same questions that your professor asks during class! The best way to prepare for the Socratic Method (where professors ask questions during class) is to read cases carefully and with professional curiosity. With each case, try to understand what new thing the court is saying about the law.

Lawyers read critically. We also read for context. Lawyers have a sort of index in their minds. That index arranges issues according to topic.

For example, when a client shares facts with a lawyer, the lawyer thinks, *this sounds like a personal injury (tort).* The lawyer then goes to the "commonplace" in her mind where she has stored rules and cases concerning tort law.

In the same way, when you read a case, first, look at the context. What casebook are you in? Torts or contracts, for instance. What section of the casebook are you in? For example, intentional torts or negligence? Which particular cause of action or specific element of a cause of action are you studying? For example, the type of damages needed to prove "intentional infliction of emotional distress."

To determine context, we also need to look at the "procedural history." Is the case on appeal or is it a trial court decision? If it is on appeal, what is the claimed legal error? For example, is the appellant arguing that the judge gave an improper jury instruction. (The appellant is the "loser" at the trial court level who brings an appeal.)

Context is key.

> *TIP: When you intern with a law firm, or as a law student, try to provide your supervising attorney or professor with context when you ask a question. This approach will be greatly appreciated!*
>
> *When speaking to a lawyer or law professor, try to include the following information along with your question: who are you, what is this all about, what do you want, why does it matter. Professor Collier adds: "Please try to answer your own question before arriving at my office. Then we can discuss the problem intelligently."*

Learning the law is difficult. Reading cases is hard.

As a law student, you may feel like you don't have enough time to read cases for class. You might be tempted to "skim" through a case. You might think you can "brief" a case using a highlighter and making notes in the margins.

You'd be wrong.

The best way we have found to read cases is to make a "case brief."

Case Brief

You might think about a case brief as a series of questions we ask of a case. Or you might think about the case brief as a way of dissecting the case. As law students, you want to learn how to "reverse engineer" a judicial decision because you want to learn how to recreate the reasoning employed by legal experts. This will help you do legal analysis and create legal arguments.

A case brief is like a form that we fill out. As we read a case, we ask a series of questions about the case. We then answer those questions in the guise of a case brief. For example, we ask questions like: what are the facts of this case? What is the court's holding?

This method of asking questions comes from the ancient Greek canon of "invention." Greek philosophers like Socrates invented questions till they fully understood a matter.

For example, when the ancient Greeks wanted to define what it means to be a "human being," they asked a series of brilliant questions. They allegedly arrived at the following result: a human being is a "hairless chicken"!

Here's a list of questions lawyers ask about a case:

- Case Name
- Case Citation
- Facts
- Procedural History
- Judgment
- Issue(s)
- Rule of Law for each issue
- Holding(s)
- Rationale/Reasoning
- Important Dicta
- Concurrent or Dissenting Opinions

1. Case Name

A case name tells us the name of the parties involved in the dispute.

If it is a trial court case, the first party is usually the plaintiff and the second party is the defendant.

However, on appeal, the party names can sometimes change positions. For example, if a defendant loses the trial, the defendant would be the one bringing appeal. Then, the defendant's name would come first.

To make matters even more confusing: if the defendant wins the appeal, and the plaintiff appeals that decision to the Supreme Court, the plaintiff's name would again come first!

This highlights a simple rule: the party bringing a claim or appeal comes first.

In our example, *McBoyle v. United States*, Mr. McBoyle was a criminal defendant at the trial court level. His conviction was affirmed by the appellate court. He then challenged the conviction at the U.S. Supreme Court. Hence, in the Supreme Court decision, Mr. McBoyle's name comes first.

2. Case Citation

The case citation contains a lot of information.

We learn which jurisdiction the case comes from, the level of court, and the date of the decision.

Each of these is a crucial factor when determining how much "weight" to give the decision. For example, whether the case is "binding authority."

For example, when we see *McBoyle v. United States*, 283 U.S. 25 (1939), we learn the following: The parties were named McBoyle and the United States. The case can be found in volume 283 of the United States reporter. A reporter is a publication that prints cases. As you will learn, the U.S. reporter only prints cases from the Supreme Court. So, we know that this is a U.S. Supreme Court decision. We also learn that the Supreme Court decided the case in 1939.

This Supreme Court decision would be "binding" authority on all federal courts including circuit courts and district courts. It would also be binding on state courts as to U.S. Constitutional issues.

Although we don't learn this tidbit from the caption, this particular case became very "persuasive" authority for all courts when deciding how to interpret an ambiguous, criminal statute.

3. Facts

We need to understand the facts that gave rise to the legal dispute. What happened? Who did what to whom?

As a beginning legal reader, you might simply tell the "story." As you become more sophisticated, you might limit your summary to the relevant (or material) facts—that is, only the facts that affect the legal analysis.

Facts that are legally relevant are those that help determine whether the "elements" of a law apply.

Put another way: a rule of law is a legal remedy that attaches to a specific set of legal facts. We call those facts "elements."

For example, an *intentional, offensive* touching that causes *harm* may result in money damages. We call that rule of law: "battery."

We might also refer to this rule as a "cause of action." When an attorney says a client has a "cause of action," the attorney means the client's factual situation seems to match a set of legal facts that trigger a legal remedy.

Therefore, if the issue before a court is whether there was a "battery," you would want to focus on facts that demonstrate "intent" or "offensive touching" or "harm." These would be the relevant facts. Other facts, like the color of the defendant's shirt, would not be relevant.

Focus on the cause of action and its elements when you summarize the facts. This will help you identify legally relevant facts.

Sometimes it can be a good idea to note any emotionally significant facts. These are facts that, while not legally relevant, might affect the outcome of the case. Judges are human beings and may be affected by the equities of a case.

The facts of a case determine the outcome of a case. For this reason, professors may ask "hypothetical questions" in class.

When asking a fact "hypothetical," the professor will change a fact. The student's job is to determine whether the fact that was changed was a relevant fact—that is, does the change affect the application of the rule? Does it affect the outcome of the case?

The use of hypothetical questions builds a student's legal reasoning skills—particularly in the area of analogous logic.

4. Procedural History

Procedural history tells us where the case came from. Is the case being decided by a trial court? Is it on appeal to a Circuit Court or to the U.S. Supreme Court? What was the legal error?

Some students simply note the procedural history alongside the facts; other students prefer to have a separate procedural history section.

5. Judgment

The judgment is the actual disposition of the case. For instance, an appellate court might reverse a trial court decision.

An appellate court can do many things. For example, it can reverse a decision or it can remand for additional consideration.

We suggest you *begin* your legal brief by skipping to the end of the case and noting the judgment.

Put simply, a case is only binding authority as to language that is directly related to the judgment.

Sometimes a novice legal reader gets confused by "dicta" or a minor point of legal reasoning that does not relate to the outcome (the "judgment") of the case.

Ask yourself, is this point critical to the judgment? If not, it is "dicta."

Hence, consider starting at the end of the case, by noting the "judgment." This will help you on other portions of your case brief.

6. Issue

The issue is the specific legal question the court must answer.

Sometimes a decision will involve more than one issue. Usually, the decisions in your casebooks have been edited to focus on one issue. Additional or unrelated issues may be omitted. This convention saves space in your textbook but is an artificial way of reading cases. Students sometimes get overwhelmed when they are confronted with long, unedited case decisions in legal research class.

There are several tips for extracting the issue from a case.

First, most courts will "spell it out" for you. The court will write something like: "the issue before us is whether . . . ." Whenever you see that language or the word "whether," make a note. That is probably the issue.

For example, in *McBoyle v. United States*, the court writes, "A writ of certiorari was granted by this Court on the question whether the National Motor Vehicle Theft Act applies to aircraft."

Second, try to narrow the issue. A poor issue statement for *McBoyle* might read: "the issue is whether the defendant is guilty." Or "the issue is whether the National Motor Vehicle Theft act has been met."

Rather, a narrow statement of the issue may focus on the *element* at issue and may *include a few key facts*. For example, "whether an *airplane* is a *vehicle*."

Your case brief might also include a reference to the law like: The issue is whether an airplane is a "vehicle" for the purposes of the National Motor Vehicle Theft Act.

7. Rule of Law for each issue

When a professor talks about a "rule," he could mean: the legal rule (law) the court is applying (for example, the National Motor Vehicle Theft Act) or the rule that this case stands for ("the holding").

For purposes of the case brief, we mean, please write down the rule (the actual law) that the court is applying. For example, in the *McBoyle* case, you should copy down the language of the National Motor Vehicle Theft Act.

Sometimes a court looks not only at a general rule, like the National Motor Vehicle Theft Act, the court also looks at a sub-rule. We might call this a specific rule.

Recall, a rule of law is a legal remedy that attaches to a specific set of legal facts that we call "elements."

For example, the court in *McBoyle* creates a sub-rule that defines the element "vehicle" in the National Motor Vehicle Theft Act.

You should list the general rule and any specific rules utilized by the court.

8. Holding

The holding is the most important part of your case brief. The holding is sometimes confused with the judgment. Instead, a proper statement of the holding explains the judgment.

What we mean by holding is—what authority or proposition does this case stand for.

Put another way, what is the court teaching through this decision.

Or you might say, in what new way is the court combining the facts and the legal principles? What new thing is the court doing? How does this decision apply outside this case?

A holding is the court's answer to the legal issue.

The holding may later become "authority" for a rule or an interpretation of a rule. The holding could also become an "analogy" to show how a rule should be applied in a factually similar situation. As a lawyer, it will be up to you to convince a judge what the "holding" of a case is and whether it applies to your case.

In order to do this, we need to get good at extracting holdings from cases.

A good rule of thumb is that a holding is only binding *authority* to the extent the language cited relates directly to the judgment.

In addition, a holding is only a binding *analogy* when the facts of your case fit the same class or category as (are "similar to") the facts in the decision.

Finally, when we read decisions, the court sometimes summarizes the holding of another case. For example, a Court might write, "in *Smith v. Jones*, we held . . ." or "*Smith v. Jones* stands for the proposition . . . ." That is an example of a legal expert taking a "holding" from a case.

Pay close attention to that language. That is what you must learn to do.

As legal readers, we must be able to pull a holding from a case and apply that holding to our client's factual circumstances either as an authority or by way of analogy.

9. Rationale or reasoning

In the western legal system, court decisions are legitimated by their legal reasoning. Hence, a court might "overrule" an earlier decision if the court no longer agrees with the legal reasoning.

For example, in 1986, the U.S. Supreme Court said there was no constitutional protection for sodomy and that states could criminalize such behavior as they have throughout most human existence.

Then, in 2002, in *Lawrence v Texas*, the U.S. Supreme Court completely changed its opinion. What happened in the intervening 16 years? The U.S. Constitution did not change. No new law was passed. The U.S. Supreme Court simply changed its mind.

Then again, Constitutional Law might best be described as bad public policy masquerading as legal reasoning. (Don't tell your Con Law professor I said that.)

Usually, a court decision has to follow certain accepted forms of analytical patterns. Some of those patterns employ logic. Deductive logic is prominent as is inductive and analogous logic. We will study these forms of logic at length in a following chapter.

Other, valid analytical patterns do not necessarily employ logic. For example, public policy arguments may be based on cultural norms. Juridical arguments, meanwhile, employ reasoning about what the law should be: critical race theory, gender theory, or economic theory, for instance.

These are all acceptable forms of legal reasoning. Other forms of reasoning are not acceptable. For example, direct appeals to emotion are not used in the law.

We may not always agree with a court's reasoning. But we should be very interested in why a court made a particular decision. We may want to persuade a court to do likewise for our client.

10. Dicta

When explaining its rationale or reasoning, a court might sometimes include dicta. "Dicta" is language in the decision that is not directly related to the judgment. For example, a court might talk about what it would do if the facts were different.

Dicta is not binding authority, but it might be used to persuade a future court.

Don't confuse dicta (or a minor point of legal reasoning) with the actual holding of the case. If language in the decision does not relate directly to the judgment, it is dicta. If you are having trouble, try going straight to the judgment and working backwards.

11. Dissenting or concurring opinion

A decision might also include a concurring opinion or a dissenting opinion. These are not binding authority and usually shouldn't be cited as authority. However, at times they might be persuasive and might be cited as persuasive authority—for instance, if they include strong legal reasoning that might later be adopted by another, more sympathetic court.

HOW WE USE THE CASES WE READ

When we read cases, we are looking to use them in one of two ways: as authority for a rule (authority) or to show how a rule was applied in a factually similar situation (analogy).

1. Authority

Sometimes a case decision might announce a new rule. For example, in *Daubert*, a federal court created a new rule concerning the qualifications for "expert" witnesses. Courts must be careful before they tell the jury that someone is an "expert." The *Daubert* decision sets forth a test to see if a so-called "expert" qualifies. Thus, *Daubert* is cited as "authority" for the rule about expert witnesses.

More commonly, a court will interpret a word or phrase from a statute. That decision then becomes a sub-rule that has to be considered when applying the rule.

For example, the Tennessee "dram shop law" says that a store can be sued if it sells alcohol to a "known minor" (a young person) who causes a traffic accident.

The Tennessee Supreme Court was called upon to determine the level of knowledge required. Could a store be sued if they failed to check a young person's ID?

The Tennessee Supreme Court held that a store cannot be liable unless the "seller [actually] knew that the purchaser was a minor and sold intoxicating beverages to him or her anyway."

Every court in Tennessee must now use the Tennessee Supreme Court's definition of "known minor" when applying the dram shop law.

Hence, when we read cases in the real world, we may use those cases as authority for a rule.

On the other hand, when you are reading a case for class, the goal is, almost exclusively, to determine what the holding or "rule" is—that is, what new thing is the court saying about the law.

However, in the real world, lawyers are often reading cases in light of their own case and trying to determine how those cases impact the outcome of their own case.

2. Analogy

We also read cases to determine how courts have applied rules in factually similar situations. We call these analogies or case precedent.

Analogies are based on the principle of *stare decisis*. Similar cases should be decided in a similar way.

We use analogies to *predict* what a court is likely to do, given the facts in our case. Or we use analogies to *persuade* a court as to what it must do, given factually similar case precedent.

In class, professors will test your analogous reasoning. Professors may ask you a hypothetical question. The professor might change the facts and ask whether a similar decision would have been reached based on those hypothetical facts.

These hypothetical questions prepare students to use analogous case precedent by determining which facts are legally relevant and which facts are "similar" to the facts in our case.

Case Sequences

In casebooks, you will sometimes read two or three cases in a row. These cases share a similar fact pattern or show the development of a particular area of the law.

When you read those cases, and as you brief them, you should consider them in context. What new thing is the court doing in each case? How does the law change from case to case?

Reading case sequences will teach you how to read a new case in the context of case precedent. You are also learning how to synthesize cases.

When reading a casebook, do not focus only on learning the substantive, black-letter law! Learn to read the law and think like a lawyer.

Otherwise, you might get frustrated.

For example, on occasion, a casebook will have you read a case, only to tell you afterward that the decision has been overruled or superseded by statute. You might wonder why the author made you read that case?

That's the right kind of question to be asking.

Online Case Briefs and Commercial Outlines

You can find case briefs for many casebooks online. Should you use those? Technically, it is not considered "cheating." However, you might be cheating yourself of a valuable experience. You must learn to read and brief cases.

In private practice, no one is going to help you. Moreover, even if they did help you, in the end, you are responsible for your own work. You sign your own name on every court filing.

Therefore, you must become confident in your own ability to read, interpret, and apply the law. Many lawyers become overconfident, thinking they can read a case better than anyone and not fully trusting anyone else's opinion. (That's one reason we cite to every source we use in a court filing, because the court and opposing counsel want to read the sources for themselves.)

Frankly, if you use an online or a commercial outline, you don't know if the person briefing that case is correct or what grade that person received on the course!

If you must use an online source or commercial outline, please consider using it only as a supplement. Do your own work first, then check your work against another source.

Christian Case Briefing

As lawyers, we must learn to read cases. But as Christians, we should approach cases differently. All lawyers ask things like, what are the facts and what is the holding.

Christians should ask other questions of a case. As one church leader said, a true question reaches into the pierced side of Christ. It partakes of the water and the blood. This is a graphic way of saying we need to relate everything to Christ.

"For in [Christ] all things were created, things in heaven and on earth, visible and invisible, whether thrones or dominions or rulers or authorities. All things were created through Him and for Him. He is before all things, and in Him all things hold together" (1 Corinthians 1:16-17).

As Christians, we might ask:

- What is the mind of Christ about this case?
- Where is the sin in this case?
- What does true reconciliation look like?
- Do the rules or policies announced in this case encourage people to live in the way God created them?

As Christian lawyers, we encourage you to think about the cases you read from a Christian perspective. This shouldn't be an afterthought. It should be our initial and immediate approach.

[7]

Reading and Briefing Cases: An Example

Introduction

Let's read through the case together. First, we will show in the annotations how a lawyer thinks when he reads a case. Second, we will show a sample case brief.

Case Reading

McBoyle v. United States
283 U.S. 25 (1931)

We see the party names and the case caption

MR. JUSTICE HOLMES delivered the opinion of the Court.

The petitioner was convicted of transporting from Ottawa, Illinois, to Guymon, Oklahoma, an airplane that he knew to have been stolen, and was sentenced to serve three years' imprisonment and to pay a fine of $2,000. The judgment was affirmed by the Circuit Court of Appeals for the Tenth Circuit. 43 F.2d 273. A writ of certiorari was granted by this Court on the question whether the National Motor Vehicle Theft Act applies to aircraft. Act of October

Facts and procedural history: copy and paste this into our brief

"whether..." legal issue: copy and paste it

29, 1919, c. 89, 41 Stat. 324, U.S.Code, Title 18, § 408. That Act provides: "Sec. 2. That when used in this Act: (a) The term 'motor vehicle' shall include an automobile, automobile truck, automobile wagon, motor cycle, or any other self-propelled vehicle not designed for running on rails." "* * * *""Sec. 3. That whoever shall transport or cause to be transported in interstate or foreign commerce a motor vehicle, knowing the same to have been stolen, shall be punished by a fine of not more than $5,000, or by imprisonment of not more than five years, or both."

Here is the general rule

Section 2 defines the motor vehicles of which the transportation in interstate commerce is punished in Section 3. The question is the meaning of the word "vehicle" in the phrase "any other self-propelled vehicle not designed for running on rails." No doubt etymologically it is possible to use the word to signify a conveyance working on land, water or air, and sometimes legislation extends the use in that direction -- e.g., land and air, water being separately provided for, in the Tariff Act, September 21, 1922, c. 356, § 401(b), 42 Stat. 858, 948. But in everyday speech, "vehicle" calls up the picture of a thing moving on land. Thus, in Rev.Stats. § 4, intended, the Government suggests, rather to enlarge than to restrict the definition, vehicle includes every contrivance capable of being used "as a means of transportation on land." And this is repeated, expressly excluding aircraft, in the Tariff Act, June 17, 1930, c. 497, § 401(b), 46 Stat. 590, 708. So

Another, narrow statement of the issue. Replace the one above.

The court considers the legislative scheme

Plain language reasoning

Here is the government's interpretation

here, the phrase under discussion calls up the popular picture. For, after including automobile truck, automobile wagon, and motor cycle, the words "any other self-propelled vehicle not designed for running on rails" still indicate that a vehicle in the popular sense -- that is, a vehicle running on land -- is the theme. It is a vehicle that runs, not something, not commonly called a vehicle, that flies. Airplanes were well known in 1919 when this statute was passed, but it is admitted that they were not mentioned in the reports or in the debates in Congress. It is impossible to read words that so carefully enumerate the different forms of motor vehicles and have no reference of any kind to aircraft, as including airplanes under a term that usage more and more precisely confines to a different class. The counsel for the petitioner have shown that the phraseology of the statute as to motor vehicles follows that of earlier statutes of Connecticut, Delaware, Ohio, Michigan, and Missouri, not to mention the late Regulations of Traffic for the District of Columbia, Title 6, c. 9, § 242, none of which can be supposed to leave the earth.

How to read items in a list, legal reasoning

Legislative history aids interpretation

More on reading items in a list

Other similar statutes aid interpretation

Although it is not likely that a criminal will carefully consider the text of the law before he murders or steals, it is reasonable that a fair warning should be given to the world, in language that the common world will understand, of what the law intends to do if a certain line is passed. To make the warning fair, so far as possible, the line should be clear. When a rule of conduct is laid down in words that evoke in the

Principle of Law: interpret criminal statutes narrowly, give public "fair warning"

common mind only the picture of vehicles moving on land, the statute should not be extended to aircraft simply because it may seem to us that a similar policy applies, or upon the speculation that, if the legislature had thought of it, very likely broader words would have been used. *United States v. Thind,* 261 U. S. 204, 261 U. S. 209.

Court adopts defendant's interpretation of the rule

Judgment reversed.

Judgment; cut and paste

Case Brief

Please try to make a brief of the *McBoyle* case. Include the following line items in your case brief:

- Case Name:
- Case Citation:
- Key Facts:
- Procedural History:
- Judgment:
- Issue(s):
- Rule of Law for each issue:
    - General
    - Specific
- Holding(s)
- Rationale/Reasoning
- Important Dicta
- Concurrent or Dissenting Opinions

[8]

Reading and Briefing Cases: An Exercise

Introduction

Please prepare a case brief for *Garratt v. Dailey*, a case you will eventually read in your Torts class. This case appears in the section on "Intentional Interference with Person or Property" under the subheading "Intent."

Case Reading

Garratt v. Dailey

Supreme Court of Washington, 1955

279 P.2d 1091

The liability of an infant for an alleged battery is presented to this court for the first time. Brian Dailey (age five years, nine months) was visiting with Naomi Garratt, an adult and a sister of the plaintiff, Ruth Garratt, likewise an adult, in the backyard of the plaintiff's home, on July 16, 1951. It is plaintiff's contention that she came out into the backyard to talk with Naomi and that, as she started to sit down in a wood and canvas lawn chair, Brian deliberately pulled it out from under her. The only one of the three persons present so testifying was Naomi Garratt. (Ruth Garratt, the plaintiff, did not testify as to how or why she fell.) The trial court, unwilling to accept this testimony, adopted instead Brian Dailey's version of what happened, and made the following findings:

> "III.... that while Naomi Garratt and Brian Dailey were in the back yard the plaintiff, Ruth Garratt, came out of her house into the back yard. Some time subsequent thereto defendant, Brian Dailey, picked up a lightly built wood and canvas lawn chair which was then and there located in the back yard of the above described premises, moved it sideways a few feet and seated himself therein, at which time he discovered the plaintiff, Ruth Garratt, about to sit down at the place where the lawn chair had formerly been, at which time he hurriedly got up from the chair and attempted to move it toward Ruth Garratt to aid her in sitting down in the chair; that due to the defendant's small size and lack of dexterity he was unable to get the lawn chair under the plaintiff in time to prevent her from falling to the ground. That plaintiff fell to the ground and sustained a fracture of her hip, and other injuries and damages as hereinafter set forth.
>
> "IV. That the preponderance of the evidence in this case establishes that when the defendant, Brian Dailey, moved the chair in question *he did not have any wilful or unlawful purpose* in doing so; that *he did not have any intent to injure the plaintiff, or any intent to bring about any unauthorized or offensive contact with her person* or any objects appurtenant thereto; that the circumstances which immediately preceded the fall of the plaintiff established that the defendant, *Brian Dailey, did not have purpose, intent or design to perform a prank or to effect an assault and battery upon the person of the plaintiff.*" (Italics ours, for a purpose hereinafter indicated.)

It is conceded that Ruth Garratt's fall resulted in a fractured hip and other painful and serious injuries. To obviate the necessity of a retrial in the event this court determines that she was entitled to a judgment against Brian Dailey, the amount of her damage was found to be eleven thousand dollars. Plaintiff appeals from a judgment dismissing the action and asks for the entry of a judgment in that amount or a new trial.

The authorities generally, but with certain notable exceptions (see Bohlen, "Liability in Tort of Infants and Insane Persons," 23 Mich. L. Rev. 9), state that, when a minor has committed a tort with force, he is liable to be proceeded against as any other person would be. [citations omitted]

In our analysis of the applicable law, we start with the basic premise that Brian, whether five or fifty-five, must have committed some wrongful act before he could be liable for appellant's injuries.

The trial court's finding that Brian was a visitor in the Garratt backyard is supported by the evidence and negatives appellant's assertion that Brian was a trespasser and had no right to touch, move, or sit in any chair in that yard, and that contention will not receive further consideration.

It is urged that Brian's action in moving the chair constituted a battery. A definition (not all-inclusive but sufficient for our purpose) of a battery is the intentional infliction of a harmful bodily contact upon another. The rule that determines liability for battery is given in 1 Restatement, Torts, 29, § 13, as:

> "An act which, directly or indirectly, is the legal cause of a harmful contact with another's person makes the actor liable to the other, if
>
> (a) the act is done with the intention of bringing about a harmful or offensive contact or an apprehension thereof to the other or a third person, and
>
> (b) the contact is not consented to by the other or the other's consent thereto is procured by fraud or duress, and
>
> (c) the contact is not otherwise privileged."

We have in this case no question of consent or privilege. We therefore proceed to an immediate consideration of intent and its place in the law of battery. In the comment on clause (a), the Restatement says:

> "Character of actor's intention. In order that an act may be done with the intention of bringing about a harmful or offensive contact or an apprehension thereof to a particular person, either the other or a third person, the act must be done for the purpose of causing the contact or apprehension or with

> knowledge on the part of the actor that such contact or apprehension is substantially certain to be produced."

. . .

We have here the conceded volitional act of Brian, i.e., the moving of a chair. Had the plaintiff proved to the satisfaction of the trial court that Brian moved the chair while she was in the act of sitting down, Brian's action would patently have been for the purpose or with the intent of causing the plaintiff's bodily contact with the ground, and she would be entitled to a judgment against him for the resulting damages. [citations omitted]

The plaintiff based her case on that theory, and the trial court held that she failed in her proof and accepted Brian's version of the facts rather than that given by the eyewitness who testified for the plaintiff. After the trial court determined that the plaintiff had not established her theory of a battery (i.e., that Brian had pulled the chair out from under the plaintiff while she was in the act of sitting down), it then became concerned with whether a battery was established under the facts as it found them to be.

In this connection, we quote another portion of the comment on the "Character of actor's intention," relating to clause (a) of the rule from the Restatement heretofore set forth:

> "It is not enough that the act itself is intentionally done and this, even though the actor realizes or should realize that it contains a very grave risk of bringing about the contact or apprehension. Such realization may make the actor's conduct negligent or even reckless but unless he realizes that to a substantial certainty, the contact or apprehension will result, the actor has not that intention which is necessary to make him liable under the rule stated in this Section."

A battery would be established if, in addition to plaintiff's fall, it was proved that, when Brian moved the chair, he knew with substantial certainty that the plaintiff would attempt to sit down where the chair had been. If Brian had any of the intents which the trial court found, in the italicized portions of the findings of fact quoted above, that he did not have, he would of course have had the knowledge to which we have referred. The mere absence of any intent to injure the plaintiff or to play a prank on her or to embarrass her, or to commit an assault and battery on her would not absolve him from liability if in fact he had such knowledge. [citation omitted] Without such knowledge, there would be nothing wrongful about Brian's act in moving the chair, and, there being no wrongful act, there would be no liability.

While a finding that Brian had no such knowledge can be inferred from the findings made, we believe that before the plaintiff's action in such a case should be dismissed there should be no question but that the trial court had passed upon that issue; hence, the case should be remanded for clarification of the findings to specifically cover the question of Brian's knowledge, because intent could be inferred therefrom. If the court finds that he had such knowledge, the necessary intent will be established and the plaintiff will be entitled to recover, even though there was no purpose to injure or embarrass the plaintiff. [citation omitted] If Brian did not have such knowledge, there was no wrongful act by him, and the basic premise of liability on the theory of a battery was not established.

It will be noted that the law of battery as we have discussed it is the law applicable to adults, and no significance has been attached to the fact that Brian was a child less than six years of age when the alleged battery occurred. The only circumstance where Brian's age is of any consequence is in determining what he knew, and there his experience, capacity, and understanding are of course material.

From what has been said, it is clear that we find no merit in plaintiff's contention that we can direct the entry of a judgment for eleven thousand dollars in her favor on the record now before us.

Nor do we find any error in the record that warrants a new trial.

. . .

The cause is remanded for clarification, with instructions to make definite findings on the issue of whether Brian Dailey knew with substantial certainty that the plaintiff would attempt to sit down where the chair which he moved had been, and to change the judgment if the findings warrant it.

. . .

Remanded for clarification.

Case Brief

Please include the following in your case brief:

- Case Name
- Case Citation
- Facts
- Procedural History
- Judgment
- Issue(s)
- Rule of Law for each issue
  - General
  - Specific
- Holding(s)
- Rationale/Reasoning
- Important Dicta
- Concurrent or Dissenting Opinions

[9]

Introduction to Legal Reasoning

IRAC in General

IRAC is an abbreviation that means Issue, Rule, Analysis, and Conclusion.

Sometimes we use IRAAC which means Issue, Rule, Analogous Case(s), Analysis, and Conclusion.

IRAC represents one of the most basic structures of legal reasoning. You can use this structure on law school essay exams. You can use the same structure on your bar exam.

The decisions in your casebook follow IRAC. As you read through the cases, you see the judges identifying issues, applying rules and analogous case precedent in order to reach an ultimate conclusion.

In fact, most genres of legal writing follow the IRAC formula (including client letters, office memorandum, and argumentative briefs). That is because IRAC is a simplified expression of a deductive logic syllogism.

Deductive logic proceeds from generalities, or broad statements that are presumed to be true, and applies those rules to specific circumstances. (Another major type of reasoning, inductive logic, starts with specific, small-scale observations and looks for patterns from which general theories can be inferred.)

A deductive logic "syllogism" consists of two premises that, if true, result in a conclusion.

Put another way, assuming that the first general principle (or premise) is true and that the second, more specific premise is also true, then the conclusion simply must follow.

Consider the following, classic syllogism:

> Major premise: All men are mortal
>
> Minor premise: Socrates is a man.
>
> Conclusion: Therefore, Socrates is mortal.

Assuming the first premise is true and the second premise is also true, the result necessarily or "logically" follows. This can almost sound machine-like. Certainly, computer programmers use similar logic. However, a poor premise can lead to an incorrect result. We should also be careful not to assume a premise. Each premise has to be proven.

Now, consider the following legal syllogism:

> Major premise: A remedy results from intentional, offensive, harmful touching.
>
> Minor premise: Ashley hit Ben.
>
> Conclusion: Ben is entitled to a remedy.

In a legal syllogism, the rule of law becomes the major premise. The facts of our case become the minor premise.

We call this: *building a legal proof.*

Remember, a rule of law is a legal remedy that results from certain legal facts (elements). The question, then, is whether the facts in our case fit into the same class or category as the elements.

In our syllogism, if Ashley's striking of Ben is "intentional, offensive, and harmful touching," a legal remedy will automatically follow.

To construct a deductive logic syllogism, both the main premise and the minor premise must be proved. As to the main premise, lawyers must prove which rule(s) should apply. As to the minor premise, lawyers must prove that the facts of a case are in the same class or category as the elements. For example, is the way Ashley hit Ben "intentional, offensive, and harmful"?

In order to prove this point, lawyers rely on analogous cases—cases that are factually similar.[1] In this manner, analogous case precedent helps define the class or category. This type of analogous logic represents the "heavy lifting" of legal reasoning.

Defining the class or category of a particular legal element is crucial to winning a case. Sometimes it is done using analogous case precedent. Sometime other forms of analysis are used. For instance, in the *McBoyle* case, the lawyers on both sides attempted to define the class or category of the word "vehicle."

The government argued that the term "motor vehicles" covered all self-propelled vehicles with motors not running on rails. From the government's perspective, an airplane has a motor, is self-propelled, and does not run on rails.

However, the court found the criminal defendant's argument more convincing. McBoyle argued the term "motor vehicle" was limited to self-propelled vehicles with motors that move primarily on land but not on rails.

Both were possible interpretations. However, after applying various rules of statutory construction, examining similar statutes, and applying principles of law, the U.S. Supreme Court agreed with McBoyle's assertion. The Court said, even if it "seem[s] to us that a similar policy applies, or upon the speculation that, if the legislature had thought of it, very likely broader words would have been used," still, criminal statutes must give fair notice and be interpreted narrowly.

---

[1] Of course, the real challenge is how to define "factual similarity." (Similar in which ways?)

Elements

As aforementioned, the general rule becomes the major premise. However, sometimes the general rule consists of several sub-rules. (We might call these specific or processed rules.) For example, the general rule "battery" consists of several elements. Each of these elements might have their own rules.

For instance, we learn from case law like *Garratt* that an "intentional act" is one that is purposefully done or where the actor knows or has reason to know an offensive touching will result.

Sometimes it is necessary to "unpack" a general rule and to examine each element in turn. Each element might require its own deductive logic syllogism.

Thankfully, in most cases only one or two elements are at issue. The other elements are not in dispute, meaning they are obviously met by the facts in the case. For example, in *McBoyle*, the court did not analyze every element. It only analyzed the element that was in dispute: the term "motor vehicle."

Inductive Logic

In addition to deductive logic and analogous logic, lawyers use inductive logic.

First, as to the common law, the general rule comes from court decisions. You have to read many cases and use inductive logic to synthesize a general rule from those cases.

Thankfully, the experts who wrote the Restatement of the Law have done that for us. The Restatements of Law are like a codification of the common law.

Second, lawyers commonly use inductive logic when reading cases to synthesize a sub-rule concerning a particular element.

Although the general rule comes from the statute or from the common law, the courts may have created a sub-rule concerning a particular element. Sometimes there are multiple sub-rules for an element.

That is—sometimes several binding court decisions have interpreted a particular element. Each of these cases must be considered when applying that element in the future.

For example, in your Tort casebook you will encounter a case sequence that shows the development of the element "intent." Each past case added something new to our understanding of the term of art "intent."

Third, in addition to synthesizing rules from cases, we use inductive logic to synthesize factually analogous cases.

Remember, we read cases in two ways: as authority for a rule and to show how a rule was applied in a factually similar situation.

For example, in *McBoyle* the court said the term "vehicle" does not include aircraft. However, what if another court decision later added to that understanding? For example, what if a court decided that a "hovercraft" is not a vehicle?

If so, you may need to synthesize the aircraft and hovercraft cases. It might be tempting to think you are creating a new "rule." You are not.

Rather, you would draw from those cases to define the class or category of the element "vehicle." You want to know, what the statute means when it says "vehicle." You want to predict what a court is likely to do or to persuade a court to take action.

In synthesizing *McBoyle* and our hovercraft hypothetical, one might say the court is looking for vehicles that "run primarily on land," and neither an aircraft nor a hovercraft "run" primarily on land.

Hence, there are two types of synthesis: rule synthesis and analogous cases synthesis. Both of these utilize inductive logic.

Reason for the Rule

To interpret an ambiguous rule, one must know the reason for the rule. What bad thing was the rule enacted to prevent? What good thing was the act written to accomplish? Why does the law exist and what does it do?

If you don't understand the reason for the rule, you don't understand the rule.

For example, the National Motor Vehicle Theft Act in *McBoyle* was intended to stop the interstate transport of vehicles that are known to have been stolen, including "automobile, automobile truck, automobile wagon, motor cycle, or any other self-propelled vehicle not designed for running on rails."

The U.S. Supreme Court determined that Congress intended to limit the NMVTA to vehicles moving on land and refused to extend the statute to cover aircraft.

Under the Supreme Court's interpretation, a hovercraft might not be "a self-propelled vehicle not designed for running on rails"; however, a four-wheel All-Terrain Vehicle (ATV) might.

Inductively, we would say the ATV has tires, an engine, runs exclusively on land just like the other items in the list; whereas, the hovercraft uses an engine and may sometimes run on land, however it uses air instead of tires and is mainly designed for running on water. The goal is to distinguish similar from dissimilar.

The *McBoyle* case also illustrates a rule of statutory construction. If a general item follows a list of specific items, the general item should be interpreted in the same class or category as the specific items.

It is almost as if the specific items in the list became analogies, like one of those children's picture games, where you look at two very similar pictures and try to circle the differences.

When faced with two possible, reasonable interpretations of a statute, as the court was in *McBoyle*, it must utilize every principle of statutory interpretation and must strive to understand and to effectuate the reason for the rule.

Preliminary Conclusion

Deductive logic, inductive logic, and analogous logic form the basis for most forms of legal reasoning.

Of course, not all legal reasoning is logical. We often rely on policy arguments or arguments that cite to Principles of Law—like the rule of lenity articulated in *McBoyle*. We also rely on arguments about what the law should do—such as protecting against racial discrimination. These arguments are not logical arguments, but are acceptable nonetheless.

Still, logical reasoning may be the most acceptable form of legal reasoning. The preference for logic may be based on the notion that logic is the best form of persuasion.

At law, we prefer dialectic reasoning (logic) to an appeal to bias or passion (rhetoric). Judges who decide impartially based on logic are seen as good judges, while judge who judge partially based on personal feelings or politics are seen as bad judges.

The most basic form of logic is the deductive logic syllogism—as demonstrated above.

To reiterate: at law, the most basic form of legal reasoning goes like this: inductive logic is used to ascertain a rule; deductive logic applies the rule to the facts; then analogous logic is used to prove that the rule is being properly applied based on the principle of *stare decisis*.

Consider the rule of law for battery. In most states, battery is a common law rule. The rule comes from court decisions. You might have to read and synthesize many cases inductively to create a good rule statement. Usually, however, the courts or legal experts have already done the hard work for you.

Once you obtain the rule by inductive logic, you would apply that rule deductively. You would apply the rule (major premise) to a set of facts (minor premise), to see if they necessitate a particular legal remedy.

Many legal remedies might flow from the same locus of facts. For example, there could be a battery and an assault based on the same facts.

It is up to the lawyer to inform the clients of the possible legal remedies and allow the client to choose the preferred manner of proceeding. Whether to bring one or many causes of action is a strategic decision.

Finally, not everyone is enthusiastic about IRAC legal reasoning. Some may have gotten "a bad taste in their mouth" from drilling IRAC in law school. Perhaps the underlying logical structure and link to classic Greek rhetoric was never properly explained or appreciated.

Others might take a skeptical approach, noting the inherent "sophistry" of legal arguments—that arguments, seemingly of equal weight, can be constructed by talented lawyers on both sides of a case!

Logic is never enough in and of itself. You need to know the reason for the rule. You need to know the legislative intent.

Moreover, you will move beyond IRAC to more complex reasoning structures as your legal training advances. Regardless, as simple as it is, IRAC is great for writing exams and is used in nearly every court document. We want to encourage you to learn it well.

Applying IRAC

IRAC is derived from the deductive logic syllogism. Faced with a legal ISSUE, we take a RULE, and APPLY it to the facts in our case to reach a CONCLUSION.

Our rule statement must be correct. Our application must be defensible with reference to analogous cases. Our application must also be reasonable in light of policy, common sense, and other juridical considerations.

When lawyers write, we consciously think: what is the issue, what is the rule, are there any analogies; therefore, what conclusion.

Practice Exercise

Apply the rule of battery to the facts given below. Try to focus on the element(s) in dispute in this argument. What is the unstated "issue" in this case? What conclusion would you reach? Explain why these facts are (or are not) in the same class or category as the legal facts. How do the facts match the elements of battery?

> Rule: Common-law rule of battery
>
> Facts: A parent is visiting her daughter at elementary school. She is talking to another parent in the stairwell. The school has a fire drill. A teacher tries to get the parent to move out of the way by tapping the parent on the shoulder. The parent falls down the stairs.
>
> Conclusion: ?

Writing an IRAC Paragraph

Let's turn the *McBoyle* logical syllogism into a short IRAC essay. First, we will state the overall *issue* that was before the court. Next, we will describe the *rule(s)* the court applied. Then, we will summarize and paraphrase the court's *analysis*. Finally, we will describe the conclusion reached by the court.

Starting out, students usually want to include facts from the case. Typically, key facts are included in the issue statement that begins your paragraph. If you want to include additional facts, you may do so after the issue statement and before the rule statements.

Summarizing a case is different analyzing a legal problem on your own. The first two steps are similar. You would describe the issue and the rule(s), then you would apply the rules to the facts of your case.

Your application of the rule to fact should reference any analogous cases, include any public policy concerns, and utilize rules of statutory interpretation or other general principles of law. Put simply, you must explain the rationale for your own conclusion. Finally, you would state your conclusion using language of probability rather than certainty (i.e. using "likely" or "probably" rather than must, will, shall).

In addition, as you read the paragraph below. Please consider circling the "transition words," the words that help the reader move between sentences. Transition words assist the reader in following the logical progression of thought.

IRAC PARAGRAPH EXAMPLE

McBoyle v. United States IRAC Paragraph
Student ID No. 215005531

The issue is whether an airplane is considered a "self-propelled vehicle not designed for running on rails" under the NMVTA's definition of "motor vehicle." The NMVTA defines a motor vehicle as an "automobile, automobile truck, automobile wagon, motor cycle, or any other self-propelled vehicle not designed for running on rails." The court examined several factors when applying this rule. First, it looked at the plain meaning of the term "vehicle." The court found the ordinary meaning of the word might not include airplanes. The court also examined other state statutes and other sections of the U.S. Code, which did not include airplane in the word "vehicle." Moreover, the court found that an airplane did not fit into the same category as the other specific items listed in the statute. In addition, the court considered that the legislative history never mentioned aircraft in conjunction with the NMVTA. Finally, the court held that a criminal statute should be interpreted give "fair warning" and should be narrowly interpreted. The court concluded that the clause "self-propelled vehicle not designed for running on rails" only includes vehicles that run on land, not ones that fly. For all these reasons, the court concluded that an airplane is not considered a "motor vehicle" under the NMVTA.

[10]

LEGAL REASONING: AN EXERCISE

WRITING EXERCISE 1 (W1)

Please read the following case.

The goal of this chapter is to summarize legal reasoning from an expert, the judge who wrote this case. You are to create an IRAC paragraph like the *McBoyle* example in the preceding chapter.

This is Writing Assignment number 1. "W1" in your syllabus.

CASE READING

Port Huron Machinery Co., Limited, v. Wohlers

Supreme Court of Iowa, 1928

207 Iowa 826

DE GRAFF, J. This case involves an alleged contract containing a stipulation for liquidated damages. If a contract did result, there can be no question that the plaintiff is entitled to recover, since the terms of the alleged contract clearly fixes the amount recoverable by plaintiff in case of a breach. *See Pace v. Zellmer, 194 Iowa, 516, 186 N. W. 420.*

This appeal presents but one question. It is a question of law and calls for the statement of the applicable legal principle. But, like every other case, the governing principle arises out of a fact situation. It is said in *Steffes v. Hale et al.*, 204 Iowa, 226, 215 N. W. 248:

> "It is almost a legal maxim that 'out of the facts the law arises,' since, if there be no state of facts, there can be no question of law."

We necessarily first turn to the factual side.

On July 18, 1927, a written order signed by the defendant was delivered to plaintiff's agent, and in that order the plaintiff was directed to deliver immediately, or as soon thereafter as possible, to the defendant on board cars consigned to the order of plaintiff at Neola, Iowa, defendant's place of residence, certain described goods (farm machinery). The order further states that the defendant will receive the machinery, pay the freight charges, and also pay to the plaintiff on or before the arrival of the machinery the sum of $1,562.50 in the manner and form recited in the order. Further:

> "If, for any reason, the purchaser fails to accept and settle for the machinery order, he will, if the company so elects and demands, pay to the company, in lieu of the enforcement of this contract, as liquidated damages, a sum equal to ten percent. of the list price, and, if shipment has been made, freight from the factory and return, demurrage, cartage, loading and unloading expense and all other similar expenses actually incurred by reason of the shipment and attempted delivery of said machinery; if suit is commenced to enforce the performance of any part of this contract the purchaser agrees to pay a reasonable attorney's fee."

The plaintiff's agent immediately, upon the signing of this order by defendant, telephoned the plaintiff at Des Moines the receipt of the order and requested that the goods be loaded and sent forthwith to the defendant. On July 20, 1927, the plaintiff filled the order in accordance with its terms and shipped the goods. On July 22, 1927, the plaintiff received a telegram from the defendant bearing date July 21, which said:

> "Delivery date specified on thresher deal now past and order is hereby cancelled."

The plaintiff, as a result of defendant's attempt to revoke and cancel the order and his refusal to accept the goods, was obliged to recall the goods and reship them to the point of delivery, thereby incurring certain expense which was established by competent proof upon the trial of this case. True, the defendant in his answer alleged a condition precedent, but the allegation continued to rest in the answer. It finds no support in the evidence. When the plaintiff rested its case, motions for a directed verdict were made respectively by the parties. The plaintiff's motion was sustained. The question, therefore, at this point, is whether the plaintiff established a prima facie case. The contention of the defendant on appeal is that the plaintiff failed to prove a contract for the reason that there is no showing that the plaintiff accepted the offer of the defendant and communicated the acceptance of the offer prior to its revocation by the defendant.

The point is now reached that we may discuss the law involved under the undisputed facts. Did a contract result? It is not practicable, or is it necessary, in a definition of contract, to state all of the operative facts, or all of the legal relations that are created by such facts. A "contract" may be defined as a promise, the performance of which the law recognizes as a duty and for a breach of which a remedy is given. A contract, therefore, does not contemplate simply the act of promising, but obligations arising therefrom. The law recognizes, as a matter of classification, two kinds of contracts--unilateral and bilateral. In the case at bar a typical example of unilateral contract is found, since it is universally agreed that a "unilateral contract" is one in which no promisor receives a promise as consideration, whereas, in a "bilateral contract" there are mutual promises between the two parties to the contract. This matter of definition has recently received careful consideration by the American Law Institute and may be found in the restatement of the law of contracts. Proposed Final Draft No. 1 (April 18, 1928) p. 17, § 12.

In the instant case the offer of the defendant must be viewed as a promise. It is promissory in terms. The rule is well stated by Prof. Williston: A promise which the promisor should reasonably expect to induce action or forbearance of a definite and substantial character on the part of the promisee, and which does induce such action or forbearance, is binding if injustice can be avoided only by enforcement of the promise. *See Williston on Contracts*, vol. 1, § 139. Clearly the instant offer signed by the defendant was of this character. Appellant, however, contends that there was no acceptance of the offer. Words are not the only medium of expression of mutual assent. An offer may invite an acceptance to be made by merely an affirmative answer or by performing a specific act. True, if an act other than a promise is requested, no contract exists until what is requested is performed or tendered in whole or in part. We are here dealing with a unilateral contract, and the act requested and performed as consideration for the contract indicates acceptance as well as furnishes the consideration. The sending of an order for goods to a merchant is an offer of a promise for an act. 13 C. J. p. 266, § 57. In the same text it is said that an acceptance of an offer may be by acts, as where an offer is made that the offerer will pay or do something else if the offeree shall do a particular thing. In such a case performance is the only thing needful to complete the agreement and to create a binding promise. *Id.*, p. 275, § 73. It must be kept in mind that there is a distinction in regard to communication of acceptance between offers which ask that the offeree shall do something, as in the instant case, and offers which ask that the offeree shall promise something. In offers of the latter kind communication of the acceptance is always essential. *Id.*, p. 284, 285, §§ 88, 89.

The decisions of this court are in accord with the general rule. In *Hankins v. Young*, 174 Iowa, 383, 156 N. W. 380, it is said:

> "In the case of an order for goods, the delivery of the goods in pursuance of the order is an acceptance of the order."

To the same effect is *Petroleum Products Distributing Co. v. Alton Tank Line*, 165 Iowa, 398, 146 N. W. 52; *Rock Island Plow Co. v. Meredith*, 107 Iowa, 498, 78 N. W. 233; *McCormick Harvesting Machine Co. v. Markert*, 107 Iowa, 340, 78 N. W. 33. Pertinent language is used in *McCormick Harvesting Machine Co. v. Richardson*, 89 Iowa, 525, 56 N. W. 682, wherein it is said:

> "We do not say that the acceptance must be a formal one. The acceptance might be shown by proving an act done on the faith of the order, such as the shipment of the goods ordered."

An especially clear expression of the rule is found in *McDermott v. Mahoney*, 139 Iowa, 292, 115 N. W. 32, 116 N. W. 788, wherein the written instrument was recognized and held to be a unilateral contract, as it was signed by one party only and by him delivered to the other and accepted as a contract between the parties. It is said:

> "Where a written agreement signed by one party is accepted and adopted by the other, and acted upon, it becomes their contract in the same sense as though both parties had signed it."

See, also, *Reynolds et al. v. Johnson*, 199 Iowa, 1055, 202 N. W. 881.

A typical case adopting the same rule is *Kingman et al. v. Watson*, 97 Wis. 596, 73 N. W. 438. See, also, notes in 19 A. L. R. 476, and 29 A. L. R. 1352.

Certain cases are cited by appellant in brief, but they are distinguishable from the case at bar on the fact side. For instance: In *Thompson & Sons Mfg. Co. v. Perkins & Son*, 97 Iowa, 607, 66 N. W 874, the order was given in November, 1892, for goods to be shipped February 14, 1893. The offeree made no acceptance, either formal or by shipment, and two weeks before shipment date the offer was revoked. The revocation was held legally permissible under the facts. The same is true in *Hargrove v. Crawford*, 159 Iowa, 522, 141 N. W. 423; *Durkee v. Schultz*, 122 Iowa, 410, 98 N. W 149; *Doll & Smith v. A. & S. Sanitary Dairy Co.*, 202 Iowa, 786, 211 N. W. 230.

The instant appeal primarily has an educational value. The applicable legal principle is well settled on both reason and authority.

The judgment entered by the trial court is *affirmed*.

STEVENS, C. J., and ALBERT, MORLING, and WAGNER, JJ., concur.

GRADING RUBRIC

Please follow your professor's instructions.

In general, writing assignments are graded out of 25 points. Five points allotted for each of the following five categories: (1) format (2) grammar; (3) IRAC organization; (4) paraphrasing, synthesizing, summarizing; and (5) IRAC Reasoning.

Other professors may grade along the same lines but emphasize different categories, for example: (1) formatting and IRAC organization; (2) overall readability; (3) issue and rule; (4) analysis and conclusion; and (5) citations and quotations.

As for the format, in general, papers should be one page only; one paragraph only; 12-point font Courier New; double-spaced; with 1 inch margins (2.54 cm). Your paper should include a title line. Finally, your name should not be on the paper. Rather, your student ID should be on the paper.

As for grammar or readability, the grader will look for fluency in English as well as control of vocabulary and number and significance of grammar errors. Because this is only 1/5 of the grade, one's grammar can be weak and one can still receive a decent score on the assignment. However, if a paper lacks basic comprehensibility, that might affect the score in other categories.

As for organization, the grader looks for the following types of things: is there a topic sentence (usually an issue statement); has the student summarized the rules and ordered them from general to specific; has the student included analogous cases if any; has the student summarized the court's holding (in the case of *Port Huron*) or explained the student's own prediction as to what a court is likely to do; has the student made a conclusion at the end. Finally, has the student used good signal or transition words to guide the reader between points.

As for paraphrasing, summarizing, and synthesizing, let's first look at some definitions. Paraphrasing means putting someone else's writing in your own words. Summarizing means taking a long or complex writing and making it shorter. Synthesizing means combining two or more different sources to form a whole or singular idea.

When it comes to paraphrasing, we will look at how well the student expressed the key idea from the original source. For example, did the student distort or change the main idea? Did the student mistake any legal terms of art? Did the student cut and paste big chunks or use quotes poorly?

As to synthesis, did the student identify key commonalities between similar sources?

As to summarizing, did the student use significantly fewer words (a 1 to 3 ratio is common).

Finally, as to logic, the grader will examine whether the student has built a "legal proof." When summarizing cases, like *Port Huron*, did the student properly describe the court's reasoning. In the alternative, if presented with a new factual situation, like a research problem, did the student show how the client's facts satisfy the rule of law using case analogies where possible?

Did the student properly state the issue? Did the student properly summarize the rules? Where applicable, did the student include analogous case descriptions? Did the student apply the rule to client's case, utilizing analogous cases to do so? Did the student articulate a reasonable conclusion using language of probability?

Grading Example

See the *McBoyle* IRAC paragraph in the preceding chapter.

[11]

Researching Secondary Sources

Introduction to Secondary Sources

Secondary sources are distinguished from primary sources. A primary source is the law itself: a statute, a case, a regulation. Meanwhile, a secondary source is a writing about the law: for example, an encyclopedia, a treatise, or a law journal article.

You might think about it like this: the Bible is the primary source of God's law for protestant Christians. However, there are many helpful commentaries, concordances, and other writings about the Bible. These writings might help you understand the Bible better.

Of course, there is no substitute for actually reading the Bible itself.

Similarly, a legal reader might start with a secondary source. A secondary source might explain a complex area of law. However, it is always a reader's responsibility to read and understand the primary source.

Primary sources may be binding authority. Secondary sources almost never are.

Unless a secondary source has been adopted as the law in a jurisdiction, as sometimes happens with the Restatements of Law, it is persuasive only.

Introduction to Authority

Another distinction between primary and secondary sources is their usefulness as authority.

The following discussion might be too "theoretical." If you find it helpful, great. If not, that's okay. You might consider marking this page and coming back to it at the end of your 1L year.

Some primary authority is binding. Everything else is persuasive.

Secondary sources are, almost always, merely persuasive. Therefore, they are rarely cited in documents to the court.

Why?

Because the courts don't have to obey secondary sources.

The only reason you would cite to a persuasive, secondary source is if the citation somehow made your argument sound more persuasive. For instance, you might cite to an expert treatise like Prosser and Keaton on Torts.

The reasons we cite to authority in the first place is to tell the court what the law says in order to convince the court of what it must do.

Authority isn't binding till you convince the judge that it is.

You might think about there being a range of authority. The closer a statute, case, or policy is to your case, the more likely a court is to apply it.

As a new law student, you might naively think courts have to follow every statute and case. However, consider the approach advocated by one famous judge, Richard Posner:

> My approach in judging a case is therefore not to worry initially about doctrine, precedent, and the other conventional materials of legal analysis, but instead to try to figure out the sensible solution to the problem or problems presented by the case. Once having found what I think is the sensible solution I ask whether it's blocked by an authoritative precedent of the Supreme Court or by some other ukase that judges must obey. If it's not blocked (usually it's not—usually it can be got around by hook or by crook), I say fine—let's go with the commonsense solution."
>
> . . .

> The time to look up precedents, statutory text, legislative history, and the other conventional materials of judicial decision making is *after* one has a sense of what the best decision should be for today's society.[1]

In Judge Posner's approach, a judge decides the right thing to do, then finds legal precedent to justify his decision.

Similarly, in the 2017 fight over President Trump's executive orders on immigration, it seemed as though certain lower courts cared more about the mental state of the President than the actual language of the order or the plain language of the statute. The Supreme Court's decision, thankfully, preserved the appearance of the rule of law in America.

Even then, a district court judge in Hawaii seemingly ignored the Supreme Court order.

If a federal judge can ignore federal statutes and Supreme Court precedent—two primary sources of law—what's the point of citing to secondary sources?

Regardless, as for secondary sources, there's usually no question. They are not binding. A court does not have to follow them.

The only question is whether citing to a secondary source will make your brief more persuasive. If not, you might consider "borrowing" the argument without revealing the source.

You might ask, *isn't that plagiarism*?

In law school, we ask you to cite your sources and not to plagiarize. By plagiarize, we mean taking someone else's ideas or exact wording and presenting them as your own. We are testing your ability to reason as well as write.

However, in the real world, there's no copyright on an argument. People might disapprove of you borrowing an argument—as they do of comedians who steal another's jokes. There may be some copyright in the words themselves. Some law firms try to copyright the briefs they file in court.

---

[1] Richard Posner, *The Federal Judiciary* 18 (2017)

The only time I can recall a lawyer getting in trouble for cutting and pasting is a case where the lawyer copied an entire brief. The lawyer did not get in trouble for plagiarism though. The lawyer got in trouble because he charged the client as if he'd written the brief himself.

Even when using primary authority, one might consider whether it is a good idea to cite to it in your legal writing. For example, imagine you found a good argument from a trial court in South Dakota in the year 1915. Would it be persuasive to cite that decision to a federal circuit court? If not, steal the argument and move on.

Just don't overbill your client.

About Secondary Sources

Secondary sources are helpful for when you need to learn a new area of law.

For example, you might read a code concerning the tax burden of non-profit organizations that reads something like the following:

> For purposes of paragraph (3), an organization described in paragraph (2) shall be deemed to include an organization described in section 501(c)(4), (5), or (6) which would be described in paragraph (2) if it were an organization described in section 501(c)(3).[2]

You might not be familiar with non-profit tax law. Even if you were, you might need help understanding that piece of code.

Secondary sources are useful for understanding an unfamiliar area of law. Sometimes, you won't even know how to generate an effective keyword search. You might not know the terms of art for a particular area of law. In such instances, you might begin your legal research by consulting a secondary source.

Secondary sources are also helpful if you are looking for similar statutes or similar cases from other jurisdictions.

---

[2] 26 U.S.C. § 509(a).

In the alternative, you might be dealing with a new or novel area of law. For instance, how the law should regulate crypto-currencies like Bitcoin.

However, please be aware that secondary sources may not be up to date. For example, a law review article from five years ago would not include the most recent judicial or legislative action. Hence, you must always read the primary sources yourself.

COMMON SECONDARY SOURCES

Let's consider a list of sources in light of the following factual problem:

> You work for KIA Motor Company in Korea. They are launching a new car line in America. The car is aimed at young millennials. Marketing wants to call it the "Kia Kickass" sports utility vehicle. As their lawyer, you are concerned about whether you can obtain trademark protection for the word "Kickass" because it might be considered a scandalous word (bad word).

The applicable statute, 15 U.S.C. § 1052(a), reads as follows:

> No trademark by which the goods of the applicant may be distinguished from the goods of others shall be refused registration on the principal register on account of its nature unless it—
>
> (a) Consists of or comprises immoral, deceptive, or scandalous matter; or matter which may disparage or falsely suggest a connection with persons, living or dead, institutions, beliefs, or national symbols, or bring them into contempt, or disrepute . . . .[3]

Is Kia Kickass "immoral" or "scandalous"?

The answer might be clear from the plain language of the statute. Or you might need to learn more about offensive trademarks. Or you might be completely unfamiliar with the area of trademark or intellectual property law.

---

[3] This statute will be before the U.S. Supreme Court in the 2019 term over the trademark name "FUCT." Jan Wolfe, *U.S. Supreme Court to Hear Challenge to Ban on Profane Trademarks*, Reuters, Jan. 4, 2019.

Secondary sources can help.

Many secondary sources not only explain the law, they also link you to primary sources like statutes and cases. Many will also link you to other helpful secondary sources!

1. The Internet

Anything you read online about the law is a secondary source. Usually, you wouldn't cite to internet sources. For instance, you'd never cite to Wikipedia. However, these sources can be very helpful in understanding the law.

An Internet search is usually the first step in any legal research project.

Considering our Kia Kickass example above, you might be surprised how much you can learn online without access to a commercial database.

You might have to! If you practice with a Korean law firm or company, you may not have access to Westlaw or Lexis Advance.

2. Legal Encyclopedias

There are two main legal encyclopedias: American Jurisprudence and Corpus Juris Secundum.[4] Many states have their own legal encyclopedias.

Like normal encyclopedias, legal encyclopedias are organized alphabetically. They provide a broad overview of a particular area of law.

Legal encyclopedias may include references to a few, important primary sources of law. Usually these cases are older than your professors: really ancient stuff.

In our trademark hypothetical above, a legal encyclopedia might help you understand the basics of trademark law and might include a brief mention about immoral or scandalous marks. If you are lucky, it might include a citation to a primary source that you can use to

---

[4] Literally, "body of law, second."

expand your legal research. For example, it might point you to a key case.

3. American Law Reports

Commonly abbreviated as A.L.R., the American Law Reports contains annotations on specific areas of law compiled by a legal expert. They usually begin with a bit of commentary. Then they aggregate and summarize cases from across multiple jurisdictions.

Research geniuses (like Dean Enlow) suggest starting your legal research by looking for an applicable A.L.R. If you find one, you are "golden." You can easily find factually similar cases from your jurisdiction and from across the country.

However, unlike a legal encyclopedia, not every legal topic has an annotation.

In our Kia Kickass trademark problem above, an A.L.R. annotation, if one exists, might compile summaries of cases where a trademark has or has not been found to be immoral or scandalous. What a goldmine!

In print, A.L.R. annotations are updated with "pocket parts"—supplements printed and placed in the back of the volume. A.L.R. annotations online may also be updated from time to time.

4. Restatements of Law

Restatements of Law are helpful when researching common law issues.

The Restatements of Law consist of a series of publications written by legal experts at the American Law Institute. The Restatements are a compilation or "restatement" of the common law rules in a particular area of law like torts, contracts, property, etcetera.

You might think about the Restatement as a codification of the common law. Because they are written like statutes, legislatures sometimes adopt them. The highest courts of some jurisdictions have adopted sections of the Restatement, making it their primary, binding law.

The Restatements usually summarize the "majority rule"—that is, the rule as it is found in most jurisdictions. However, it might also note the "minority rule" or emerging legal trends.

The Restatements may provide citations to a few, important authorities that can be used to expand your legal research. They also provide commentary on the law as well as illustrations—factual hypotheticals—that might be used in the same way you would use an analogous case precedent.

As to the Kia Kickass trademark issue, the Restatements probably wouldn't help much since trademark is a federal statutory issue and not a common law problem.

5. Treatises

In a treatise, legal experts systematically share everything they know about an area of law. A treatise may consist of a single book or it might be a multi-volume series, for example Prosser and Keaton on Torts or Williston on Contracts.

If you begin to practice in an area of law, it would be wise to pick up the corresponding treatise and read it cover to cover. For example, students who become immigration lawyers are encouraged to read Kurzban's excellent treatise on immigration law.

Treatises may be cited to a court. For example, you may see Prosser and Keaton on Torts cited in the cases you've read for Torts class. In such instances, the expert's opinion might be consulted as an authority concerning a contentious or ambiguous question of law.

In our Kia Kickass example, a treatise on trademark law (similar to Nimmer on copyright) would be very helpful in understanding both trademark law and our particular issue. You could expect to find a detailed analysis of the statute as well as citations and explanations of the most important cases.

6. Legal Periodicals

Every law school publishes a legal journal or two. Most legal journals in America are run by students. There is no peer review process. (Professors in Asia who are unfamiliar with student-led journals may be uncomfortable finding themselves being edited by students.)

Law review students often have to write an article to get course credit. Law professors have to publish law review articles in order to get tenure.

Law review articles usually cover emerging areas of law. They might address problems or conflicts in the law; propose solutions; identify new legal theories; advocate for change; offer insights to practitioners; or provide practical and substantive advice.

Judges and practitioners may publish for the sheer joy of it. Theirs are some of the more helpful law review articles.

Regardless, hundreds and hundreds of articles are published each year. A few manage to say something useful.

Law journal articles can be found in print in your law library. Nobody reads journals cover to cover anymore. Like building a good "mix-tape," there used to be an art to compiling an issue of a law review. Now, we read individual, isolated articles, usually in a commercial online database. Westlaw and Lexis Advance publish many journal articles. SSRN offers law articles online for free. However, the best commercial database for journal articles may be Hein Online.

In addition to articles written for law reviews, articles written for professional publications, like state bar journals, can be even more helpful from a legal research perspective.

Blogs and articles online even more so.

Be careful though. There's no way to update law articles. The reader is responsible for making sure that the primary sources haven't changed.

Considering our Kia Kickass challenge, you might find numerous articles writing about immoral and scandalous trademarks. Intellectual property law is always a hot topic. You should find articles that discuss the statute as well as some of the key cases. This particular statute is before the U.S. Supreme Court in 2019; hence, there's bound to be tons of law journal articles discussing and debating it.

7. State Practice Guides

Many states publish their own practice guides. These guides may include the elements of a cause of action as well as key cases.

As Professor Seefried notes, for many practicing lawyers, the first (and last) step is to look up the issue in the state practice guide.

Many of these guides are available online on Westlaw and Lexis.

Researching Secondary Sources

In the next two chapters, you will get a chance to research using secondary sources.

Remember, the goal of legal research is to find mandatory, binding (primary) authority in answer to your legal question.

Secondary sources are a means to find and understand primary sources.

Commercial databases like Westlaw and Lexis Advance feature many secondary sources. These databases also link directly from secondary sources to primary sources, making it even easier to find helpful materials.

Sometimes there are so many sources that it might feel a bit overwhelming.

First, we need to think about using the right tool for the job. Consider which secondary source is a good fit for the type of research you are doing. For instance, if you need general information about an area of law, look up a legal encyclopedia or state practice guide.

If you are researching a novel area of law, try searching law journals. If you need to locate factually similar cases across multiple jurisdictions, try American Law Reports.

When it comes to *print* research, make sure to *update your research* by looking for a pocket-part in the back of the book. Pocket parts are small pamphlets that law library use to update hardbound volumes. They are placed in the back of the respective volume. Then, when the next series of the encyclopedia comes out, those updates are included in the book itself.

Whichever source you choose, when it comes to *print* research, there are three basic ways to proceed (after locating the source in your law library):

1. Find by citation

If you know the citation where the material is located, you can simply look it up.

In our law library, this is the only way to find law journal articles. Maintaining an index for the hundreds of journals published each year is too much trouble. Meanwhile, we don't carry enough journals to justify keeping a commercial law journal index. Nevertheless, if you know the name of the journal as well as the volume and page number, you can look it up.

2. Find by table of contents

If you are using an encyclopedia, the subjects are arranged alphabetically. For example, trademark would be covered in the volume(s) covering the letter "T."

If you are using another source, like a Restatement of Law or a treatise, you can use a table of contents (usually located in the front of each volume) to locate the subject you are searching for.

3. Find by keyword

Most commonly you will start with a keyword search in an "index."

An "index" is a book or series of books that point you to a particular topic. For example, you could look up "trademark" in the index for American Jurisprudence.

As for American Law Reports, you *must* use the index. The A.L.R. publishes annotations chronologically, not by subject. Hence, to find an annotation on your topic, it would take ages if you tried to page through every volume. You should use the index.

Print research can present unusual difficulties. For instance, A.L.R. is published in a multi-volume series, for example: A.L.R; A.L.R.2d; and A.L.R.3d.

You can think about this like a comic book reboot. Imagine D.C. got tired of Batman #829 and reset the series to #1!

That happens with legal volumes too.

The problem is, each A.L.R. series might have its own index!

Therefore, in order to search all of the A.L.R., back to the very first annotation ever published, you might have to consult several indexes. (Anticipating this problem, the A.L.R. includes a "Quick Index" that indexes some of the most popular annotations from every series.)

Conclusion

Electronic research mirrors print research. For example, if you know a citation to a source, you can look it up directly. Or you can search an index online or execute a keyword search.

Aren't you glad that computers came along?

The reason we do research in print is that, for now, most online legal research is based on print sources. You need to understand the print sources to get the most out of online research. That is slowly changing and, with yearly improvements to Westlaw and Lexis Advance, the analogies between print research and electronic research are growing weaker.

Two final notes.

One, secondary sources can be wrong. Don't fully trust them. They are a crutch for understanding the primary sources. Maybe they're not wrong *per se*, but as you come to fully understand the law, you might find yourself disagreeing with them. Read the primary sources for yourself.

Two, *the ebb and flow of legal research is from secondary sources to primary sources*. Secondary sources should be used as a starting point for finding or understanding primary, mandatory authority. A good secondary source will point you to other secondary sources. It will also point you to primary source, which in turn, might lead to other primary or secondary sources, and so on and so forth until you've exhausted every source.

[12]

Secondary Sources: Research & Writing Exercise

Writing Exercise 2 (W2)

Please read the following facts. Answer the problem assigned to you by your professor. Please follow your professor's instructions for turning in the assignment.

Finally, please note that, while the following fact pattern may seem complicated, it is very similar (in length and scope) to what you might see on a law school final exam.

Recall these three steps from the preceding chapter when it comes to researching secondary sources in print:

1. **Use an index (word search) or table of contents search;**
2. **Locate the material in the main text;** ***and***
3. **Update your research (pocket parts).**

Game Night, Inc.

It is an early Monday morning in the sleepy little town of San Jacinto, the capitol of the new state of Tex-Mexico.

You have just gotten your second cup of coffee and are settling into the ergonomically designed chair behind your desk, when your secretary pages you, informing you that a client is waiting outside your office. You haven't even had time to check your e-mail yet. Cursing your rotten luck and Mondays, you tell your secretary to show in the client.

In walks Clint East. You recognize Clint from the legal work that you did for him on a real estate deal—when Clint renovated and ran a historic old inn called the Ramrock Inn.

Clint says that he wants to talk to you about his newest business venture. Turning his hobby into a business, Clint opened Game Night, a store that sells board games and card games.

Game Night is located in a strip mall in a part of San Jacinto that is undergoing gentrification.

Normally, you'd be happy to see Clint, but he looks troubled. His eyes are bloodshot and dark circles have formed underneath them.

You nod, thoughtfully. Pulling out your trusty Parker Pen and yellow legal pad, you say to Clint, "What brings you to my office."

Clint's Story

I am getting sued by a bunch of people and charged with various crimes.

I thought running a game and toy store would be awesome. But it's turning into such a headache.

Sure. Parts of it are fun. I get to play all the latest games before they come out.

Each night of the week, we host a different game night. Mondays are Magic: The Gathering. Real old school.

Tuesday nights feature the Game of Thrones card game. Wednesdays are for Settlers of Catan. Thursdays features miniatures games like Warhammer or Star Wars: X-wing Fighter.

Fridays are for special events. Next week, we're having a Keyforge tournament.

Saturdays, of course, are for Pokemon card players—the young types.

You get the idea.

I even got into creating and promoting new games.

For example, I think I told you about the time I spent in Korea? I was working as an English teacher in Busan.

I wanted to introduce some Korean games to America.

I designed a version of a classic Korean game: Yut Nori. It is a lot like the board game "Sorry." You move your pieces around a board and try to finish first. But instead of dice, you use wood sticks.

Well, on a Friday night last month, I hosted a Yut tournament. To enter the tournament, players had to purchase a game of Yut from my store, valued at $5. Then, the winner of the tournament got a $100 cash prize.

Two people dressed in suits and wearing dark sunglasses joined the tournament.

Afterward, they identified themselves as local detectives and said they were arresting me for gambling. According to them, the law says that a person "engages in gambling when he stakes or risks something of value upon the outcome of a contest of chance."

Well, I told them Yut was not a game of chance. Sure, you throw the sticks, but you have to use skill and strategy.

They told me to "Tell it to the judge."

If only that was the end of my problems.

I also developed a collectible card game. I call the game Mudang-mon. It is based on Korean shamanism. The players control spirits, called shins, and battle each other. My game, Mudang-mon, is played exactly like the Pokemon card game.[1]

We have been promoting the heck out of Mudang-mon.

But after my arrest, I have become wary. I had announced a tournament for Mudang-mon at my game store. For a small entry fee of

---

[1] https://hobbylark.com/card-games/PlayPoketcgDummy.

$10, participants would get a chance at winning a cash prize for the winner of $10,000.

The announcement blew up on social media. People were going to come from all over the country.

But now I'm a bit worried that I might get in trouble.

The state prosecutors might charge me again with gambling, saying that Mudang-mon is a game of chance.

I don't think they're right. I think it's a game of skill like bridge or hearts. In fact, maybe even more skill than poker. You have to play smart and analyze your opponent psychologically. Does he like water spirits or earth spirits?

Each player creates his own card deck of 60 cards. However, they shuffle their decks before playing.

You get the idea.

What do you think?

The reason that I am asking is that I've already had some legal issues with Mudang-mon that are costing me a small fortune to defend.

A buddy of mine who runs a game store up in Las Vegas, Nevada held a small Mudang-mon event. The cash prize was $10,000.

Each player had to play with an official 60 card deck purchased brand new from the store.

For the final round, the players were given, free of charge, a brand new, 60 card Mudang-mon deck from the store.

Unfortunately, one of the card decks from the final round didn't have the requisite number of "level-up" cards. The defect wasn't discovered till the end of the tournament.

The player with the defective deck lost the tournament.

He wants to sue me, as the manufacturer of the cards, for breach of warranty.

In addition, I am being sued by my friend, Chuck Turpen. Chuck agreed to invest some money to help us trademark and copyright the game as well as to help manufacture the first run of the card game. We had a contract that said he would get twenty-percent of the net profit as well as his name on the product. Every edition of Mudang-mon would say "Created by Clint East" followed by "a Chuck Turpen Production."

Chuck thought the publicity would help him promote his own board game called "Crafty Carpenter."

But Chuck never ponied up the cash. Nada. Zip. He defaulted. He never paid for anything.

So, when the game came out and became super popular, I didn't pay him anything. I also didn't put his name on it. Why should I?

Chuck is suing me. He wants money, sure. But he also wants to force me to put his name on every pack of Mudang-mon cards.

As if!

Well, that's all the exciting stuff. I got another run-of-the-mill type problem.

One of my part-time workers, Kate Kinney—you know her, the one who was supposed to be marrying Zeke? Remember, she has been working on her women's study degree at the University of Tex-Mexico for the past 6 years, with no end in sight.

She had a slip and fall in the store and is blaming me for it. Even though she was the one doing the mopping and made the floor wet.

Well, I got service of process from the federal courthouse. The federal courthouse! Since when is a slip and fall a federal offense?

I called her out on Facebook!

She says she is from out of state. She intends to return to Georgia whenever she finishes her degree. As if that is ever going to happen.

Anyhow, she says that her attorney told her she can sue me in federal court.

Sure, her hometown is in Georgia. But she came here six years ago to go to college. As her employer, I even have a copy of her driver's license. It's from right here in Tex-Mexico.

She's not the only employee that is suing me.

I hired some Youtube vloggers to make some videos reviewing and showing walkthroughs on how to play Mudang-mon.

One of the guys, his username is OldGuyPlays. He made some videos. I paid him a contingency fee for each video posted. There were incentives if the videos got more views. But he uses his own computer, his own equipment. I don't pay taxes or health insurance on him. It's a straight-up commission assignment.

Well, I had to let him go because he used some bad language in one of his videos.

But now, he says he is going to sue me for "age discrimination" saying I am firing him because he is too old and uncool. Well, maybe he is, but that's not why I'm firing him. And how can he sue me for employment discrimination when I'm not his employer? Riddle me that, Batman!

And, gosh, I haven't even gotten to the good stuff yet.

Remember how I was telling you about Mudang-mon? Well, just last week I got a cease and desist letter from Nintendo USA. To be honest, I kind of geeked out a little. How cool is that?

What was uncool about it is that they want me to stop using Mudang-mon as they say it is too close to their trademark for Pokemon.

Whatever!

Oh, and there's one final thing, but it's kind of personal. After the Friday night game nights, we take our volunteers, our employees, and certain valued customers to "Smartys," the restaurant next door. We buy them food and have a good old time.

Except, one of my business partners feels very strongly about alcohol. He doesn't want any business money being spent on drinks. So, I always end up buying the drinks out of my own pocket.

Is there any way I can deduct that for income tax purposes? I know you're not a licensed CPA, but what do you think, old buddy, old pal?

Your Assignment

After listening to Clint's story, you tell him that you will look into his case and will have an answer for him soon.

You may use any facts from Clint's story as well as any facts included in the question itself. If you infer a fact, please let the reader know that it is an inference rather than a known fact.

To answer the question, you must use the *print* copies of American Jurisprudence Second Series and/or American Law Reports located in the law library. Initially, **you *may not* use online sources**.

If you start with online sources, you may fail this assignment. (Your professor may allow you to use an online source *after* you've located the correct secondary source in print. Please follow your professor's instructions.)

You should answer one question below, as assigned by your professor.

Your answer should be in the form of a one page, one paragraph IRAC writing assignment. Assignments should be in 12-point Courier New font, double spaced, with one-inch margins. Your paper should include a title. Your paper should also include your student ID number, not your name.

Your IRAC paragraph must include a rule as well as at least one helpful case or comment that you find as a result of that secondary source research.

Please return the library books to the exact location as soon as you locate the proper secondary source.

> Question 1: According to American Jurisprudence 2d on Gambling, when it comes to the definition of chance or skill, is Yut Nori a game of chance? How does a New York case (involving mahjong) from 2009 impact your answer?

> Question 2: According to American Law Reports Second Series, is Mudang-mon, a card game like bridge, a game of chance? How does a California case from 1962 impact your answer?

> Question 3: According to American Jurisprudence Second Series, regarding damages for contracts, and injunctions in particular, what equitable considerations apply in general to someone like Chuck who defaulted on their obligations? Can Chuck force performance on the contract even though he himself is in default? How does the Washington state case from 1923 impact your answer?

Question 4: According to American Jurisprudence Second Series, regarding diversity of citizenship, is an out-of-state college student like Kate likely to be considered a resident of Tex-mexico or of her home state Georgia? How does a 1976 case from the federal district court in Rhode Island impact your answer?

Question 5: According to the American Law Reports Fourth Series, when it comes to Toys and Games and recovering tort damages for legal card games, can the Mudang-mon tournament loser from Nevada sue the Mudang-mon card manufacturer (Clint) for breach of warranty? How does a case a federal court case in Nevada from 1981 impact your answer? (Please read to the end of that case.)

Question 6: According to American Jurisprudence Second Series, what is the rule about job discrimination concerning independent contractors? How does a case concerning a salesman named *Kirby v. Robby Len Swimfashions* from 1990 affect your answer?

Question 7: According to the American Law Reports, Federal Series, what is the Trademark rule when it comes to famous marks? According to that annotation, as to toys & games, how does the *Toys R Us* case from 1996 impact your answer?

Question 8: According to the America Law Reports First Series, what is the rule concerning income tax and entertainment expenses? How does the case of an actor named *Blackmer* from 1934 affect your answer? (That case is actually located as the preceding entry to your ALR annotation in case you want to read it in full.)

Sample Assignment

Sample problem: Using American Jurisprudence second series, will a Mudang-mon tournament at Clint's store likely be defined as gambling? Is it a card game that, like poker, is a game of chance rather than a game of skill? How does the North Carolina appellate court case from 2007 impact your answer?

Sample answer: Students should write a 1 page, IRAC paragraph similar to the sample below. To do this, students would need to find the "index" for the print edition of American Jurisprudence 2d.

Students should look in the index under volume G for "Gambling." Students may look up the sub-topic "Card Games" and, under that, "Poker." The index points students to "Gambling § 35."

Students should then locate the Am. Jur. 2d title on Gambling (browsing alphabetically). Locate and read section 35 of that title.

Section 35 may provide some rules and examples. For instance, a footnote in that section cites to *Joker Club, LLC.* That case is found in volume 183 of the North Carolina appellate court reporter on page 92. It is a 2002 case.

Students should do an internet search to locate and read the *Joker Club, LLC* case. For example, students could enter the following search terms: joker club llc 183 nc app 92.

Students should write an IRAAC paragraph based on this research. Meaning: state the issue; give the rule along with any sub-rule(s) from the case; describe the facts and holding of the case; apply the rules with reference to the analogous case (comparing its facts to the facts of our case); then, make a predictive conclusion.

GRADING EXAMPLE

What follows is an example from the ***first draft*** of a student paper. The font and line spacing have been altered. You should double space and use 12-point Courier New font.

Writing Assignment 2
Student ID # 21305501

The issue is whether defendant is liable. Extreme and outrageous conduct is the conduct that has been so outrageous in character, and so extreme in degree, as to go beyond all possible bounds of decency, and to be regarded as atrocious, and utterly intolerable in a civilized community. It is for the jury to determine whether the conduct has been sufficiently extreme and outrageous to result in liability. The first example of outrageous conduct is that A, the president of a company, summons B and in the presence of an intimidating group of associates tells B that B has been collecting rubbish in territory which the association regards as exclusively allocated to one of its members. A

Issue statement too broad, try to drill down to element at issue. Also please indent your paragraph. And please use a transition word to move to rule sentence.

If you use exact language you must use quotation marks !!!!!!

Have you properly stated the rule here? Also, please use transition words to move into the rule!!!

Good analogies, but (1) your examples are too long. Need to synthesize these two cases. Cut this part in half.

(2) Also, use descriptive terms not A and B

demands that B pay over the proceeds of his rubbish collection, and tells B that if he doesn't do so the association will beat him up, destroy his truck, and put him out of business. B suffers severe emotional distress. In the second example, A is invited to a swimming party at an exclusive resort. B gives her a bathing suit which he knows will dissolve in water. It dissolves while she is swimming, leaving her naked in the presence of people whom she has just met. A suffers extreme embarrassment. These two examples are different from our case: their acts were carried out on the basis of the certain knowledge of their results; in our case, the school and the church did not know the results of firing the plaintiff and shunning her. Thus, the church's conduct was not outrageous per the Restatement. Restatement (Second) of Torts § 46 (1965).

Don't use contractions -- like "doesn't"-- in formal writing

Good transition here.

What is "knowledge"?!! If you apply a rule, you must mention it in the rules

Would people say "outrageous" at these two instances? What about in our case? Careful fact comparison!

Finally, use language of probability: "likely," or "probably," not "was not"

GRADE:

Format: 5 (title, font, margin, line spacing all correct; indent your paragraph)

Grammar: 4 (pretty good job, but you "borrowed" a lot of language)

IRAAC Organization: 3 (issue statement needs improvement, needs signal words between points, use short sentences)

Paraphrasing / Synthesizing / Summarizing: 1 (this part was the weakest, no more plagiarism. Use quotation marks.)

IRAAC Reasoning: 3 (Didn't apply the rule you gave me to the facts in our case.)

Total: 16/25

TOP TEN TIPS

Do you want to make the best score on your IRAC paragraph? Then don't neglect these very common mistakes!

1. When giving a case name, try saying: "In the <u>Smith</u> case," or "In <u>Smith</u>." Never say, "In <u>Smith</u> case,"; omitting the article "the" is a big no-no!
2. When referring to case precedent, use past tense verbs.
3. When referring to a case precedent, always say in "that" case. When referring to the facts of your own case, always say in "this" case. Never use "this" case to refer to a case precedent. It will confuse a legal reader! When legal readers hear, "in this case," they are mentally ready to hear an analysis of the facts of our case.
4. When referring to our case always use the word "here." Never use the word "there." Actually, use the word "there" or "in that case" when referring to case precedent.
5. When you make a quotation, always put the final quotation mark on the outside of the punctuation like this: "I am quoting a sentence from a case." Do you see how the period is inside the quotation mark? This is the American way. British people use a different system. I prefer the British way. But Americans will think it is "wrong." The only exception is when using a "semicolon"; the semicolon will go outside the quotation marks. Don't ask me why!
6. When you list a series of items, separate each item with a comma. Like if I tell you to always write clear phrases, sentences, and paragraphs, I must use a comma between sentence and paragraph. Do you see that comma? It is called a serial comma or Oxford comma: X, Y, and Z. News journalists don't use it. But lawyers do. We use it to avoid ambiguities.

7. When you use the phrase X of Y, try changing it to Y's X and see if that works better. Nine times out of ten, that construction will work much better. For example: the "brief of the plaintiff" becomes the plaintiff's brief.
8. Finally, many Korean students use the phrase: "it is difficult to say that. . . ." Don't do it. Usually students use it to soften a prediction such as: it is difficult to say that the rule applies in our case. This construction is almost always awkward and incorrect. We do have a similar expression in English, but I encourage you to avoid it altogether for now.
9. Go back and check your articles: a, an, and the. Is it a noun that you can count? If so, you probably need an article in front of it. If you are struggling, ask your professor for a handout on articles.
10. Underline case names.

Bonus Tip! Use short, simple sentences. This is technical drafting, not a creative writing class.

[13]

Secondary Source: Electronic Research Exercise

Electronic Research Exercise Number 1 (R1)

Instructions

- Please type your answers. Answers should be **single-spaced** in **Courier New Font size 8**. Pages should be numbered.
- Your paper must have a header on the first page (not needed on subsequent pages) including the following: a title; your Professor's name; and your student ID number. Do not write your name; use your student ID number.
- Please e-mail your answers prior to class or hand them in at the beginning of class according to your professor's preference.
- If you cut and paste, you must use quotation marks!
- There are *8 total questions* in this assignment. Please do not miss any.

The Assignment

Researching secondary sources online is like researching in print.

However, on Westlaw[1] and Lexis Advance[2] there are many more secondary sources than you will find in the library.

At first, the sheer number of sources on Westlaw and Lexis can be a bit overwhelming. However, as you get used to online research, you may prefer it. Certainly, the majority of legal research is now done online.

Because you are likely a "digital native" and have been using search engines for a long time, it should be easy to transition into electronic research. In the past, Westlaw and Lexis featured complex user interfaces. However, with recent changes, doing legal research online feels like using a regular search engine.

During this exercise, we will learn to use free internet sources as well as paid, commercial sources like Westlaw and Lexis Advance.

The internet is always changing. Because we are preparing this exercise before the semester begins, there is a chance that pages may change slightly. Please try to be flexible. Let your professor know if there appears to be some change that affects your assignment.

As to secondary sources, we will focus on the most commonly used secondary sources: legal encyclopedias, A.L.R., Restatements, treatises, state practice guides, and law journal articles.

There are many additional secondary sources on Westlaw and Lexis Advance that you can explore on your own time or via a tutorial. During your research, if you see a source that looks interesting, feel free to come back and check it out later.

For the following research exercise, let's consider the following fact scenario:

> You are interning at a law firm in California. Your supervising attorney asks you to research the following case.

---

[1] Westlaw is a registered trademark of Thomson Reuters.
[2] Lexis Advance is a registered trademark of LexisNexis.

Your client is Mary Smith. She lives in Orange County, California. Mary runs an online blog named theoriginaltradwife.blogspot.com.

Mary has always had problems with online trolls. Two months ago, a troll with the user name "Anti-Phoenician" began posting harassing messages to the comment section of her blog.

Mary noted Anti-Phoenician's IP address. The IP address came from a user located in San Francisco, California. Mary blocked the user's comments. Mary also announced via a blog post that Anti-Phoenician was not welcome to post on her blog anymore.

Anti-Phoenician began posting under different user names, using the same IP address. Many of the new messages included shockingly obscene language that deeply offended Mary. None of the messages threatened physical harm.

Mary blocked all messages from that IP address.

Last week, a new user, logged into the IP address of a public library in San Francisco, began posting similarly worded messages. Mary thinks it is Anti-Phoenician.

Mary came to your law firm to seek advice.

Let's begin our research! Before we log on to a commercial research website like Westlaw or Lexis Advance, let's check the largest and most helpful secondary source—the internet itself.

The Internet

Open up a search engine of your choice like Google, Bing, or DuckDuckGo. If using Google, please use google.com and not google.co.kr as the former will return better results!

Let's do a word search. We want to find background reading on cyberstalking and harassment. Let's run a search for online and harassment in California.

1. **What is the criminal law in California for online harassment? (A website from privacyrights.org is a top Google search. If you use a different website, please include a link to that website in your answer.)**

2. **Based on your reading of that website, do you think Anti-Phoenician violated the California Penal Code?**

When you do an internet search, a website may give you a citation to primary law.

For example, the privacyrights.org website refers to California Penal Code 653m.

If so, one of the best ways to continue your research is to look that law or case up directly. If you look up the case or statute on a commercial database like Westlaw or Lexis Advance, you will get helpful research annotations. We will do that together in a moment.

Remember, the goal of secondary source research is to move from secondary sources (about the law) to mandatory, primary sources (the law itself).

BLAWG RESEARCH (USING LEGAL BLOGS)

Searching law blogs can also be a good source of information. It just so happens there is a good, free resource out there: http://blawgsearch.justia.com

Blawgsearch aggregates many hundreds of law blogs in one place.

Go to blawgsearch.justia.com and enter "online harassment laws" (without the quotation marks). Use the information to answer the following question.

3. **Please give a brief summary of the Electronic Frontier Foundation blog post from 8 Jan 2015. As of the date of that blog, how many states had online harassment laws? Is the EFF positive or critical of these laws? Why?**

An interesting this about the blog article from the Electronic Frontier Foundation are the public policy arguments.

In the summer oral advocacy course or the advanced legal writing course, students often complain that they do not know how to find public policy arguments.

We can see many such arguments in the EFF blog.

Finally, please note that you can search specific blogs directly on search engines like Google. For example, I love to start legal searches at The Volokh Conspiracy. Professor Eugene Volokh and his cohort of bloggers usually have something interesting to say.

Lexis Advance®

Please log onto your personal Lexis Advance ("Lexis") account.

You can also access Lexis through the public account available on campus, via the law school library website: lawlibrary.handong.edu (I think you have to be on university Wi-Fi to use the public Westlaw account.)

It is better to use your private account. Your private account will store your research history. The public account stores the research history of everyone who is using it!

Research history can be helpful if you need to pause your research and come back to it later.

Lexis is a wonderful place to begin your research. It has a nice, clean user interface that looks a lot like a search engine. However, as you become more familiar with it, you will see that the simple front page hides a wealth of powerful search tools.

In a nod to Professor Seefried, let's begin our search using a state practice guide!

Try typing California Criminal Law into the search box. You should see a pop-up suggesting sources, including Matthew-Bender Practice Guide to California Criminal Law. *Unfortunately, our subscription doesn't cover that source*! Sorry, Professor Seefried.

Let's use Witkin California Criminal Law instead. This is a "treatise" on Criminal Law. Remember from the previous chapter, a treatise is a comprehensive volume or multi-volume set covering a specific legal topic.

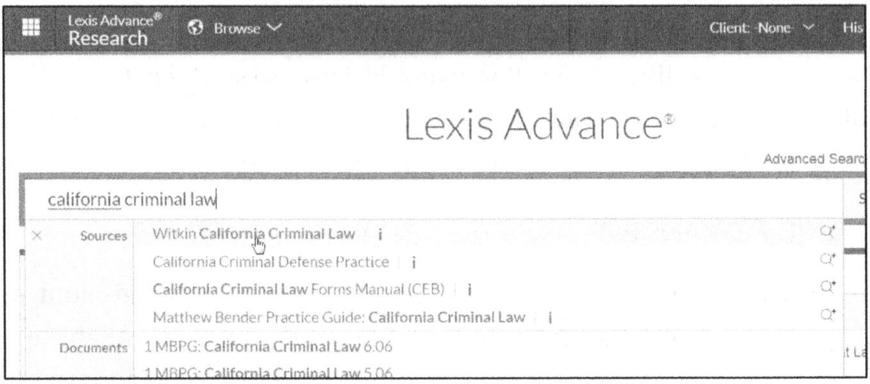

In Witkin, let's run a search in All Documents for: annoying electronic communication.

In Lexis, you can search just the Table of Contents only or you can search All Documents (every word) in that source. Sometimes, searching All Documents can return too many results. Let's try it anyway.

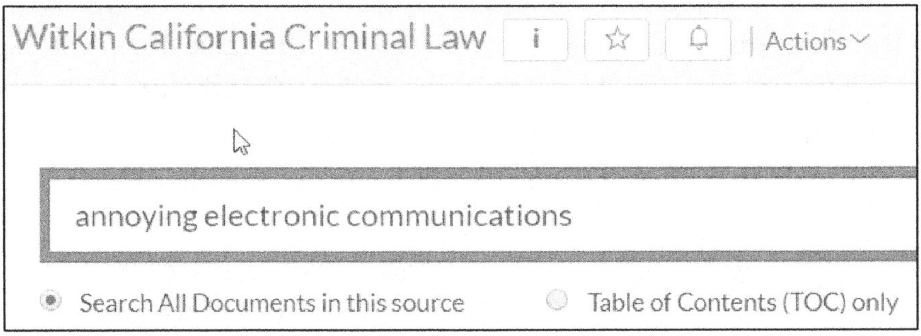

4. **Please explain your answers in a full sentence, not in one or two words: According to 7 Witkin Cal. Crim. Law Crimes - Pub § 521, what level of crime is it (felony or misdemeanor) to make repeated online contact with the intent to annoy or harass? According to the case *People v. Astalis,* cited in Supplement (2), is that section of the statute still good law?**

When researching secondary sources on Lexis, you can always jump directly into a Secondary Materials search or even go directly into searching Treatises & Practice Guides.

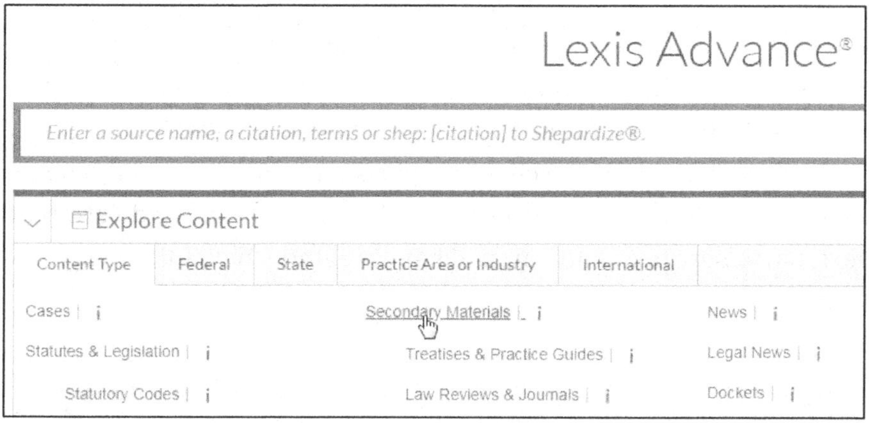

Let's click on and search Secondary Materials. We can search American Law Reports or American Jurisprudence.

We can search law reviews and law journals.

We can even drill down to secondary materials by state.

However, in this instance, let's search all secondary materials for the terms: online harassment

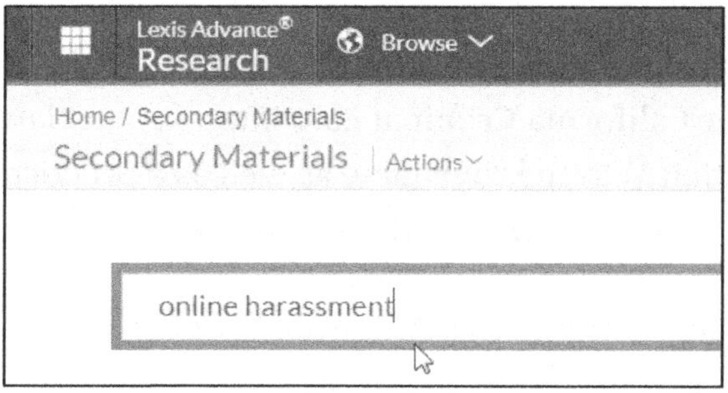

5. **According to a top result, 51 Cornell Int'l L.J. 297, under section IV subsection b (near the end of the article) what does the author suggest the United States can learn from Canada's attempts to curtail online harassment?**

WESTLAW®[3]

Let's now turn to Westlaw. Again, it is better to use your private account.

When you log on to Westlaw, you may be prompted to choose a Client ID. That is how real lawyers manage their client research and client billing. A lawyer can check how much time she spent researching for client "Mary Smith" and bill the client accordingly.

If prompted to name a client ID, please use "Mary Smith." If some text is already highlighted in the dialogue box, simply delete that text, write new text, and you will have created a new Client ID. Click "continue" to proceed.

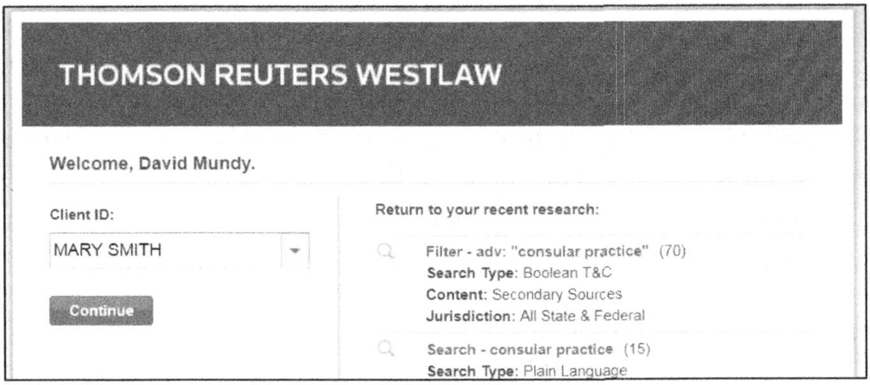

Westlaw also has a clean user interface.

If we enter California Criminal Law into the Westlaw search engine, we see that Witkin is available as well as a practice guide from The Rutter Group. Let's choose their Criminal Practice Series.

[3] Westlaw is a registered trademark of Thompson Reuters.

Let's search that database for: annoying electronic communication.

One thing I immediately noted, is that I don't see an entry dealing with California Penal Code 653m(b). However, there is an entry for Penal Code 653m(a).

That is a good reminder that we may need to search multiple secondary sources. One source may not cover everything.

6. **Please explain your answers in a full sentence, not in one or two words: According to The Rutter Group-California Criminal Law § 7:56, what is the definition of an "obscene" communication?**

By now, it may be clear that California Penal Code 653m is the primary source of law for our client's case.

We can look that statute up directly.

If we look it up on Lexis or on Westlaw, you will get annotations that include links to helpful secondary sources.

Please go to the Westlaw home page.

Then, type the following into the Westlaw search box: California Penal Code 653m. Hit enter.

You should now be looking at California Penal Code 653m.

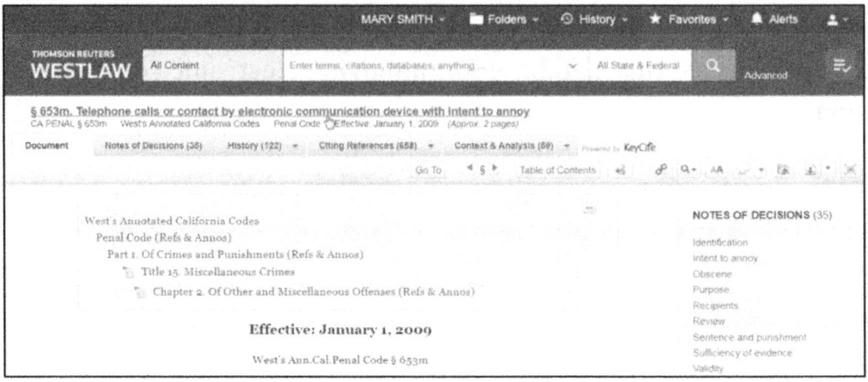

You will notice there are tabs at the top of the page that provide links to helpful sources. There is a "Notes of Decisions" tab that links to cases that discuss this statute. There is a history tab that shows the legislative history of the statute.

As to secondary sources, there is a "Citing References" tab that contains links to secondary sources and other sources that cite to the statute. Finally, there is a "Context & Analysis" tab that links to sources that discuss or explain this statute in greater detail.

Please click on the "Context & Analysis" tab.

Scrolling down to the section on Encyclopedias, note there are links to California Jurisprudence Third Series.

That is a state specific legal encyclopedia for California!

Let's click on the encyclopedia entry entitled: 19 Cal. Jur. 3d Criminal Law: Miscellaneous Offenses § 292, Prohibition Against Obscene, Threatening, or Annoying Contact by Telephone or Electronic Communication Device.

Hint: when you click on a link to a source in Westlaw, try right-clicking and open in a New Tab.

7. **According to that encyclopedia entry, does the California statue recognize freedom of speech protections guaranteed in the state and federal constitutions? What case is cited in support of this proposition?**

You might wonder why we didn't simply start our research at Westlaw or Lexis. It used to be that a simple internet search was arguably a better place to start. In addition, when you are in private practice, Westlaw and Lexis Advance cost money. The internet is a low cost option for legal research. Moreover, if you are practicing in a country other than the U.S., you might not have access to Westlaw or Lexis Advance.

Nevertheless, using the research tabs attached to a case or to a statute is my favorite way to expand legal research, to find secondary sources and factually analogous cases.

If you can find your statute online or find a case that is factually similar to yours, even just a little bit, you can often find secondary sources that will link you to cases that are even better!

Other Secondary Sources

Westlaw and Lexis have a wealth of secondary sources available. We don't have time to cover them all.

One of those sources the "50 States Surveys." The 50 State Surveys database does exactly what it sounds like—it compiles similar laws of all 50 states in one place.

Unfortunately, I couldn't find a 50 State Survey for online harassment law, although a Google search revealed some websites that had done the hard work of aggregating such laws.

Other key secondary sources include Am. Jur. Proof of Facts which outlines the elements for causes of action. Westlaw has "Words and Phrases" which is like a concordance for legal terms of art.

We hope you will take some time to explore all that Westlaw, Lexis, and the world wide web have to offer as you become legal research experts!

8. **What is your best advice for Mary Smith based on all your research? Would you advise her to contact her local police? Do you think she has a case? Why or why not?**

[14]

READING RULES OF LAW

INTRODUCTION

In the coming chapters, we will practice finding the law.

This chapter focuses on reading the law.

Rules of law come from statutes; or, with common law, rules come from court decisions.

Rules can also come from administrative regulations or from court-adopted rules of procedure, like the Federal Rules of Civil Procedure.

Rules tell people what they cannot do or tell them what they must do.

The goal of legal research is to locate the rules that apply to your case and to interpret those rules correctly. To do this, we first need to understand the "Reason for the Rule."

REASON FOR THE RULE

Let's try to find the "Reason for the Rule" for the following section of legal code:

> If a man take a wife, and have her, and she find not favour in his eyes, for some uncleanness: he shall write a bill of divorce, and shall give it in her hand, and send her out of his house (Deuteronomy 24:1).

Is that passage easy to understand? It seems like simple computer programming logic: "if this, then that."

However, that passage has resulted many disputes over time. Amazingly, Christians still disagree about the meaning of this verse.

This leads to our first point. If you want to understand the rule, you have to understand the reason for the rule.

Let's see how a wonderful counselor interprets this rule:

> And Pharisees came up to him and tested Jesus by asking, "Is it lawful to divorce one's wife for any cause?" Jesus answered, "Have you not read that he who created them from the beginning made them male and female, and said, 'Therefore a man shall leave his father and his mother and hold fast to his wife, and the two shall become one flesh'? So they are no longer two but one flesh. What therefore God has joined together, let not man separate." They said to him, "Why then did Moses command one to give a certificate of divorce and to send her away?" He said to them, "Because of your hardness of heart Moses allowed you to divorce your wives, but from the beginning it was not so. And I say to you: whoever divorces his wife, except for sexual immorality, and marries another, commits adultery (Matthew 19:3-9).

The Pharisees read the Bible, but they didn't understand it. They didn't recognize the Person who wrote the Bible. Not even when He was standing right in front of them.

In the passage above, the Pharisees didn't remember the reason for the rule. Jesus reminds them how marriage came to exist and how important it is. He reminds them how God joins people together in marriage with a piece of his own Sprit (Malachi 2:15).

Let's look at Jesus's interpretation again, this time from Matthew 5:31-32:

> "It was also said, 'Whoever divorces his wife, let him give her a certificate of divorce.' But I say to you that everyone who divorces his wife, except on the ground of sexual immorality, makes her commit adultery, and whoever marries a divorced woman commits adultery."

Look at the simple word "if" in Deuteronomy or the word "whoever" in Matthew.

Moses did not "command one to give a certificate of divorce" as the Pharisees said.

Moses said, "if" a man divorces his wife, or as Jesus says, "whoever" divorces his wife.

Divorce isn't the intent or the heart of the Lawgiver in the Old Testament. Rather, the law protects the weaker party from a wrong.

It's like saying: "If a man murders another..."

God is not commanding murder. Neither does God condone divorce. But people had hard hearts, so God made a rule to protect the weaker party.

Of course, God's rules are much wiser than human rules. The Psalmist says, "The unfolding of your words gives light; it imparts understanding to the simple" (Psalm 119:130).

God takes an active role in human law as well. Human law can help teach people right from wrong. Murder, stealing, and cutting in line are wrong both in South Korea and in North Korea.

Sometimes we have laws that are written, but not enforced. Adultery in Korea used to be like that. It was good to have those laws "on the books," even if they weren't enforced, because those laws taught people right from wrong.

Some people didn't like being told that they were doing a wrong thing, so they got that law taken off the books. In Korea, they are trying to do the same thing with abortion.

The main point is that in order to properly read a rule, you have to understand the reason for the rule. Or, in the case of biblical law, the Reason.

To understand the Bible, you have to have the help of the Holy Spirit. You have to have the mind of Christ. Of course, this also helps in understanding secular law.

Structure of a Rule of Law

A rule of law is defined as: a legal consequence that attaches to a specific set of legal facts.

For example, if you have legal facts that include an intentional, harmful physical contact without consent, the legal consequence is money damages.

We call that rule of law "battery." Some lawyers call that a "cause of action." If a client came to them with similar facts, the lawyer might say, "You have a good case" or "You have a good cause of action."

The same set of legal facts might give rise to multiple causes of action. For example, if you made the person afraid that you were going to hit them, just prior to hitting them, that would be called "assault." Or if your offensive and harmful touching improperly detained someone, that might be called "false imprisonment."

In each instance, legal facts are present that compel the court to grant a remedy.

We call those legal facts "elements."

The elements for battery are: intentional *and* offensive touching *and* causes harm.[1] If a lawyer spots those facts in a client's story, that client can ask the court for a legal consequence: money.

Did you see the "and" in the rule for battery? We call that a conjunctive rule of law. Each element must be present. If one element is not present, the legal consequence will not result.

As we will see below, sometimes a rule will include the word "or." We call these rules "disjunctive." That means, a legal consequence will follow if one legal fact occurred *or* if another legal fact occurred.

Although I am trying to speak plainly, it may be better to look at some examples.

Reading a Statute

Like the rules from the Old Testament, human rules define our relationships with each other and with the authority.

Justice Oliver Wendell Holmes offers a more cynical view:

---

[1] The rules of some states add another element: without consent. However, consent is usually better understood as an affirmative defense: for instance, a boxer consented to being hit.

> "When we study law we are not studying a mystery but a well-known profession. We are studying what we shall want in order to appear before judges, or to advise people in such a way as to keep them out of court."[2]

According to Justice Holmes, whom you might remember as the author of the *McBoyle* case, people read the law for a reason. They want to know when the power of the state will force them to do something or to punish them for not doing something, like baking a cake for a gay wedding.

Other legal scholars think laws are verbal constructs of a patriarchal hegemony used by the powerful to oppress minorities. Put another way, they are a word game, the goal of which is to prevent the ascendance of competing power structures.

Christians have a different view of the law. We think God is intimately involved in the formation of law.

Regardless of one's perspective, in order to advise a client or argue in court, we need to know how to read a rule of law.

1. Ask the Holy Spirit

God wants to be involved in everything you do. Studying law is an act of worship.

God is always communicating to you. God is Spirit. God usually speaks to us through thought impressions or a still small voice.

Even when you are reading secular statutes, you should ask the God what He thinks about the statute. You may be surprised how often He answers.

Sometimes people think God is silent. That may be because they haven't been taught how to distinguish their thoughts or impressions from other sources (like demonic influences or familiar spirits) or from the voice of God.

If you want to practice hearing the voice of God, there is an easy way. Pick a passage of the Bible and read it carefully. Wait for a word

---

[2] Oliver Wendell Holmes, Jr., *The Path of the Law*, 10 Harvard Law Review 457, 457 (1897), available at http://www.constitution.org/lrev/owh/path_law.htm.

or phrase to "pop out" at you. Sometimes you will remember another similar passage and want to go read it. Sudden connections or insights may form in your mind.

Maybe you've had that experience before. Did you think it was your own brilliance or insight?

Usually that is God talking to you. That's one of the way God speaks to us.

If you want to learn more, you might consult this book: *God Speaks: Perspectives on Hearing God's Voice.*[3] Dozens of Christians share how they hear God's voice. Some of their stories are quite unique.

How does God speak to you?

Consulting God about a particular rule or statute should not be an afterthought. For a Christian lawyer, it should be the first thing we do.

2. Outline the Rule

There are different types of rules. Some rules contain elements that must be met before a legal consequence is triggered.

Other rules consist of factors that a court can consider in reaching its decision: for example, criminal sentencing guidelines require a court to consider many factors when deciding how long a criminal should be imprisoned.

Some rules contain *mandatory* language like "must," "will," and "shall." Other rules are *discretionary*: using words like "can" or "may."

As mentioned above, some rules are *conjunctive*, meaning the elements are joined by the word "and." This means every element has to be met. For instance, a battery has to have intentional *and* offensive *and* harmful touching.

---

[3]https://www.amazon.com/God-Speaks-Perspectives-Hearing-Voice-ebook/dp/B071H3GNVZ.

Some rules are *disjunctive*, meaning the word "or" is used. This means either element can be met and the rule still applies. For example, in Tennessee, a store can be liable for selling alcohol to a known minor *or* to a visibly intoxicated person.

As lawyers, we are responsible for *understanding every word and every punctuation mark.*

This might sound obvious, but some important cases have hinged on comma placement.[4]

One tool lawyers use to make sure we understand every word of a rule is to break a rule into an outline.

An outline is a diagram of a statute. If you are visually oriented, you might create a flowchart. If you are a computer programmer, you might organize the statute as a series of "if...then..." clauses.

There are many ways to outline a statute. We will focus on the simplest format below.

For example, the Tennessee dram shop law reads as follows:

> Notwithstanding the provisions of § 57-10-101, no judge or jury may pronounce a judgment awarding damages to or on behalf of any party who has suffered personal injury or death against any person who has sold any alcoholic beverage or beer, unless such jury of twelve (12) persons has first ascertained beyond a reasonable doubt that the sale by such person of the alcoholic beverage or beer was the proximate cause of the personal injury or death sustained and that such person:
>
> (1) Sold the alcoholic beverage or beer to a person known to be under the age of twenty-one (21) years and such person caused the personal injury or death as the direct result of the consumption of the alcoholic beverage or beer so sold; or

---

[4] A million dollar contract dispute hung on lack of a comma, http://www.nytimes.com/2006/10/25/business/worldbusiness/25comma.html. Here a company lost 10 million dollars over placement of a comma, https://www.bostonglobe.com/business/2017/03/16/lack-oxford-comma-costs-maine-company-millions-overtime-dispute/BIxK837fA2C06qavQMDs5J/story.html.

> (2) Sold the alcoholic beverage or beer to a visibly intoxicated person and such person caused the personal injury or death as the direct result of the consumption of the alcoholic beverage or beer so sold.

This rule might seem complicated. As we break it down into an outline, the meaning becomes more clear.

First, we *omit language that describes the nature of the cause of action.* It is not necessary to put these phrases into our outline because they don't describe a legally significant fact that leads to the result.

For example, "A person is guilty of battery when..." We can safely omit language like that.

We want to *focus on facts that, if met, lead to a result.*

Let's look at the opening paragraph. I will highlight the words that jumped out as I read the opening paragraph and put my thoughts in brackets.

> Notwithstanding the provisions of <u>§ 57-10-101</u> [*I better read that statute*], no judge or jury may pronounce a judgment awarding damages to or on behalf of <u>any party</u> [*I wonder if that includes the drunk person too*] who has suffered personal injury or death against any person who has [*I can* almost *ignore all previous language, which essentially says there is no liability unless someone:*] sold any alcoholic beverage or beer, unless such jury of twelve (12) persons has first ascertained <u>beyond a reasonable doubt</u> [*this is the burden of proof, and it is <u>higher</u> than most civil causes of action*] that the sale by such person of the alcoholic beverage or beer was the <u>proximate cause</u> [*I need to analyze proximate causation, which you will learn in Torts class*] of the personal injury or death sustained <u>and</u> [*conjunctive*] that such person . . .

Here's how I summarize or outline that opening paragraph:

1. Where that sale of alcohol is the proximate cause of injury or death,
2. Beyond a reasonable doubt
3. Any person who sold alcohol or beer is liable if:

Note that I did not separate "any person" and "sold any alcohol or beer" into different parts of the outline. I could have written: 1. Any person who; 2. Sells; 3. Alcohol or beer

You could do that. It wouldn't be wrong. But it doesn't help much.

Next, her is my outline the two subsections:

A. The sale was,
B. To a person known to be under the age of twenty-one OR to a visibly intoxicated person, AND
C. Such person caused the personal injury or death
D. As the direct result of the consumption of the alcoholic beverage or beer so sold.

First, note that I combined both subsections. Element B is disjunctive. It has two options, either a sale to a known minor or a sale to a visibly intoxicated person.

Again, you could break each element down individually. But that may not be very helpful.

You can see there is no exact science to creating outlines. Two people might outline a statute different ways.

Often, courts that have applied a rule will give an outline!

The court will say something like, "This rule or statute has three elements (1), (2), and (3)." Pay careful attention to that kind of language. That is a legal expert outlining a rule for you.

Sometimes different courts will give the elements for the same rule but will use slightly different words!

That is okay. Don't be confused. Different judges might outline the statute a bit differently. They might emphasize or de-emphasize certain phrases or words.

If that happens, the best advice is to use the language from the highest court's most recent case. Or you might choose language that sounds best for your client.

For example, try taking the rule from a case where the ruling is favorable to your client. Courts don't want to be reversed on appeal.

The court will phrase the rule as favorably as possible to the courts position. That should be the best phrasing for your client as well.

We will come back to the Tennessee Dram Shop Law in a later chapter.

Let's look at what our final outline of the Tennessee dram shop law looks like:

1. Where a sale of alcohol is the proximate cause of injury or death,
2. Beyond a reasonable doubt,
3. Any person who sold alcohol or beer is liable if
   A. The sale was,
   B. To a person known to be under the age of twenty-one OR to a visibly intoxicated person, AND
   C. Such person caused the personal injury or death
   D. As the direct result of the consumption of the alcoholic beverage or beer so sold.

Exercises

Let's try outlining a few different rules of law.

1. The National Motor Vehicle Theft Act

> That when used in this Act: (a) the term "motor vehicle" shall include an automobile truck, automobile wagon, motorcycle, or any other self-propelled vehicle not designed for running on rails . . .

2. Illinois Residential Burglary Statute

> A person commits residential burglary when he or she knowingly and without authority enters or knowingly and without authority remains within the dwelling place of another, or any part thereof, with the intent to commit therein a felony or theft.

3. Uniform Probate Code § 2-508

> If after executing a will the testator is divorced or his marriage annulled, the divorce or annulment revokes any disposition or appointment of property made by the will to the former spouse . . . unless the will expressly provides otherwise.

4. Immigration and Nationality Act, exclusion for political and national security

(A) In general.-Any alien who a consular officer or the Attorney General knows, or has reasonable ground to believe, seeks to enter the United States to engage solely, principally, or incidentally in-

(i) any activity (I) to violate any law of the United States relating to espionage or sabotage or (II) to violate or evade any law prohibiting the export from the United States of goods, technology, or sensitive information,

(ii) any other unlawful activity, or

(iii) any activity a purpose of which is the opposition to, or the control or overthrow of, the Government of the United States by force, violence, or other unlawful means, is inadmissible.

5. National Vaccine Injury Compensation Program

[A] vaccine set forth in the Vaccine Injury Table which is administered after October 1, 1988, if a vaccine-related injury occurred as a result of the administration of such vaccine, no petition may be filed for compensation under the Program for such injury after the expiration of 36 months after the date of the occurrence of the first symptom or manifestation of onset or of the significant aggravation of such injury . . . .

6. Immigration and Nationality Act, Suspension of entry or imposition of restrictions by President

Whenever the President finds that the entry of any aliens or of any class of aliens into the United States would be detrimental to the interests of the United States, he may by proclamation, and for such period as he shall deem necessary, suspend the entry of all aliens or any class of aliens as immigrants or nonimmigrants, or impose on the entry of aliens any restrictions he may deem to be appropriate.

Rules of Statutory Interpretation

Statutes can often be difficult to read. For example, as you read the statutes above, consider the following questions.

> In the Immigration and Nationality Act, how did you interpret the phrase "any other unlawful activity"? If an immigrant intended to jaywalk, could the government exclude him from entering the country?
>
> In the National Vaccine Compensation Act, what does "manifestation of onset" mean?

Did you have any similar questions when reading the statutes above?

Judges have developed legal tools for determining what a statute means.

1. The Statute Itself

A statute usually consists of a preamble, the law itself, and any exceptions or provisos. Some statutes have titles that explain the subject of the statute. The preamble and the titles are not authoritative but may help you interpret the statute.

Moreover, some statutes contain definition sections that will define key terms.

For example, a definition provision from the National Motor Vehicle Theft Act above defines the term "motor vehicle" for the purposes of that act.

If a term is not defined in your statute but has been defined in a similar statute, courts may consider that as evidence of what the legislature intended.

Remember, the guiding principle when reading statutes is to *understand the legislative intent*. How did the legislature intend for this statute to be applied?

2. Rules of Interpretation

Courts have adopted a number of helpful guidelines for reading ambiguous statutes. Sometimes these are called "canons" of statutory interpretation.

Other times courts refer to broad principles of law.

For example, in the *McBoyle* case the court employed many canons of statutory construction. The court also referred to a broad rule of law when it said criminal statutes should give fair warning and be narrowly construed.

Canons and rules are only used as guides. In fact, one can often find contradictory or competing canons. Let's look at a few canons of statutory construction and principles of law:

a. Plain language

Words are presumed to bear their ordinary meanings. Moreover, the plain, uncontradicted language is the best indicator of legislative intent. However, sometimes a word or phrase is a term of art and must be understood as such. An ordinary dictionary won't do. For example, the phrase "manifestation of onset" in the National Vaccine Compensation Act is a medical term.

b. Avoid absurdity

Statues should be read to avoid absurd results.

c. Same words, same meaning

A word or phrase is presumed to have the same meaning throughout a statute. Similarly, if a new word is used, it is presumed to have a unique meaning.

d. Silence

Judges assume that, "When Congress speaks it means as much as it says, not less." If Congress didn't say something, the silence might be considered significant: the proverbial "dog that didn't bark."

e. Notice

Criminal statutes should give fair warning in plain language.

f. Rule of Lenity

Similarly, if a criminal statute is ambiguous, it should be interpreted in favor of the criminal defendant. Put another way, criminal statutes should be narrowly interpreted.

g. Every word, every statute counts

"No interpretation should be adopted that renders the provision in question - or any other provision — superfluous, unlawful, or invalid."

h. Expressio unius est exclusio alterius

The inclusion of one implies the exclusion of others. This involves a negative implication. For instance, a sign that reads "for sale to persons 19 and over" implies alcohol is not sold to persons under 19.

i. Ejusdem generis

General words or phrases following a list should be read in the context of the particular items of the list. They should be read as being "of the same kind." For example, the phrase "any other self-propelled vehicle not designed for running on rails" should be analyzed in the context of the specific items listed including automobile truck, automobile wagon, and motorcycle.

If the statute read "staples, rivets, nails, pins, stakes, and other items," can "other items" include balloons? What about screws?

j. Noscitura sociis

This phrase means, "A word is known by the words with which it is associated." Put another way, the meaning of a word in a list is colored by the other words in that list. For example, in the clause "staples, rivets, nails, pins, stakes, and other items," nails would not be read to mean "fingernails."

k. Ut magis valeat quam pereat

This rule means, "So that it may survive rather than perish." Plainly stated, it means an ambiguous provision should be interpreted in a way that makes it valid rather than invalid.

Final Note

Statutes must be read in the context of the statutory scheme, including any preamble or definition section or similar statutes within the code.

Statutes must be understood in light of any mandatory, binding court decisions that interpret or add additional meaning to the words of the statute.

Statutes often must be understood in light of the administrative code. For example, the U.S. Code authorizes the U.S. Department of Agriculture to make labeling requirements for food. The U.S. Code does not say that GMO foods must be labeled. Rather, the USDA made that rule on its own, based on the broad enabling legislation from Congress.

[15]
Researching Statutes

Introduction

The United States federal government has no common law. Every law is written in a code.

Each state government has a legislature and administrative agencies that write codes. Many local governments, like cities, counties, and municipalities, have codes as well.

Although the U.S. is known as a common law jurisdiction, the law is primarily code based and becoming more so every year.

For the most part, when you begin legal research, you will begin by looking for a statute. Only afterward will you read cases that interpret the statute.

For this exercise, we will use the United States Code (U.S. Code) as our primary example. State codes are similar.

The Legislative Process

Most Americans of a certain age are familiar with a cartoon called "I'm Just a Bill" that came out on the program *Schoolhouse Rock*. This cartoon taught us how a bill becomes a law: youtu.be/FFroMQlKiag.

The cartoon is surprisingly informative.

The cartoon ends with the bill becoming a law. If the cartoon continued, it would show "Bill" being cut apart and put into various titles of the U.S. Code. =)

At the start, a bill is introduced into the U.S. House of Representatives or into the U.S. Senate. After the bill is introduced, it is given a bill number. Bills introduced into the Senate start with an "S." Bills introduced into the House start with an "H.R."

The bill is then sorted by subject and sent to the appropriate committee. The committee may refer it to a subcommittee.

The subcommittee holds hearings on the bill and may invite experts or other witnesses to testify. Witnesses may submit reports. The subcommittee may revise the original bill.

If the subcommittee likes a bill, they may refer it to the full committee. Otherwise, the bill dies.

The full committee also has hearings. Witnesses may submit written reports. The full committee may revise the bill.

At the end of the process, if the full committee likes a bill, it sends the bill to the floor of the House or Senate to be debated and voted upon. It will also write a committee report.

If a committee doesn't like a bill, the bill dies (it is never reported out of committee).

Once on the floor of the House of Representatives or of the Senate, the Representatives or the Senators can debate the bill. They can make speeches. In the Senate, they might even "filibuster" a bill—that is, talk for such a long time that the bill cannot be brought to a vote.

If a bill is voted upon by the Senate, it will then be sent to the House of Representatives, where it will go through the same process. Likewise, if a bill is passed in the House, it will be sent to the Senate, where it will undergo the same process.

Occasionally, a bill will go to the House and to the Senate at the same time.

Regardless, if the bill passed by one of the chambers differs from the one passed by the other chamber, they will hold a "Conference

Action" to work out the differences. The Conference will issue a report and will send a compromise version of the bill back to each chamber for a vote.

All of this legislative history is published daily in the Congressional Record. It is available for free at Congress.gov.

As you can see from the discussion above, the most important legislative history comes from the following:

1. **The text of the bill itself (along with any changes)**
2. **The committee and subcommittee reports**
3. **Floor debates (especially by the bill's sponsors)**
4. **Any conference action report**

Some committee reports are also published in a source called the United States Code Congressional and Administrative News (U.S.C.C.A.N.).

We will learn how to research the legislative history in a later chapter.

Finally, if the Senate and the House pass the compromise bill, that bill is sent to the President.

The President can either sign the bill or veto the bill. If the bill is vetoed, it is returned to Congress. Congress can override the veto with a 2/3 majority vote.

If a bill is signed by the President, it becomes a law.

Codification

A bill signed by the President becomes a law. It is given a public law number, and is published as a slip law.

A citation to the public law might look like this: Public Law 115-97. The number indicates that the law was passed in the 115th session of Congress. It was the 97th law passed.

A bill or an act might also have a popular name. Public Law 115-97 is known as the "Tax Cuts and Jobs Act of 2017."

Public laws are published individually as slip laws.

Public laws are then grouped chronologically, by session of Congress into a multi-volume set called the Statutes at Large.

This process might seem redundant to people who grew up in the age of the Internet. But you can imagine during the days of print, a public law would be printed separately and distributed. Then, at a later time, the laws from an entire Congressional session would be taken and bound together as the Statutes at Large.

For example, the Patient Protection and Affordable Care Act (Obamacare) can be found at the following citation in the Statutes at Large: 124 Stat. 119.

This means it is in volume 124 of the Statutes at Large, beginning on page 119.

Finally, the law is divided by subject and placed into the U.S. Code.

The U.S. Code is organized by subject. It is divided into as many as 54 different titles, each of which covers a different area of law. For instance, Title 28 covers criminal statutes while Title 8 covers immigration law.

Titles may be broken into chapters, and chapters into sections.

For example, 8 U.S.C. § 1158 is the section of code that covers asylum in the United States. This citation tells us that asylum law can be found in Title 8 of the U.S. Code.

After we found Title 8, we would then turn to section 1158.

That odd squiggly mark "§" means section. You can easily write it by holding Alt while entering 0167 on your keyboard's number pad: Alt+0167.

Some titles of the U.S. code span more than one volume. For example, the U.S. tax code is in multiple volumes under Title 26.

State codes are also organized by subject. Many states number their codes. Their subjects and numbers might not match the U.S. Code.

Some states organize their codes alphabetically, like California.

Back to our original example, the Patient Protection and Affordable Care Act covers many different subjects including health care (Title 42) as well as taxation (Title 26). (You might find it strange that Obamacare is incorporated into the U.S. Tax Code, yet the Supreme Court said it isn't a "tax." Oh well.)

Therefore, the Affordable Care Act was split up into many different sections of the U.S. Code.

If you want to read an act in its entirety, you cannot do so in the U.S. Code.

If you want to read the entire law, before it is split up into the U.S. Code, you need to look it up using either the Public Law Number (PL 111–148) or the Statutes at Large citation (124 Stat. 119).

You can easily find these. Most publications of the U.S. Code will include a reference to their Public Law Number and Statutes at Large citation.

When I say "most publications of the U.S. Code" you should know that there are two types of code. There is the official code and commercial code books.

Official codes are published by the government. They don't have annotations.

Commercial codes are published by a commercial publisher like West or Lexis. They usually have annotations.

For example, the U.S. Code is published by the government. A citation to the U.S. Code official reporter might look like this: 8 U.S.C. § 1158.

Meanwhile, West publishes the U.S. Code Annotated (U.S.C.A.) while Lexis publishes the U.S. Code Services (U.S.C.S.).

That is why you sometimes see a citation to the code that looks like this: 8 U.S.C.A. § 1158 (West) or 8 U.S.C.S. § 1158 (LexisNexis).

Don't get confused. All of these are citing to the same section of the U.S. Code.

Annotated versions of the U.S. Code also come with volumes entitled "Tables."

Tables for the U.S. Code serve as cross-references: connecting the code to Public Laws and to Statutes at Large. Tables also connect key cases to sections of code. If you know the name of a key case, you can easily find the code provision using the Table.

This was all before computer research, you understand.

Meanwhile, the Statutes at Large will also include a reference to its final location in the U.S. Code.

Researching Statutes in Print

It is easy to find a statute if you know the citation. For example, in our chapter on secondary sources, we located California Penal Code 653m.

We often find citations to the code while reading secondary sources including the internet.

For example, if you were researching about North Koreans seeking asylum in the United States, you might come across a citation to 8 U.S.C. § 1158.

In addition, you might come across a Public Law Number or a citation to the Statutes at Large. Those normally include a reference to their location in the U.S. Code. Or you can use the Tables to connect a Public Law or a Statute at Large to the U.S. Code.

Another table links statutes to the popular name of the act. This is called the "Popular Name Table."

For instance, if you were looking for the statute dealing with the North Korean Human Rights Act of 2004, you could look it up alphabetically in the Popular Name Table.

However, the most common way of researching the statutes in print is to use the index.

The general index to the U.S. Code consists of many volumes and is organized alphabetically.

The index will point you to a particular section of the code, sometimes followed by "et seq." Like, 8 U.S.C. § 1158 et seq.

"Et seq." literally means "and following." It means you should read multiple sections, starting with section 1158.

Once you find the code, you have to read it.

In a commercial code publication, like U.S. Code Annotated (West), you will be provided with annotations.

For example, in addition to the text of the code itself, West will provide you with "Historical Notes": how has the language changed over time.

You might be given "Notes of Decisions": how have courts applied the code. The Notes of Decisions section might contain its own index if there are a lot of cases.

In addition, you might be given "Cross-References" to other similar portions of the code. You might be given "Library References and Law Review Articles": links to secondary sources that discuss the code.

Hence, the first step for a statutory law research problem is to find the annotated code. Once you find it, you can expand your research using the annotations.

A brief note: it is not a good idea to start researching the U.S. Code by browsing the table of contents. Use the index.

However, after you have found an applicable section of code, it is highly recommended that you take a moment to look at the table of contents and to familiarize yourself with the surrounding sections.

For example, there might be a nearby section containing definitions. Or there might be a preamble that states the legislative purpose.

Statutes cannot be read by themselves. They have to be understood in the context of the entire statutory scheme. For example, one could not understand the National Motor Vehicle Act section 3, without reading Section 2, which defines the term "motor vehicle." In addition, the court in *McBoyle* looked to other portions of the U.S. Code to see whether similar statues included the term aircraft.

Finally, the U.S. Code is published every six years. Therefore, in order to update your research, you need to check the pocket part in the back of the volume where your statute appears. These pocket parts are updated every year.

In addition, some law libraries might receive quarterly updates in softbound volumes. These are separate books and are usually located at the end of the code. They cover any updates that take place before the pocket parts come out.

Conclusion

It may seem difficult to keep a huge source like the federal code up to date in print format. It may also seem difficult to research the print version for this reason. Things are always changing.

However, understanding the legislative process and print research will be very helpful when it comes to researching statutes online.

[16]

STATUTES: RESEARCH & WRITING EXERCISE

WRITING EXERCISE 3 (W3)

Please read the following facts. Answer the problem assigned to you by your professor. Please follow your professor's instructions for turning in the assignment.

Finally, please note that, while the following fact pattern may seem complicated, it is very similar (in length and scope) to what you might see on a law school final exam.

When researching statutes in print, recall these three steps summarized from the preceding chapter:

1. Use an index (word search);
2. Locate the statute in the main text; and
3. Update your research (pocket parts).

Something about Smitty

Your old pal Smitty keeps trying to make good but just can't seem to stay out of trouble. He's come to you again to ask for your advice on how to get out of the sticky situations in which he finds himself. *What has he gotten himself into this time*, you wonder as he shambles into your Washington DC office. If he wasn't your best friend since elementary school, you would've long ago stopped trying to help him. At least with Smitty things are always entertaining. Smitty tells you the following story.

Smitty's Story

With the money I got back from that e-mail from the Nigerian prince, I invested in the next thing. Virtual Reality video games. VR!

I came up with an idea, a first-person shooter based on the Korean war. I called it KOWO: The Frozen Chosen. It's based on the battle of Chosin Reservoir.

I put an ad on Craigslist looking for programmers and for promoters.

I put together a team of about twenty people. Most everyone works from home except for me and my secretary Shanise and our IT security team, Carl and Max. Hackers are a real big deal, stealing trade secrets. I wanted a top-notch team. I even had the IT team take a polygraph test to make sure they were each honest people who weren't working for Blizzard, Rockstar, or some other video game company to steal my intellectual property.

Like I said, everyone else on the team works from home. But the whole team meets up every Wednesday morning at our office in Fairfax, Virginia. We have a briefing session from 9 a.m. to 12 p.m. Eastern time. Some team members don't live nearby, so they come to the meeting by video conference.

KOWO turned out great.

We did a pre-sale on Steam. Players can buy and play the beta version of the game.

KOWO generated a lot of industry buzz. Well, I had to pay a few Gizmadoo.com reporters to write some nice blog posts, but I heard everyone does that. At least I didn't have to resort to other means like that one developer, Literally Who, a few years back.

I had some of the top streamers on Twitch playing the pre-release to generate even more buzz. Games like ChocoTaco and Viss (but not Shroud, he's still wasting his talents on Fortnite).

Well, anyways, we were getting good pre-sales. We were gearing up for a big holiday season release.

Then everything went south.

One of the promoters that I hired through Craigslist said she's going to file a Title VII sex discrimination lawsuit against me.

Juanita, she's the one with the purple hair and rather *ahem* large frame, she said I was giving all the good sales leads to "cisnet males."

Well, it's true I was giving some good leads to Jimmy and James. But that's because they'd proven their ability to close sales. Juanita, meanwhile, well, I don't know how many sales pitches she made a day, but her returns were quite weak. Sometimes when I asked her "how's it going," she told me that the question made her uncomfortable and that she needed a "me day" to recover.

That's fine because, like I said, all of the sales promoters work as independent contractors. They get paid a straight commission on each sale. If a sales lead comes in online, I send those out. Maybe I sent some good ones to Jimmy or to James. But I sent plenty of leads to Juanita and to other members of the team. I don't care about gender or race or none of that, as long as you perform.

Juanita works from home or a coffee shop or wherever. She uses her own computer. I don't pay any health insurance or benefits or taxes. I'll give her a 1099 tax form at the end of the year.

So, what I am saying is that Juanita is an independent contractor and, like everybody else, I treat her fair and square.

But that's not the end of my problems. Some website located in Texas is already selling a hack for my game.

Players can buy the hack from the website and install it on their computer. Then, when they are playing the game, the player can see through walls and shoot other players through walls. They call it "KOWOllhax."

Isn't that, like, violating my intellectual property rights in the video game I created? It changes the way players see the game on their screen. Doesn't that violate my copyright?

Speaking of intellectual property.

I got a trademark problem.

I made the KOWO logo look real cool. I want to make a whole line of KOWO video games, just like Call of Duty.

But the Korean Embassy is causing a fuss because they say my symbol looks like the Korean flag.

That's true. But so does Pepsi. And so does Korean Air for that matter.

I made the Os in KOWO look like the yin-yang symbol used on former national flag of Korean. It's from an old Korean flag and it looks sweet.

The mark consists of the letters K and W as well as images. The images are red and blue swirls covered by a crosshair. I made a print out for you. I know it's black and white, but you get the idea?

KOWO

That KOWO symbol can't possibly violate rules on trademark, can it? I've already put a lot of money into promoting that mark. I was just waiting for it to be registered with the Patent and Trademark Office. But, like I said, the Korean consulate heard about it and is raising a stink.

That's not the only stinky thing in this mess.

I got a question for you. I think some of the beta players have been giving their passwords to other people. That is a straight-up violation of the Terms of Use. Beta is supposed to be for a select few, elite gamers and cool people. They are not allowed to share passwords.

So, the other day, I asked my IT security team to watch the servers. There is a user who is supposed to be in Washington, D.C., but he was logging in from Alaska!

I went online as my character and approached him in game. I said, "Oh, hey Jeremy, what's up?"

But he responded in a British accent, this isn't Jeremy, I'm just borrowing his account to check out the game.

I said, oh cool, what's your name bro, and he said "Devin." And I was like, do you live near me and Jeremy in D.C., your accent doesn't sound very Foggy Bottom. And he said, no, I'm British, but I live in Fairbanks, Alaska.

I was thinking to myself. Gotcha.

I googled him and found his facebook account and mailing address, which matches up with the location of the GPS.

I'm so smart, it took me, maybe an hour to do that.

Then I cancelled Jeremy's account. Natch.

But I want to go after that annoying-sounding Devin guy. Can I sue him for hacking?

Speaking of hacks, do you remember Jon Jakes who used to develop video games back in the 80s?

I got a license to use an old video game character named "Donic the Ledgedog." The copyright owner is Jon Jakes.

Do you remember him? He lives in Arlington, Virginia now. Right nearby me in Fairfax, Virginia.

Now that my game is famous, Jon wants more money. We made a contract giving me a full license to use the character. I paid him good money.

Now he is claiming that license was only for the game and not for any advertising materials. He is also threatening to file DMCA take down notices against any streamers using his characters.

Streamers are the big promoters of the game!

Jon is saying that he is going to sue me, but the joke's on him. We have a clause in the contract saying that all disputes must be arbitrated. So, here's what I want to do. I know his attorney. A real dumb lowlife. An ambulance chaser.

I want you to sue in federal court in Virginia to force Jon into arbitration.

His attorney won't want to go to federal court. He only deals with state court issues. His attorney will pressure Jon to settle.

Well, it's like my boy Biggy says, "Mo money, Mo problems!"

Speaking of problems, I'm also getting sued by one of the IT team, Carl.

After hiring the IT team, the polygraph company told me that one of the guys, his name is Carl, while they were interviewing him, they jokingly asked him "you ever murder someone?"

He laughed, and said no, but the polygraph tech says that he was lying. Those tests aren't 100% accurate, is what they told me. Still, I was a little worried. So at the next staff meeting I told everyone to be careful, because the lie detector test said one of the security guards might be a murderer.

I didn't tell them which one, just to keep their eyes open.

Well, Carl got angry.

After a coffee break, he confronted me in front of everybody and says I must've been talking about him and that he is going to sue me for disclosing his polygraph test to everybody. Thankfully he didn't murder me! Ha ha.

Seriously, though, crimes are no laughing matter.

In fact, the government tried to accuse me of a crime.

You know how I hate to use credit cards or checks? Well, I decided to buy a new truck. But on the drive over to the dealership, I got tired. So I parked in Rock Creek Park.

Well, a forest ranger came knocking on my car window.

Then he noticed the bag of money on the seat next to me. I had $42,050. All in cash, wrapped up nice and neat in those little things the banks wrap around them.

The park ranger called a bunch of officers.

They had a dog sniffing my money.

They said the money was suspected of being intended for use in a drug crime because so many people deal drugs in the park.

They took my money. They said it was forfeit.

They said I was red-eyed and acting strange. Well of course I was red-eyed. I was tired. And anyone would act strange if a bunch of federal officers suddenly interrupt your nap.

You gotta help me get that money back.

Meanwhile, you'll never guess what happened next. I got hit with a subpoena from some bigshot law firm. Apparently one of the beta testers is going through a messy divorce. Her husband is trying to get all of her private, in-game chat messages. I guess he thinks she was cheating on him with one of her gaming buddies. The law firm wants me to turn over all of her private in-game chats from the past six months. Do I really have to do that?

Finally, I have a more technical question.

I've been giving "air-drops" to my IT guys in order to give them the proper motivation to reach certain goals. We have to get this game ready to ship and soon if we want to hit the holiday season.

Air-drops contain random items that can be used in-game, like a new piece of clothing or a custom skin for your rifle. KOWO players can buy air-drops online or earn them through online play. Some of the rare items are pretty valuable. Players buy them or trade them on the Steam marketplace.

But I gotta file my taxes soon, and I'm wondering whether the air-drops I gave the IT guys count as gifts or whether I can deduct them as a business expense.

Whoo. That's a real load off of my chest.

You got to help me out, old buddy.

QUESTIONS

After listening to Smitty's story, you tell him that you will look into his case and will have an answer for him soon.

You must use the *print* copies of the U.S. Code or the Washington D.C. Code located in the law library. Initially, **you *may not* use online sources. If you do, you may fail this assignment.** (Your professor may allow you to use an online source after you've located the correct statute in print. Please follow your professor's instructions.)

You should answer one question below, as assigned by your professor.

Your answer should be in the form of a one page, one paragraph IRAC writing assignment. Assignments should be in 12-point Courier New font, double spaced, with one-inch margins. Your paper should include a title. Your paper should also include your student ID number, not your name.

You must include the rule from the statute.

You must also include a helpful case precedent. Remember, cases can be used in two ways: (1) the case precedent might add a helpful interpretation of the rule; (2) *and/or* the case serve as a factually similar case analogy that helps you apply the statute to your fact pattern.

Sometimes a case can give you a good rule *and* be a factually similar case.

Please return the library books to the exact location as soon as you locate the proper source.

Questions begin on the next page.

Question 1:

You remember from law school that Title VII of the Civil Rights Act of 1964 makes it unlawful "for an employer . . . to discriminate," inter alia, on the basis of sex. However, you don't know whether an independent contractor is an "employee" for the purposes of the code. You need to find a definition of employer or employee. Therefore, search the U.S. Code under Civil Rights. You need to find the definition of employee under the equal employment opportunity provisions of the Civil Rights Act.

Write the title number and section here: ________________

You find and read the definitions section of the statute. If the answer is not clear, you need to find a case in the notes of decision that helps you on the sub-rule for whether an independent contractor meets the definition of employee.

From the Notes of Decision index, write the note name and number here: __________________________

Go to that section of the Notes of Decision and find a helpful court of appeals case from 2009 named *Brown*. You might have to look in the pocket part.

Write the citation of the case here:

____

Read the summary of the case in the Notes of Decisions. Then, look up the case online and read the applicable part of the case.

In your written answer, please include a citation to the statute and to the case that helps with the sub-rule. Compare the case factually to your client's case. Predict the outcome using language of probability.

Question 2:

You remember that the U.S. Code provides protection for copyright owners to create derivative works. Because the computer hack changes the appearance of your client's copyrighted work, you wonder whether it might be derivative work that violates your client's rights. You search under the U.S. Code on Copyright, for the definition of derivative works.

Write the title number and section here: ________________

You find and read the definitions section of the statute. If the answer is not clear, you need to find a case in the notes of decision that helps you on the sub-rule for whether a video game can be a derivative work.

From the Notes of Decision index, write the note name and number here: ____________________________

Go to that section of the Notes of Decision and find a helpful appellate court case from 1992 named *Lewis Galoob Toys, Inc.* You might have to look in the pocket part.

Write the citation of the case here:

____

Read the summary of the case in the Notes of Decisions. Then, look up the case online and read the applicable part of the case.

In your written answer, please include a citation to the statute and to the case that helps with the sub-rule. Compare the case factually to your client's case. Predict the outcome using language of probability.

Question 3:

You remember that the U.S. Trademark law allows people to register trademarks. But there are some limitations for registration of flags. You search under the U.S. Code on Trademark concerning the registration of marks with flags.

Write the title number and section here: ________________

You find and read the statute. If the answer is not clear, you need to find a case in the notes of decision that helps you on the sub-rule for whether the KOWO mark can be registered where the Korean flag is a subject matter of the mark.

From the Notes of Decision index, write the note name and number here: ____________________________

Go to that section of the Notes of Decision and find a helpful district court case from 2012 named *Brothers of the Wheel*. You might have to look in the pocket part.

Write the citation of the case here:

____

Read the summary of the case in the Notes of Decisions. Then, look up the case online and read the applicable part of the case.

In your written answer, please include a citation to the statute and to the case that helps with the sub-rule. Compare the case factually to your client's case. Predict the outcome using language of probability.

Question 4:

You think that a federal district court might have jurisdiction over computer fraud issues, but you aren't sure if Smitty's description about Devin's "hacking" meets the elements; for example, whether he can prove that his "losses" were enough to trigger the statute. In the U.S. Code, you look up Computers and Hacking to find out.

Write the title number and section here: ________________

You find and read the statute. If the answer is not clear, you need to find a case in the notes of decision that helps you on the sub-rule for whether Smitty can allege sufficient damages, generally, to meet the statute.

From the Notes of Decision index, write the note name and number here: ____________________________

Go to that section of the Notes of Decision and find a helpful district court case named *Global Policy Partners LLC v. Yessin* from 2010. You might have to look in the pocket part.

Write the citation of the case here:

____

Read the summary of the case in the Notes of Decisions. Then, look up the case online and read the applicable part of the case.

In your written answer, please include a citation to the statute and to the case that helps with the sub-rule. Compare the case factually to your client's case. Predict the outcome using language of probability.

Question 5:

You think that a federal district court might have jurisdiction over copyright issues, but you aren't sure about arbitration. In the U.S. Code, you look up Arbitration to find out about jurisdiction.

Write the title number and section here: ________________

You find and read the statute. If the answer is not clear, you need to find a case in the notes of decision that helps you on the sub-rule for whether the federal court has jurisdiction, generally to order arbitration.

From the Notes of Decision index, write the note name and number here: ___________________________

Go to that section of the Notes of Decision and find a helpful appellate court case named *Gibraltar, P.R., Inc.* from 1997. You might have to look in the pocket part.

Write the citation of the case here:

____

Read the summary of the case in the Notes of Decisions. Then, look up the case online and read the applicable part of the case.

In your written answer, please include a citation to the statute and to the case that helps with the sub-rule. Compare the case factually to your client's case. Predict the outcome using language of probability.

Question 6:

You know that money intended for use in a drug crime can be seized by the government. But you need to so some more research. You search in the U.S. Code for Controlled Substances looking for the forfeiture process.

Write the title number and section here: ______________

You find and read the statute. If the answer is not clear, you need to find a case in the notes of decision that helps you on the sub-rule for whether the officers had probable cause to rely on such circumstantial evidence.

From the Notes of Decision index, write the note name and number here: ______________________

Go to that section of the Notes of Decision and find a helpful appellate court case named *U.S. v. U.S. Currency, $36,060.00,* from 1994. You might have to look in the pocket part.

Write the citation of the case here:

____

Read the summary of the case in the Notes of Decisions. Then, look up the case online and read the applicable part of the case.

In your written answer, please include a citation to the statute and to the case that helps with the sub-rule. Compare the case factually to your client's case. Predict the outcome using language of probability.

Question 7:

You know that the Stored Communications Act prevents electronic communication services (ECS) from disclosing the private messages of users to third parties without express permission in the statues. But you wonder whether the KOWO game servers are defined as ECS. You need to so some more research. You search in the U.S. Code for electronic mail, evidence and disclosure.

Write the title number and section here: ________________

You find and read the statute. If the answer is not clear, you need to find a case in the notes of decision that helps you on the sub-rule for whether KOWO has to answer the subpoena.

From the Notes of Decision index, write the note name and number here: __________________________

Go to that section of the Notes of Decision and find a helpful district court case named *Crispin*, from 2010. You might have to look in the pocket part.

Write the citation of the case here:

____

Read the summary of the case in the Notes of Decisions. Then, look up the case online and read the applicable part of the case.

In your written answer, please include a citation to the statute and to the case that helps with the sub-rule. Compare the case factually to your client's case. Predict the outcome using language of probability.

Question 8:

You know that the ordinary and necessary business expenses are deductible whereas deductions for business gifts have some strict limitations. You search in the U.S. Code that covers income tax, for the section relating to gifts and the types of deductions that might qualify as exemptions.

Write the title number and section here: ________________

You find and read the statute. If the answer is not clear, you need to find a case in the notes of decision that helps you on the sub-rule that describes incentives.

From the Notes of Decision index, write the note name and number here: ____________________________

Go to that section of the Notes of Decision and find a helpful district court case named *Dobbe*, from 2000. You might have to look in the pocket part.

Write the citation of the case here:

____

Read the summary of the case in the Notes of Decisions. Then, look up the case online and read the applicable part of the case.

In your written answer, please include a citation to the statute and to the case that helps with the sub-rule. Compare the case factually to your client's case. Predict the outcome using language of probability.

Sample Assignment

Sample Question:

You think that a federal law might prevent disclosure of polygraph test. In the U.S. Code, you look up polygraphs to find out about disclosure rules.

Write the title number and section here: 29 § 2009

You find and read the statute. If the answer is not clear, you need to find a case in the notes of decision that helps you on the sub-rule for whether the federal court has jurisdiction, generally to order arbitration.

From the Notes of Decision index, write the note name and number here: There is no index, only a few cases, so no index is included.

Go to the Notes of Decision and find a helpful district court case named *Long* from 1997. You might have to look in the pocket part.

Write the citation of the case here:

Long v. Mango's Tropical Café, 972 F. Supp. 655

Read the summary of the case in the Notes of Decisions. Then, look up the case online and read the applicable part of the case.

In your written answer, please include a citation to the statute and to the case that helps with the sub-rule. Compare the case factually to your client's case. Predict the outcome using language of probability.

Grading Example

What follows is an example from a student paper. The font and line spacing have been altered. You should double space and use 12-point Courier New font.

This is the *final draft* of the assignment with only minor edits by Professor Mundy for publication in this book.

Hence, this is a very good example of what your professors are looking for. You may notice that the student's legal English is not perfect, but the analysis is quite good and thorough.

Writing Assignment #3
Student ID 21955001

The issue is whether an employer, Smitty, is liable for disclosure when he told his employees that one of the security guards might be a murderer based on polygraph test. According to the U.S. Code, 29 U.S.C.A § 2008, an employer may disclose polygraph test results to not everyone but limited people. According to a court decision in Long, the word "disclose" does not mean merely "speak about" but rather "to make known", which is opening up to public about a certain person's identity. Long v. Mango's Tropical Café, Inc., S.D. FLA. 972 F. Supp. 655 (1997). In that case, the court considered the question of whether disclosure occurred when the employer talked about the polygraph's result of a certain employee without saying his name. The court opinion is that no disclosure occurred in that case. This is because, firstly, the owner of Mango's Café, Mr. Wallack, told his staff that one of the employees had failed a polygraph exam, but he has never mentioned the employee by name. Second, before the employer's statement occurred, the employee filed a lawsuit against Mango that she was fired because of polygraph test results, which made known to others that she is the one who did not past the test. In our case, Smitty informed about the test results of the IT team member to other employees, but he did not make known the person's identity. Also, that person then confronted Smitty, so other staff knew that he is a certain person that the employer mentioned. Therefore, it is likely that Smitty is not liable under the statute because he did not make people known the person's identity as well as the team member disclosed the test results to the public by himself.

Sample Answer Grade: 24 / 25

Format: 5

Grammar: 4 (some awkward sentence structures)

IRAAC: 5

Paraphrasing/Synthesis/Summarizing: 5

Analysis: 5 (good job)

[17]

STATUTES: ELECTRONIC RESEARCH EXERCISE

ELECTRONIC RESEARCH EXERCISE NUMBER 2 (R2)

INSTRUCTIONS

- Please type your answers. Answers should be **single-spaced** in **Courier New font size 8**. Pages should be numbered.
- Your paper must have a header on the first page (not needed on subsequent pages) including the following: a title; your Professor's name; and your student ID number. Do not write your name; use your student ID number.
- Please e-mail your answers prior to class or hand them in at the beginning of class according to your professor's preference.
- If you cut and paste, you must use quotation marks!
- There are 17 total questions in this assignment. Please do not miss any.

INTRODUCTION

The process of researching statutes online is similar to researching them in print. But, in reality, it is *much* easier.

If we know the citation for the code, we can look it up directly.

As we saw with secondary source research, many times when we are reading secondary sources, we may find a citation to a statute—like to California Penal Code 653m.

If we look up that statute in a commercial database like Lexis or Westlaw, we will be given key cases that have cited to that statute. We will also be given other secondary sources that describe or discuss the statute. Amazing!

If we don't know the exact section of the code, but we know which jurisdiction we are in, we can browse the code using a Table of Contents. That is not a common research method.

More commonly, on the Internet, we can execute a keyword search on the entire code. Or we can limit our keyword search to the table of contents or to an index.

We can easily learn to locate statutes.

Being able to read, understand, and apply those statutes is a different matter.

You are learning to read the law every day in your substantive law courses. As you read cases that interpret a statute, pay careful attention to the court's reasoning!

The Assignment

For this assignment, we are going to focus on state law research.

Please use the following fact pattern when answering the questions below:

> Our law firm's client, Bella Diball, complains that a retail store breached a contract to provide a prom dress for her use in her senior prom ceremony at her high school in Trussville, Alabama.
>
> Our client, Miss Bella Diball, who is 18 years old, was going to prom with her high-school boyfriend. Bella ordered a Rewee Weeton dress. Rewee Weeton features the latest in high-tech wearables.
>
> Bella's dress was to have a built-in electronic system. Fiber optic threads sewn into the dress would change color. Bella said, "I want it to be like Katniss Everdeen."

The price gown was $3,000.

The day of the prom, Bella put on her dress. The lighting system seemed to be working well.

However, during the prom, there was a short-circuit in the dress's lighting system.

Bella and Clint were elected prom Queen and King. While Bella was doing the celebratory slow dance with Clint as Prom King and Queen, her dress began emitting flashing, strobe lights. The circuit board started smoking.

Bella was humiliated in front of the entire school. Many of her classmates posted it to social media. It went viral.

After the prom, Bella and Clint had an argument and ended their dating relationship.

Bella says that, because of the "dress situation," she was humiliated. She was angry, embarrassed, depressed, and she lost a lot of sleep, and had nightmares about the event.

There may be many possible causes of action including breach of contract, fraud, negligence. However, your supervising attorney wants you to focus on whether there was a violation of the Uniform Commercial Code for breach of warranty.

The Uniform Commercial Code, as adopted in the state of Alabama, governs the sale of goods. Your supervising attorney want to know, not only whether there was a breach of warranty, but *whether Bella can recover for emotional distress.*

FREE ONLINE RESEARCH

When you are researching state codes or the U.S. code online, you have several options. First, there are free websites available.

Cornell Law School's Legal Institute provides free access to the U.S. Code.[1]

Many states also have free versions of their code online.

Also, websites like findlaw.com are free and easy to use.

Be careful when using free, online sources. You must make sure the law has not changed or been overturned.

---

[1] https://www.law.cornell.edu/uscode/text.

Second, there are commercial (paid) services like Westlaw or Lexis Advance. Other paid services include Hein Online (especially good for international law research) and Loislaw.com.

Assuming you know nothing about the Uniform Commercial Code, it would be wise to approach this problem by first doing some background reading. Go to Google and enter the following search:

ucc buyer's damages breach of warranty

One of the first links should be to the Cornell Law School's Legal Information Institute.

1. **Please give a citation for that section of the UCC.**
2. **According to sub-sections (2) & (3), what is the measure of damages for breach of warranty? You may paraphrase or you may quote your answer.**
3. **Subsection (3) says the next section defines consequential damages?**
4. **According to that next section, what do consequential damages include (see subsection (2))? You may paraphrase or you may quote your answer.**
5. **After reading these sections of the UCC, do you think Bella can recover emotional distress damages? Why or why not? Please answer in at least one or two sentences.**

First, you may note that the UCC on Cornell's website does not have any annotations. It contains only the text of the code. It does not give any links to cases or other secondary sources that interpret the code.

Second, you may be aware that the UCC is a secondary source. The UCC is a model code. This means that a jurisdiction, like Alabama, has to adopt the model code for itself.

Sometimes a jurisdiction like Alabama makes some changes when it adopts the model code.

Let's check Alabama.

STATE CODE SEARCH

Alabama has its code online. http://alisondb.legislature.state.al.us/alison/CoA.aspx

However, that page is often unavailable for some reason. So let's just use a search engine.

Run an internet search for:

Alabama commercial code buyer's damages for non-delivery

One of the first links should be to justia.com which provides a free copy of the Alabama code.

6. **Please give a citation for that section of the Alabama Code.**
7. **Read both of the applicable sections of the Alabama code as you did for the UCC above. What differences are there, if any?**
8. **Do those differences impact your answer as to Bella's claim for emotional distress?**
9. **Does Justia.com provide any annotations or just the plain text of the code?**

USING LEXIS ADVANCE®[2]

Lexis Advance ("Lexis") and Westlaw provide annotated codes. That's why you pay them the big bucks.

Let's look at the same code on Lexis Advance®.

Open your personal Lexis Advance account.

In the search box, let's find the following citation:

Ala. Code 7-2-715

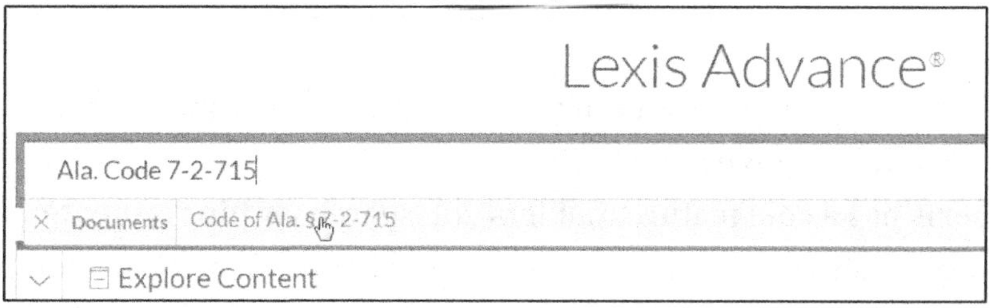

[2] Lexis Advance is a trademark of Lexis.

One major benefit of using Lexis Advance is that it provides annotations. Annotations contain helpful research information about the statute.

For example, in addition to the text of the statute, Lexis Advance provides: History (notes about changes to the statute) and Notes to Decisions (links to cases that have applied the statute).

Lexis is also home to "Shepard's."

Shepards is a citator service. Citator services tell you which authorities have cited to this source. Thus, you can determine whether a source is still good law or whether it has been overturned. You can also use a citator like Shepards to find secondary sources that have cited to your source.

Please click on the link that says: "Shepardize this document." This will show you the history of the statute, any cases that have cited to this statute, and other sources—like secondary sources.

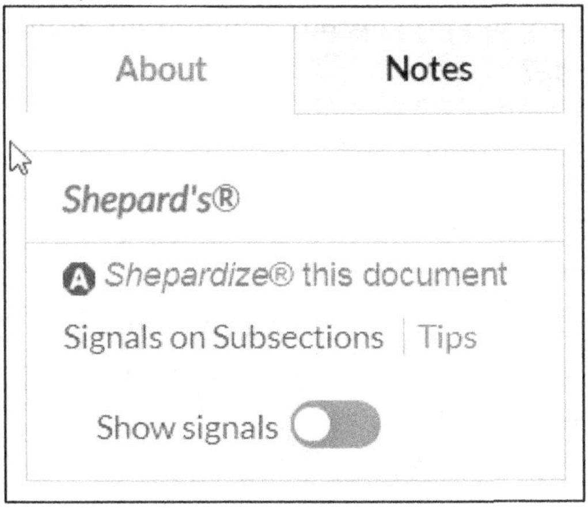

There are many cases citing to this statute. We want to limit them to cases that involve mental distress.

Lexis has a cool feature that lets you search within results. Scrolling down on the left side, please "Search Within Results" for the phrase: "mental distress".

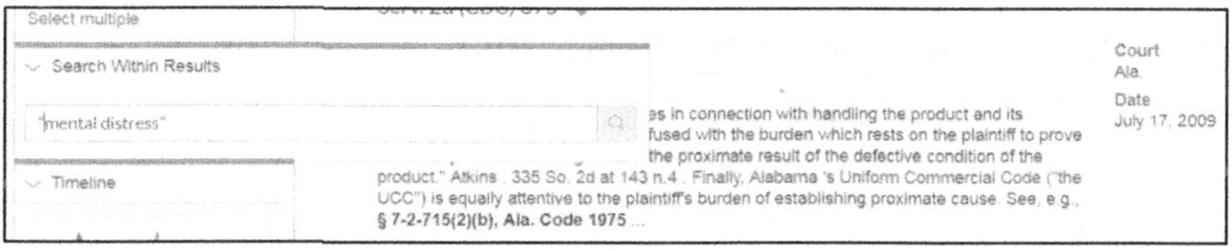

10. **Please give a citation to the top case entitled, *Volkswagen*.**
11. **Reading that case at Headnote 1, does the general rule in Alabama allow mental anguish to be recoverable for breach of contract?**
12. **Is there an exception, and if so, why?**
13. **Reading Headnote 7 through the end of the case, does the Alabama Commercial Code allow the jury to award damages for mental anguish for breach of warranty?**
14. **That case applied to the sale of a new car, do you think the same reasoning should apply to Bella's dress? Why or why not? Please answer in one or two sentences.**

USING WESTLAW®

Let's find the same statute on Westlaw. We could do a keyword search on the main page. But let's try a different route.

On the main Westlaw page, go to the State tab and click on Alabama.

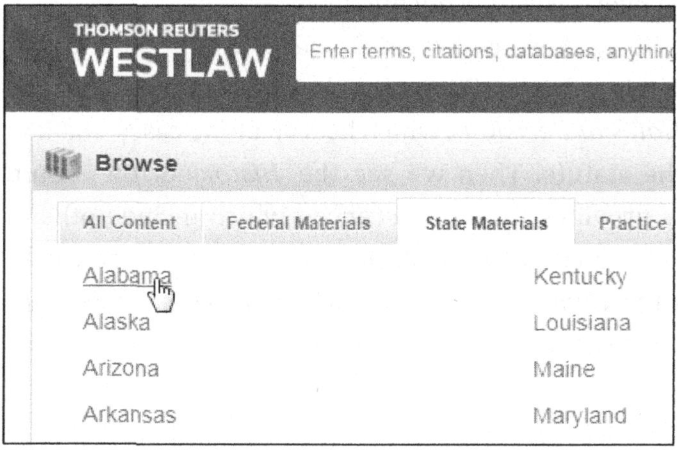

Next, we want to select Alabama Statutes & Court Rules

From this page we can search the Alabama code directly in the search bar.

We can also navigate through the table of contents. Already, you might have spotted Title 7, Commercial Code, in the table of contents.

We can even search the statute using the Alabama Statutes Index which is exactly like the print index—since Westlaw prints the code books for law libraries.

Let's searh the Alabama Code for:

damages for breach of warranty

The statute in Westlaw also has helpful annotations.

First, there is an incredibly helpful tool bar on the right hand side of almost every Westlaw document.

In addition, Westlaw provides a set of tabs at the top of the page. The first tab is for the *Document*, the actual text of the statute. Next comes *Notes of Decisions*, which lists all of the cases that have referenced the statute. Then we see the *History* of the statute. Next, Westlaw provides *Citing References*, which include other authorities that have cited to the statute, like secondary sources. Finally, there is the *Context & Analysis*, which specifically lists secondary sources and other helpful commentary on the statute.

Finally, you can open the *Table of Contents*. Or you can use the green arrows to page back and forth as if you were reading the statute in a book.

Under the Citing Refences tab, please select "Secondary Sources."

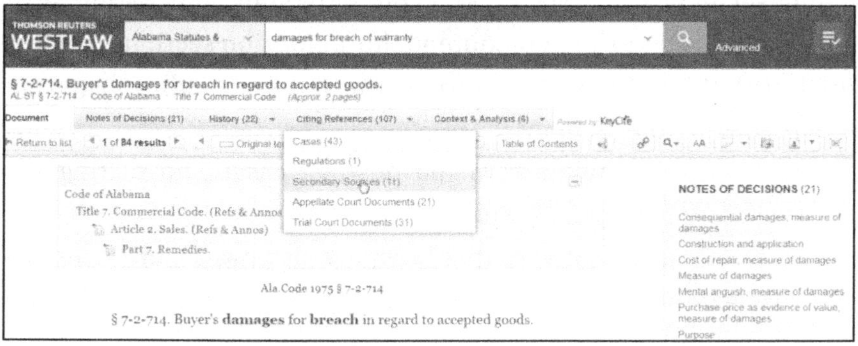

Scroll down till you find a secondary source entitled: "Alabama Law of Damages s 35:18, Buyer's damages after acceptance of goods".

15. **What does that secondary source say about "mental anguish"?**
16. **As you can see, the footnotes to this secondary source links to many additional cases. You see the *Volkswagen* case, but you also see *Barko Hydraulics*. Please read the *Barko Hydraulics* case. Please describe the holding in the *Barko* case in one or two sentences.**

We can see that, when researching a statute, we need to be aware of the surrounding legislative scheme. For example, in our present case, you would need to locate both section 2-714 and section 2-715.

To understand these sections and how they apply to the facts of our case, we have to understand case precedents like *Volkswagen* and like *Barko*.

Volkswagen is a positive case analogy for our client. Barko is a negative case analogy for our client—meaning, the outcome is not what our client would like to happen in her case.

FINAL NOTES

Friends, this is a very common pattern for researching statutes. If you don't know the statute, look it up using a secondary source.

Once you have found the statute, use the annotated code to find helpful secondary sources to help you understand the statute. Also look around in the Table of Contents for definition sections. Finally, find Notes of Decisions that interpret the statute—adding a subrule or a helpful factual analogy.

Draw positive analogies to the positive cases and distinguish negative cases from your case.

You should also be aware that Westlaw also has a citator service called Keycite which will tell you if a case or a statute is still good law.

17. Final question, looking at the rules, plus the analogous cases, both Volkswagen and Barko, how do you predict whether a court would award damages to Bella for emotional distress arising from the breach of warranty? Please answer in at least a sentence or two.

OPTIONAL WRITING EXERCISE

Write your finding from your research as an IRAAC writing assignment using the statutes as well as the two cases mentioned. The cases might be used as authority for a subrule(s) or as positive and negative analogies. Please also include a brief *public policy* argument indicating the significance in the fact that Alabama altered section 2-714 of the UCC.

Your professor might ask you to write your answer as a one page, one paragraph assignment or as a multiple page, multiple paragraph assignment.

[18]

CASE ANALOGIES: AN INTRODUCTION

INTRODUCTION

By now, you are on your way to becoming an expert in reading cases. You are reading cases every day for your substantive law courses. Hopefully you are still briefing every case.

Reading cases in casebooks is a bit of an academic exercise. When we read casebooks, we are reading edited, appellate court opinions. We are reading them in the context of a particular point of law.

However, when lawyers read a case for practice, the case is read for a specific purpose. In addition, unless the lawyer is reading a case for private amusement or continuing education, the case is being read in the context of a client's legal case.

As lawyers, we read cases in two ways:

1. As authority for a rule
2. As analogy, to show how a rule was applied in a factually similar situation

Let's explore these two functions further.

1. Authority for a rule

First, we read cases as authority for a rule (broadly defined).

We may use a case as authority for a public policy position or for a general legal principle. For instance, we might use the *McBoyle* case as authority for the principle of law that a criminal statute should be narrowly interpreted.

At common law, we may cite to a case as authority for general rule of law.

For statutory law, we may cite a case as a rule for how a particular word or phrase of the statute should be interpreted. For example, one might cite to *McBoyle* in order to interpret the word "vehicle" in the National Motor Vehicle Theft Act. In *McBoyle*, the rule itself comes from the statute. Yet, a sub-rule, the definition of the term vehicle, comes from that case.

If a decision is from a higher court in your direct line of appeal, like *McBoyle*, that court's interpretation of the statute is binding.

To those coming from a civil law background, the use of case precedent might seem strange. After all, the statute itself does not explicitly say that an "airplane" is not a "vehicle" for the purposes of the motor vehicle theft act. The government prosecutors thought it a reasonable interpretation. Why should a court be bound by one judge's interpretation of that statute?

We will leave such difficult questions to your jurisprudence or legal philosophy classes. Perhaps one reason is to ensure a uniform application of the law. The famous British jurist Blackstone articulated another theory. He thought that, as with Biblical exegesis, there is only one true interpretation. Once someone has articulated that interpretation, it may be relied upon into perpetuity.

Regardless, the fact remains: we read cases as authority for a rule.

To restate: even if the rule itself comes from a statute or from a common law case precedent, we may yet cite to another case as authority for a sub-rule. For example, in *McBoyle* the rule comes from a statute. *McBoyle* defines an element of the statute: vehicle. The case also gives, as its reason, a general principle of law: criminal statutes must be interpreted narrowly. You could use *McBoyle* as good authority for either of these points.

In a similar vein, in the *Garratt* case, the rule for battery comes from the common law. The *Garratt* case gives a sub-rule for a particular element of battery: intent.

You have the rule of law: battery.

Battery has several elements including intent.

To analyze the rule of law, you have to analyze each element. You have to see if the facts of your client's case are in the same class or category as those elements, like "intent."

But what if the statute or common law rule has not defined that term?

Then, a latter court might offer an interpretation or definition.

If that court is in your direct line of appeal, that interpretation or definition is binding. You must consider it when applying the elements of a rule of law to your client's case.

Please note, a case may be binding for a rule even if it is not factually similar to your client's case!

This is a hard point for incoming students to grasp. As stated above, *McBoyle* could be used when interpreting any number of criminal statutes from residential burglary to war crimes.

McBoyle is not factually similar to those examples, but that isn't the point. We are using it as authority for a rule, not as a factually analogous case.

Finally, a word of warning. Don't pull rules from concurring or dissenting opinions. With some limited exceptions, the rule should come from the language of the main decision.

Also, don't pull rules from dicta. Dicta is language in a court decision that does not directly affect the outcome (the judgment) of the case. Sometimes dicta can be confused with a court's holding or reasoning. If you are struggling to determine whether language in a decision is dicta (an extraneous point), consider whether it directly affects the judgment.

That being said, dicta can be cited to as persuasive authority.

2. Analogy

We also use cases to show how a rule is applied to a factually similar situation. We call this "case analogies" or "analogous cases."

If the outcome of a case precedent is in line with what our client wants, we call it a "positive analogy." If the outcome goes against our client, we call it a "negative analogy."

You might think about one of those picture games you played as a child, where you were asked to look at two pictures and to identify any differences. Likewise, we compare case precedents to our client's case.

Of course, a case can be used as both authority and as an analogy. Or it can be used for one or the other. It does not have to be used for both.

Analogy plays an important part in logical legal arguments.[1] Analogy is used to build a legal proof.

You have studied IRAAC legal reasoning. You know that IRAAC is a deductive logic syllogism in which a rule of law is applied to a set of facts. You may wonder how analogous logic fits into the context of the IRAC deductive logic syllogism.

The typical line of legal reasoning goes like this:

There is a rule of law. That rule of law gives relief to your client if certain legal facts are met. We call those legal facts elements.

In an unusual case, you might be called upon to use inductive logic to define the rule of law itself. For example, you might have to read many cases in the common law to determine the best, most accurate, most recent iteration of the common law rule. That's what the experts did in the Restatements of Law. They give a synthesis of the rule from a majority of jurisdictions.

---

[1] Not every legal argument is based on logic. Public policy arguments or juridical arguments about what the law should be or do, these are not based on logic.

Usually, however, the rule of law is given to you by the statute or by a widely accepted statement of the common law made by a higher court in your direct line of appeal.

According to that rule of law, your client is entitled to relief if the elements are met.

We then use deductive logic to apply the rule of law to your client's facts. We ask whether the client's facts are in the same class or category as the legal elements.

If it is not clear whether your client's facts meet a legal element, we look to see whether a higher court has interpreted that element (see "Authority for a rule" above).

Once any additional rules have been applied, we might still question whether our client's particular facts are in the same class or category as that element.

We then look for analogous cases, to see how a court has applied the rule to similar facts.

a. Questions of first impression

If we find no factually similar cases, we say it is an "issue of first impression." An issue (or question) of first impression is one that a court has never been called upon to decide. A question of first impression can involve either a novel interpretation of law or an application of law to a hitherto unaddressed set of facts.

In such cases, a lawyer has to convince the court that a reading of the rule as applied to her client's facts is reasonable (and that her opponent's reading is unreasonable).

That's what happened in *McBoyle*. The prosecutor argued that the National Motor Vehicle Theft Act could apply to airplanes. The defense disagreed. In that question of first impression, the court sided with the defense.

Afterward, *McBoyle* became an authority for interpreting the term "vehicle." *McBoyle* also became a case analogy. Any future interpretation of the element "vehicle" must take that holding into consideration.

For example, if a prosecution was brought for transport of a stolen hovercraft, the parties would need to argue whether the outcome in the *McBoyle* case should apply.

In the common law, this use of case precedent comes from the principle of *stare decisis*. Simply put, factually similar cases should be decided in the same way.

Questions of first impression are rare.

Normally, there are a number of factually similar cases available. The number of cases available will depend on how broadly or how narrowly we define the "factually similar cases."

Lawyers use factually similar cases to argue whether a client's facts are in the same class or category as the legal elements, thus triggering (or denying) relief.

b. Binding case precedent versus persuasive case precedent

When doing legal research, we are looking for binding case precedent: factually similar cases from a higher court in your direct line of appeal.

If a binding case precedent is exactly similar, it is "on point." The matter is settled. The rule of law has been applied to a similar set of facts; thus, the same outcome should result in our case.

However, it often happens that the facts are not "exactly" similar.

The question "what is a factually similar case," is one that every lawyer struggles with.

This is why analogy—arguing from similarities or differences—is the weakest form of logic. It is why two lawyers on opposite sides of litigation can make a convincing argument using the *same* case.

If a case is not "exactly" factually similar, it may not be binding. It is merely persuasive. Even if it comes from the highest court in your jurisdiction.

Still, persuasive cases are incredibly useful.

Lawyers use persuasive case precedent to predict what a court is likely to do or to persuade a court as to what it should do.

This brings us to an interesting point. Unlike rules, persuasive case analogies may come from courts *outside* our jurisdiction.

When we use cases as authority for a rule, that rule should, almost always, come from primary, binding authority in your jurisdiction.

For example, you would never ask a Texas court to apply a rule from California when dealing with an issue arising in Texas. The rule must come from Texas.

However, you may cite to factually similar cases from other jurisdictions. You may tell a court in Texas about a factually similar case in California.

These are not binding of course. A binding case precedent would be a factually similar case from a higher court in your direct line of appeal. Nevertheless, analogous cases from other jurisdictions could be persuasive authorities.

c. Using persuasive case precedent

Analogous cases are used when analyzing a rule of law, to determine whether your facts are in the same class or category as the elements and, thus, whether legal relief is triggered.

For example, if the legal relief is monetary damages from a breach of contract, you would have to analyze, among other elements, whether there has been an "offer" and "acceptance."

You might then turn to case precedent to determine what is meant by the term "offer" (is there a sub-rule defining the term "offer").

You might also turn to case precedent to see whether an offer has been found to have existed in factually similar cases.

Lawyers use inductive logic. Lawyers read many cases and synthesize those cases. Different strategies are employed depending on the type of analogy needed (positive or negative) or the number of case analogies available.

The goal is the same, *to distill the cases into a predictive statement*. A predictive statement sounds like this: "In *these* types of cases the courts reach *this* outcome." Put another way, "Given these types of facts, this element is met (or not met)."

A lawyer reads cases looking not only for common facts, but also for "material" common facts. A material fact is one that affects the outcome of a case. This step can be quite difficult for first year law students.

For example, some states define residential burglary as breaking into the "dwelling place" of another. A "dwelling place" might be someone's house, but courts have also applied the term to screened-in porches and to unattached garages. Those courts were not looking at the type of building: house versus garage. The material, factual commonality was whether those places were used in a residential way: did people eat there, sleep there, live there.

Some students would look at two cases, one involving a house and the other involving an unattached garage, and think, *These two cases are not factually similar. Hence, I cannot use this case as a factually analogous case.*

Those students would be wrong.

It can be especially difficult for new students to determine a "helpful" level of similarity. If you narrow the facts too much, you may not find any similar cases (unless there's a case directly "on point"). If you broaden the factual similarities too much, those cases may not be helpful in creating a predictive function.

Analogous cases are useful to the extent they help create a predictive function.

Consider a nightly weather report on the news. The meteorologist looks at hundreds of similar days and similar data points including wind direction and barometric pressure. Based on those analogous cases, the meteorologist predicts tomorrow's weather.

Lawyers use cases in the same way. We use them to predict what is likely to happen in a client's case or to persuade a court what it should do.

We read cases actively. Each new case may adjust our internal, ongoing synthesis.

As we read, we form and revise a predictive function: "in *these* types of cases, courts reach *this* conclusion."

We test that predictive function against every case to see if it helps us explain or understand what the courts are doing. We test it against hypotheticals to see whether our predictive function is reasonable.

Moreover, as we argue cases and as courts reach a ruling, those rulings become part of the next cycle of legal reasoning. In that way, we contribute to the body of the law and to the ongoing legal dialogue.

A word of warning. When students synthesize factually similar cases and create a predictive function (noting a strain of commonality), sometimes the students think they are creating a new "rule."

The student may think they are brilliant and have created something that nobody else has ever thought of before. Nope.

The rule is the rule. That is to say, the general rule from the common law or from the statute is the rule. The higher court's interpretation of an element is a rule.

A brilliant synthesis of analogous cases, awesome and creative as it may be, is not a new rule.

Case synthesis is a way of defining the class or category of the elements so as to determine whether your client's facts fit those elements.

In that way, through the principle of *stare decisis*, case precedents do affect the actual rule. However, I find it unhelpful to refer to this type of synthesis, the predictive functions we create, as "rules."

Nevertheless, the heavy lifting of legal reasoning is case synthesis—learning to recognize and categorize material factual similarities among the available case precedent both inside and outside your jurisdiction.

The easiest way to begin doing this heavy lifting is, as you read cases, to make a list of similar facts.

After making that list, look for a strain of commonality that could serve as a predictive function.

As you think about it, consider the reason for the rule. The best predictive functions explain commonalities in light of the reason for the rule.

> *Try making a statement like: "in these types of cases (define "these types") the court reaches this outcome (define it) because of this reason for the rule (define it)."*

If you are having trouble finding factually similar cases, broaden your idea of the legally relevant facts. For example, in a residential burglary case, don't focus on primary residences only—you could look at cases involving garages, porches, and vacation homes.

Or, for instance, if you were the attorney in the *Wallace v. Rosen*, a torts case where a woman was pushed down a stairwell at her daughter's school: if you only looked for cases that involved schools and stairwells, you might be out of luck.

You would want to broaden what you'd consider the legally relevant facts to include other places where touches might not be considered offensive in a given context, like crowded movie theaters.

However, if you broadened the legally relevant facts too much, say: every battery case ever written. That would be too broad and wouldn't help serve a useful predictive function.

Our main goal is to develop the skills to read cases and to apply them *individually* or to be able to *synthesize a group* of cases to form a useful predictive function.

[19]

Legislative History Research & Exercise

Electronic Research Exercise Number 3 (R3)

Instructions

- Please type your answers. Answers should be single-spaced in Courier New Font size 8. Pages should be numbered.
- Your paper must have a header on the first page (not needed on subsequent pages) including the following: a title; your Professor's name; and your student ID number. Do not write your name; use your student ID number.
- Please e-mail your answers prior to class or hand them in at the beginning of class according to your professor's preference.
- If you cut and paste, you must use quotation marks!
- There are 14 total questions in this assignment. Please do not miss any.

Legislative History

In a previous chapter, we read about the process by which a bill becomes a law.

Sometimes, the law is not written very clearly. Judges have to determine the meaning of an ambiguous word or phrase.

As with all statutory interpretation, the guiding principle is the legislative intent. What did the legislature mean by these words?

Hence, when faced with an ambiguity, judges may look to legislative history for help.

Judges might look at the following sources of legislative history:

1. The text of the bill itself (along with any changes)
2. The committee and subcommittee reports
3. Floor debates
4. The conference action report

Most judges agree that the words themselves (the text of the bill) are the best indicator of legislative intent. That's why Justice Holmes in the *McBoyle* case first tried to ascertain the plain meaning of the word "vehicle" in the National Motor Vehicle Theft Act.

Typically, judges are only interested in legislative history when the statute is ambiguous (capable of more than one interpretation). Bad judges sometimes use the legislative history to create ambiguity, to give them "wiggle room" to interpret a statute in the way they prefer.

Good judges are rightly skeptical of legislative history.

The political process and the increasing politicization of judicial decisions have created strange incentives in the creation of legislative history. For example, knowing that legislative history might be used to interpret a statute, politicians will often try to put their interpretation on record in the legislative history.

Legislative assistants, young college graduates who run the Capitol Hill offices and who have ideological agendas, will often pack congressional hearings with speakers who testify about a bill in an ideologically-charged way.

These political actions create cover for progressive judges to interpret a statute in a particular way.

Hence, legislative history is not always reliable.

Even Congressman and Senators who speak on the floor of their respective houses may later edit or amend their remarks.

Finally, who among us believes that politicians do what they do for the reasons they say? Most people suspect that politicians say one thing and do something entirely different.

For these reasons, legislative history—that is, the record created by politicians in the legislature when creating a bill—should be taken with several healthy grains of salt (an idiom meaning you should be skeptical).

The Assignment

We are going to focus on the electronic research tools that you can use to research the legislative history of a federal statute.

It is difficult to search legislative history unless you understand the process by which a bill is introduced, sent to committee, reported to the chamber, voted on, and signed into law.

Please review that Chapter 15 in this textbook before continuing.

Some free websites are maintained by the federal government. For example, we are going to focus on the Computer Fraud and Abuse Act. After being signed into law, that law was published in title 18, section 1030 of the U.S. Code.

In particular, we are interested in 18 U.S.C. § 1030(a)(5)(C) which makes it illegal to "intentionally access[] a protected computer without authorization, and as a result of such conduct, cause[] damage and loss." For instance, how is damage different than loss?

We want to know what is meant by "without authorization" or "damage and loss."

The first thing we want to search is:

The text of the bill itself & Any Changes

Changes to the language of a bill and later changes to the language of a statute by subsequent amending bills, help judges interpret the language of a statute.

Please go to: http://uscode.house.gov/

Let's look up Title 18, Section 1030.

This free government website gives us the text of the code as well as amendments.

1. **How is "damage" defined in section (e)(8)**
2. **How is "loss" defined in section (e)(11)?**
3. **How was damage previously defined in subsection (e)(8) prior to the 2001 amendment by Public Law 107-56?**
4. **Under the new statutory language, to prove "damages" does a party have to prove a "loss" of at least $5,000?**
5. **Is it fair to say that the term damage no longer incorporates but is separate from the term loss? Why or why not?**

Committee and Subcommittee Reports

After a bill is submitted to the Senate or to the House of Representatives, that bill is referred to a committee or a subcommittee that deals with that particular topic.

The committee will hold hearings. The committee will take oral and written testimony. The committee may make some changes to the bill.

The committee may then refer the edited bill to the entire chamber. If so, the committee will write a report.

That report is a good resource for determining legislative intent. Consider the Computer Fraud and Abuse Act of 1986.

Let's find the bill.

Go to: www.congress.gov.

This web site is maintained by the Library of Congress. It contains a wealth of legislative information. Some of its databases go back many years, while others contain information only since about 1996. Therefore, you need to assess this website's coverage to see if it contains the information you need.

You can also use Congress.gov to trace the progress of pending bills as they make their way through the legislative process.

In our case, we want to search "All Legislation" for "Computer Fraud and Abuse Act of 1986".

Scroll down to find the Computer Fraud and Abuse Act of 1986. We see that the CFAA was originally (1) H.R. 4718 (House of Representatives, bill number 4718); (2) it was sponsored by Representative William J. Hughes from New Jersey; (3) a similar bill was also passed by the Senate as S. 2281; and (4) the CFAA became Public Law 99-474.

Clicking on that Senate Bill, we can get a lot of information. Including, as we scroll down, we can use the tabs to locate the Senate "Committee" Report.

6. **What is the citation for the Senate Committee Report Number for S. 2281?**

Unfortunately, we cannot read that report on Congress.gov. That document is too old. However, a commercial research database should have that Senate Report.

Let's open Westlaw.

WESTLAW LEGISLATIVE HISTORY

There are many ways to find the legislative history on Westlaw. For example, you could search the for Congressional Committee Reports under the U.S. Congressional and Administrative News database.

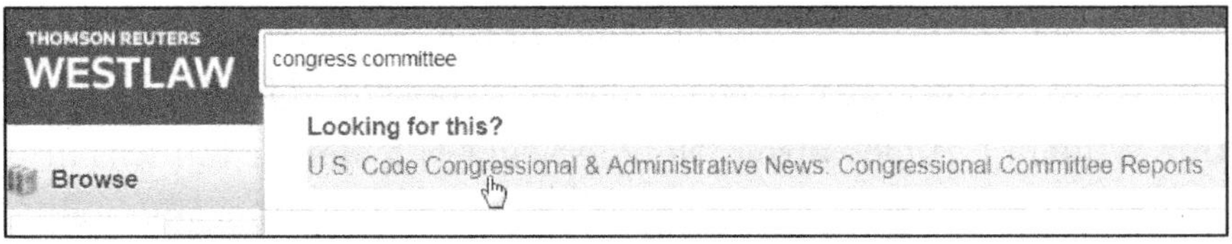

In that database, we can scroll down and search for our Senate Report number. Enter your answer from question number 6 above.

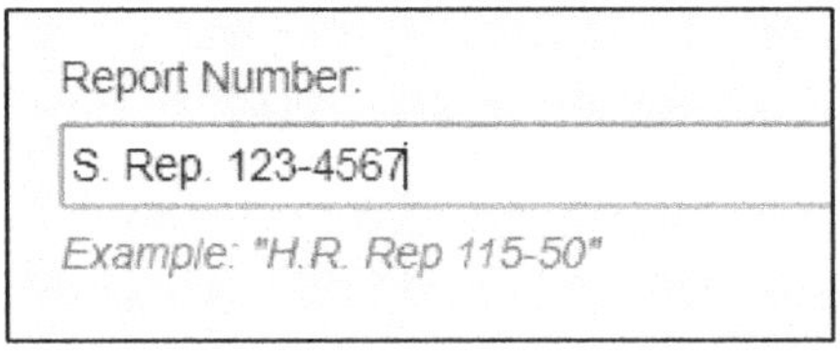

Or we can go to the statute itself and use the "History" tab to find the different versions of the statute, any Editor's and Revisor's Notes, Bill Drafts, and Legislative History materials.

Click on Legislative History Materials.

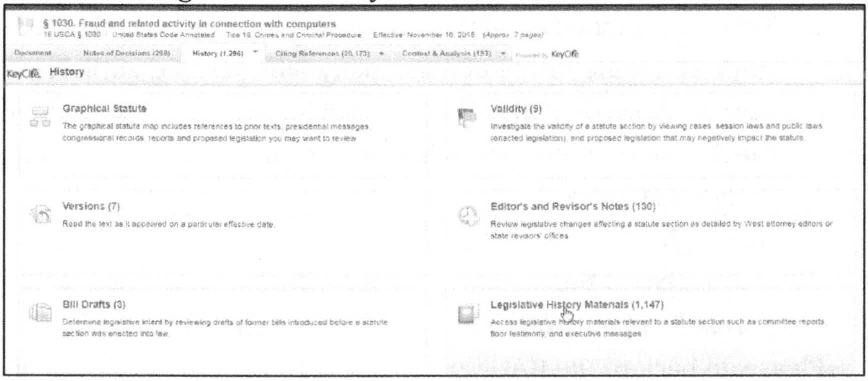

If we scroll down to 1986, we will find an entire "Compiled History" of Public Law 99-474! Here, the government accountability office (GAO) has compiled all the key legislative history documents for that bill.

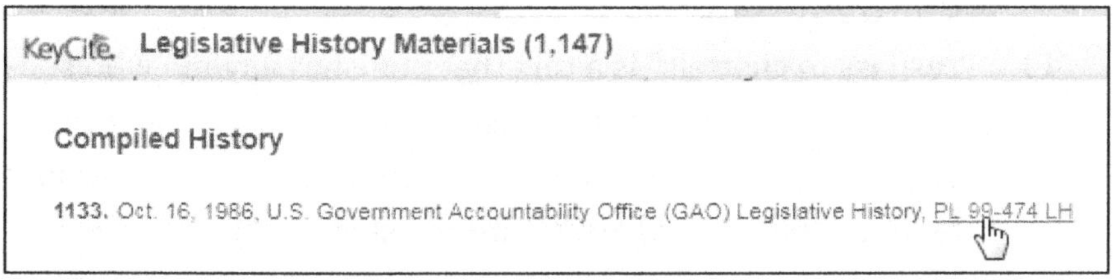

Keep this tab open. We will use it again!

Scrolling down, we can easily find a pdf version of the S. 2281 Senate Committee Report.

Having grown up in the era of microfilm and microfiche, I am still so amazed by internet search capabilities!

Click on that pdf. You should be looking at a 22-page document. Not a 10-page document. Make sure you are looking at the correct document.

7. **According to page 5 and 6, the drafters changed the mens rea from knowingly to intentionally in order to "focus federal criminal prosecutions" on whom?**

8. **This act extended liability from those "without authorization: to those on the inside of a company who "exceed authorized access." According to page 13 of that Senate Report, how does the Senate describe the definition of terms including "exceeds authorized access."**
9. **Although "exceeds authorized access" is now defined in the statute, could the Senate's characterization be applied to the phrase "without authorization"? Explain why or why not.**

Please go back to the GAO Compiled Legislative History page on Westlaw.

Let's look at House Report Number 99-612 from May 22, 1986.

10. **On Page 5 of that report, how does Congress compare "hackers" to trespassers?**
11. **"Trespass to chattels" is a tort that punishes anyone who substantially interferes with the use of another's personal property ("chattels"). Plaintiffs must show that the offender had intentional physical contact with the chattel and that the contact caused some substantial interference or damage. Based on the § 1030 statutory definition of damages, and the Committee Report language about "hackers," please make a one or two sentence analogy between the rule for "trespass to chattels" and the rule for damages under § 1030.**

Floor Debates

So far, we have looked at changes to the language of the bill or of the statute. We have looked at the language of committee reports.

Judges might also look to what was said on the floor of the House or of the Senate. Especially by a bill's sponsor or co-sponsor.

The Congressional Record is published daily. It publishes everything that happens in the House or in the Senate including speeches.

From your research, you found that Congressman Hughes made a speech on the floor of the House in support of the Computer Fraud and Abuse Act of 1986 on April 30, 1986.

Frankly, you could find this document quite easily under the GAO Compiled Legislative History perhaps.

But, let's find it by searching the Congressional Record

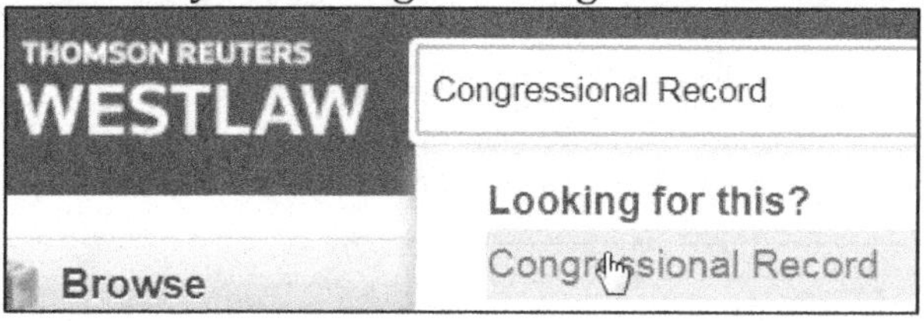

Search for:
William Hughes & "computer fraud and abuse act of 1986"

Read the Congressional Record remarks from April 30, 1986.

12. **Although subsection (a)(5) has changed somewhat over time, according to the bill's sponsor, Congressman Hughes, what type of provision was (a)(5) and what is it designed for?**
13. **Based on Congressman Hughes' statement, do you think the Computer Fraud and Abuse Act of 1986 should be used to punish people who log-in to Netflix using a friend or roommate's password?**

Conference Action Report

Finally, we learn from Congressman Hughes' floor speech, that a similar bill passed the Senate. Hence, there appears to have been no need for a joint conference of the House and Senate to "iron out" a compromise bill.

Had there been a Conference Action, that Report would be of great interest to judges seeking to interpret the language of a statute.

LEXIS ADVANCE

Finally, let's look at Lexis Advance.

Lexis Advance has a nice feature where they collect the legislative history of certain key statutes. Let's check that out.

Let's look up Legislative Histories on Lexis.

Following this link will allow you to search a number of collected legislative histories.

Let's run a search for: North Korean Human Rights.

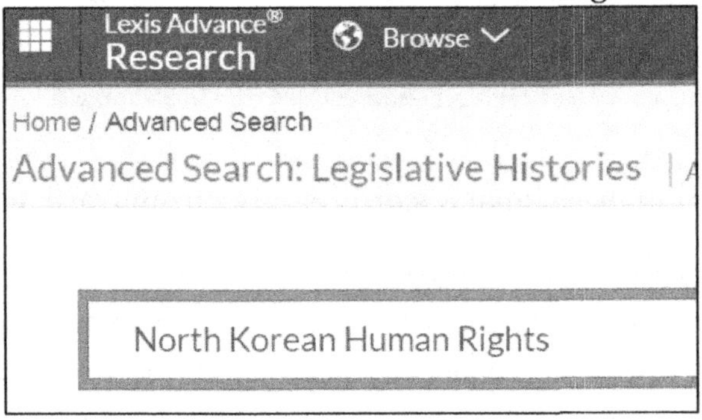

Lexis Advance lets you run a search within a search. This feature is called "Narrow By."

It is very helpful when you want to narrow the search results. Let's Narrow By Sources → "Committee Reports"

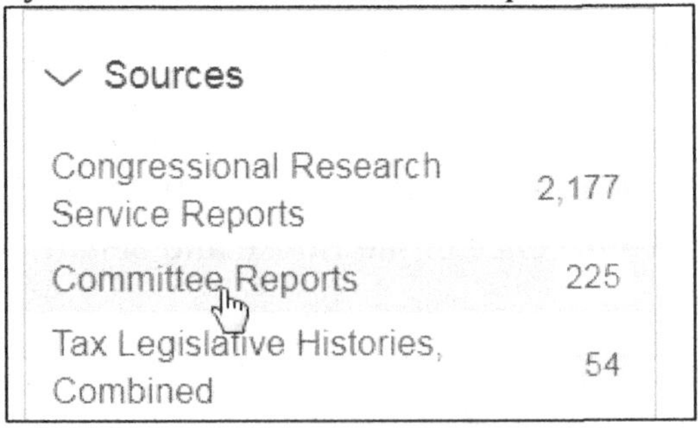

A Committee Report for the North Korea Sanctions and Enforcement Act of 2015 (House Report 114-392 Part 1) should near the top of the page.

Click on that link.

14. Under the Findings Section of the report, what did Congress state concerning North Korea and its development of nuclear weapons?

Conclusion

Legislative histories can be useful for determining the legislative intent. The strongest sources of legislative history are (1) the language of the bill itself; (2) the committee report recommending the bill to the entire chamber; (3) speeches or debates, especially by the bill's sponsors; and (4) any conference report sending a compromise bill back to both chambers.

In addition, the President will sometimes make statements when he signs a bill. Those statements could also be used as some evidence of legislative intent.

Legislative history is helpful in determining legislative intent, which is what judges are looking for when they interpret statutes. However, it is good to have a skeptical view of the value of legislative histories since they are part of the political process.

[20]

RESEARCHING CASES

INTRODUCTION

International students who study American law sometimes think legal research is all about finding cases. When faced with a research problem, they immediately execute an internet search, hoping to find an analogous case.

Their hopes are usually dashed.

Unless you are already familiar with an area of law, it is generally a bad idea to start your legal research by searching for a factually similar case.

As we've learned, most American law is codified. The first step in legal research is to locate the statute or rule.

Unlike civil law jurisdictions, our search doesn't end there. Next, we must read any cases that have interpreted that statute or that have applied the statute to a factually similar situation. Usually, the annotated code will point you toward the key cases.

Occasionally, you may be called upon to research a common law issue. If so, you might need to examine the case law to find the rule.

You may see experienced lawyers begin legal research by looking for factually similar cases in the target jurisdiction. Experienced lawyers take this approach because they already have a general idea about the law itself. If so, they might turn to case law research.

Even so, many experienced lawyers first use secondary sources.

Similarly, if you run into a common law issue, better to begin your research with a secondary source, like a state legal encyclopedia or a state practice guide.

However, international lawyers seldom get involved in common law disputes. Common law disputes often involve state law, not international or U.S. federal law.

Regardless, if one is unfamiliar with an area of law, it is a bad idea to begin your legal research by looking for cases using a keyword search. Better to navigate from secondary sources to primary sources.

Researching Cases in Print

There are many cases. More are published every year.

There are fifty states. Each state has trial courts, appellate courts, and a high court. The federal government also has more than 94 district courts as well as 13 appellate courts and a supreme court, not to mention all the federal administrative courts like tax courts and bankruptcy courts.

All of these courts publish decisions.

Prior to the Internet, these decisions could only be found in bound volumes called "Reporters."

Reporters print court decisions in chronological order.

1. Cases are published in reporters

There are many different types of reporters. They evolved to fit the practice of law. For example, there are reporters that only cover Supreme Court cases. There are reporters that only cover a particular state, like California.

There are reporters that cover multiple states. For instance, the Southern Reporter publishes cases from state courts including Alabama, Florida, Louisiana, and Mississippi.

Consider the business of practicing law prior to the Internet. If an attorney had a state court practice in New York, he could order the

New York state reporter. A state reporter includes cases from the state and federal cases within the state.

If an attorney had a multi-state practice, for instance if an attorney was located in New Jersey but also practiced in nearby New York, she might want case reports from both states. Hence, she might prefer a regional reporter.

For this reason, a case decision might be published in several reporters. In the example above, a New York court decision would be published both in the state reporter and in the regional reporter.

This could cause confusion. Therefore, when citing a case lawyers may include a citation to both the state reporter and to the regional reporter as a matter of common courtesy. We call this a "parallel citation." Although it is increasingly rare, you may still see it from time to time.

Another point of confusion is this: reporters publish cases in chronological order. Therefore, if you are looking for a case on point, how can you find it? Must you read every case in every reporter until you happen to find a similar case?

2. Cases are organized by topic in Digests

An enterprising book salesman named John B. West noticed that lawyers had an organization problem. They needed to be able to find cases quickly. He solved this problem by creating a system that organized cases by topic.

West began publishing a case reporter that also included a handy index of topics.

Although he was not a lawyer, West hired lawyers to read and summarize the cases. He published the cases along with an index that organized the cases by topic. This publication became the North Western Reporter. It was the first, among many reporters published by West.

The West publishing company is now owned by Thompson Reuters. Mr. West's brilliant, billion-dollar idea was to organize print cases by topic.

West created an indexing system called the "Key Number" system. He divided the law into more than 400 topics. Each topic was further divided into certain key numbers.

As cases were published by a court, those cases would be read by attorneys hired by West. Those attorneys would index a case—they would attach key numbers to that case. That case would then be published in a reporter. Meanwhile, a summary of that case would be placed under a topic and key number in a Digest.

A "Digest" is simply a collection of case summaries organized by topic or key number.

The West publishing company maintains the print reporters. West also maintains the digests that allow lawyers to find cases within those reporters.

As you can see, maintaining a law library is quite difficult. The librarian has to make sure the reporters remain up to date. The librarian also has to maintain the digests.

Thankfully, there aren't nearly as many digests as there are reporters.

There is a federal practice digest and a US Supreme Court digest. Almost every state has a digest. Several of the larger regional reporters have their own digests. There is also a massive digest called the Decennial Digest that summarizes state and federal cases over a ten-year period.

Law librarians face another problem. Like reporters, each set of digests has multiple *series*. You see, it is impossible to summarize every case, ever written in one volume.

Hence, the publishers decided to start a new series every ten or fifteen years. For example, the Federal Digest is now in its fifth series.

For the legal researcher, in order to find every case on a particular topic, you may need to consult several series of digests.

For example, West's Federal Practice Digest *Fifth Series* will help you find the most recent federal cases. Meanwhile, the *Fourth Series* will take you back to the early 1980s. If you wanted to search for cases before the 1980s, you would need to dig into the Third, Second, or First Series.

Hence, if you were researching a federal law problem and wanted to find cases (after exhausting secondary sources and annotated statutes) you would begin by searching the most recent, Fifth Series of the Federal Digest.

If you found enough cases, you might stop there. If not, you might move on to the Fourth Series and so on, searching for factually similar cases back through time.

This must seem strange to students who grew up as digital natives. These days, when searching Westlaw online, you can search every case, ever written with one simple click.

Truly, we live in remarkable times.

On the other hand, lawyers who learned to research before the Internet had a few advantages.

First, the digests cannot contain every case; only the most important cases are selected. Case summaries in the digest are curated by experts.

These days, the sheer number of cases returned by a keyword search can be overwhelming. (Still, Westlaw allows you to search online using the print digest!)

Second, because cases were not so easy to search, knowledge of case precedent was quite valuable. Lawyers spent a great deal of time simply reading the law; keeping up with the cases in their practice area. Experienced attorneys had a distinct advantage over new attorneys.

These days, having good research skills can lower the barrier of entry and level the playing field.

3. To find a case in a reporter, look it up using the citation or find it by using the proper digest.

If you know the exact case you are looking for, you can use the case name or citation to find the case directly in the reporter.

For instance, some students are surprised to learn they can go to our law library and pull almost every case from their textbooks. They can read the unedited case for themselves. Some students do this; then they drive the teacher crazy with questions about the case, questions that don't come from the assigned reading! Better to save your questions for after class in such instances.

The point remains, if you know the citation, you can find the case by citation. For example, *McBoyle v. United States*, 283 U.S. 25 (1931) is available on page 25 of volume 283 of the United States Reports. If you walk into our law library today, one of the first set of books you will see is the United States Reports, which reports all U.S. Supreme Court decisions.

Many companies like West vied for lawyers' business. Hence, other commercial reporters also publish U.S. Supreme Court decisions including: the Supreme Court Reporter (S. Ct.); the United States Supreme Court Reports, Lawyers' Edition (L. Ed.); and United States Law Week (U.S.L.W.).

The United States Reports is the "official reporter." That means it is published by the government. Other reporters are "unofficial," meaning they are published by a commercial, for-profit publisher.

Because reporters are expensive, most law firms (and law libraries) chose to purchase and maintain only one reporter set. For example, our library chose to carry the United States Reports.

Cases in the United States Reports are published in chronological order as they are written by the US Supreme Court.

In a similar vein, the Federal Reporter publishes all federal appellate court decisions. Meanwhile the Federal Supplement publishes federal district court decisions.

a. Use the Descriptive Word Index

Moving on, if you don't know the citation for a case, you would need to use West's Federal Digest Practice Digest. Assuming you were looking for the most recent case precedent, you would begin with the most recent series of that digest: the Fifth Series.

To find cases associated with a legal term, you can browse the digest alphabetically. Digests are organized alphabetically by topic. Certainly, you could search the digest like an encyclopedia, by alphabet.

However, every digest also comes with a set of volumes called the "Descriptive Word Index" or DWI. You can use the DWI to do a keyword search of the digest. The DWI is usually located at the end of the digest.

The Descriptive Word Index will point you to the appropriate topic and key number.

You would then locate the topic by alphabet in the digest volumes.

After finding the topic, you would turn to the indicated key number. You would then skim the accompanying case summaries, looking for a helpful case.

Sometimes the DWI uses abbreviations for the name of the topic. If you get confused, there is an abbreviation guide in the opening pages of each volume of the DWI.

b. Using headnotes from other cases

If a case is published by West, that case will have headnotes at the beginning. Headnotes are helpful summaries that help the reader find key passages in a case.

Each headnote may also include a key number.

Hence, if you find a helpful headnote, you may use the key number associated with that headnote to search the digest in order to find other similar cases.

This research strategy works online as well as in print.

c. Update your research

As with all print research, you want to check the back of the digest for a pocket part. You want to see whether new cases have come out on your topic and key number.

In addition, each pocket part will have a "Closing Table" on the inside front cover. The Closing Table tells you last volume and page number of each reporter covered. For example, if a Closing Table lists: 133 S. Ct. 499, that means cases published after page 499 in volume 133 have not yet been indexed in that digest.

4. Is every court decision published in print?

No. some cases are published and others are "unpublished."

Only some cases are important enough to be "published" by a court.

It used to be that courts would only "publish" cases that had a new interpretation or new application of the law. These were important enough to be put into a print reporter.

However, these days, nearly every court decision is posted online.

Still, the courts designate some as "published" and others as "not for publication." This has two important effects. First, an unpublished decision will never be printed in a court reporter.

Second, unpublished decisions may not be used as binding authority. In fact, in some jurisdictions, you may not cite to those decisions at all! You may not use those decisions to persuade a court of what it should do under the principle of *stare decisis.*

Needless to say, the use of unpublished cases as precedent is controversial.

Regardless, you can always use unpublished decisions informally, to help you predict what a court is likely to do in a factually similar situation.

Many jurisdictions also allow lawyers to cite to unpublished decisions as non-binding, persuasive precedent.

If you get confused by seeing an "unpublished" decision; that's all right. Remember, the "published" and "unpublished" distinction is an anachronism, a strange item that remains from the time when cases were only published in bound volumes called reporters.

Conclusion

Don't begin a legal research project by looking directly for cases, unless you already have a good working knowledge of that area of law.

Work from secondary sources (even a simple Internet website), to find primary sources like case law.

However, if you do need to research cases in print, remember to follow these steps:

1. Find the appropriate digest
2. Use the Descriptive Word Index to find a topic and key number
3. Read the case summaries under that topic and key number
4. Update your research
5. Find and read the actual cases

[21]

Researching Cases: Research & Writing Exercise

Writing Exercise 4 (W4)

Your professor will assign *one* of the following problems.

Remember the steps for researching a case in print:

1. Find the indicated federal or state digest.
2. Use the Descriptive Word Index to find a topic and key number.
3. Locate the indicated case in the case summaries under the topic and key number.
4. Using the citation, locate the case in the reporter.
5. Read the case and answer the problem.

First, you need to locate the correct digest. Second, consider the best keyword(s) to look for based on the legal terms of art found in your problem set.

Browse the digest alphabetically or use the Descriptive Word Index to find cases on your topic. It is also possible to browse the topic outline at the beginning of your topic in the digest; use the topic outline to identify the key number most relevant to your research.

Be sure to use the correct digest, and be sure to find the case referenced in your problem set. As always with print research, don't neglect the pocket parts.

Using the information from the digest, locate the case in the print reporter. Read it. *You must use the print digest to find the case in print. If you use online sources, you will fail this assignment.* Your professor may allow you to access the case online after finding it in print.

Be sure to use the headnotes at the beginning of the case to help you navigate the case.

For example, the print version of *McBoyle v. United States* includes several helpful headnotes. Headnote 1, for instance, is categorized under topic "Automobiles," key number 341. If you wanted to find similar cases, you could go to the digest topic Automobiles, key number 341.

However, if you simply wanted to learn more about that issue from the *McBoyle* case, you can easily glance ahead until you find a number 1 in brackets like this: [1].

The bracketed number refers back to the headnote.

(283 U. S. 25)

McBOYLE v. UNITED STATES.

No. 552.

Argued Feb. 26, 27, 1931.

Decided March 9, 1931.

1. **Automobiles** ⇐**341.**

Airplane *held* not "motor vehicle" within law relating to transportation in interstate or foreign commerce of motor vehicle knowing the same to have been stolen (National Motor Vehicle Theft Act [18 USCA § 408]).

National Motor Vehicle Theft Act, Oct. 29, 1919, c. 89, § 2, 41 Stat. 324 (18 USCA § 408), provides that, when used in the act, the term "motor vehicle" shall include an automobile, automobile truck, automobile wagon, motorcycle, or any other self-propelled vehicle not designed for running on rails.

[Ed. Note.—For other definitions of "Motor Vehicle," see Words and Phrases.]

2. **Automobiles** ⇐**341.**

"Vehicle" as used in law relating to transportation of stolen automobiles in interstate or foreign commerce is limited to ve-

Please write a one-page/one paragraph IRAC paragraph.

Remember that we use cases to find rules and sometimes as analogies as well. The case you read may give you the rule. It may or may not be capable of being used as a factually analogous case. You should use the case correctly and as fully as possible.

Finally, in the title of your paper, you must include the name of the *topic and key number* that you used in answering your question. For example, an appropriate title might read:

Criminal Law, Key Number 13

Please return the library books to the exact location as soon as you locate the proper source.

QUESTIONS

Question 1: Your client, Hank McCrady owns a plant nursery in Chicago, Illinois, which is in the Seventh Circuit. He handles his banking through Loanstar Bank. One day, he opened his Loanstar bank statement to discover that he had $76,000 more than he should have. He immediately withdrew the money and hid it under his mattress. The manager of his local Loanstar called Hank and requested that he return the money. The manager says that the clerk accidentally entered one incorrect digit, sending the money to Hank's account instead of to its intended recipient.

Hank called you to see what he should do. Hank believes that the money should be found money or that the bank abandoned that money and that he should not be required to repay the money. He wants to buy a new Porsche.

Under Illinois law relating to *abandoned and lost property* specifically with regards to the *rights and liabilities of a finder as to the owner*, is your client entitled to keep the money?

Using the Federal Practice 4th series digest, please answer the question with reference to a 2005 case from the United States Court of Appeals for the Seventh Circuit. This case is located in volume 400 of the Federal Reports, Third series, which is available in our library. Please do not use any online source for this assignment.

Question 2: Your client is Will Blackstone. He has a law degree from the UK but is not a practicing lawyer. He is a literary agent who represents professional authors. He lives and works in Washington DC. His standard representation contract provides that he gets 10% of his clients' earnings.

One of his clients is Tommy Tuttle, a best-selling author. Mr. Tuttle asked whether earnings meant base pay only or included signing bonuses. Mr. Blackstone told Mr. Tuttle that U.S. law defines earnings to include all monies paid, including bonuses.

Based on this representation, Mr. Tuttle remitted 10% of his base pay and bonuses to Mr. Blackstone.

Mr. Tuttle recently learned, however, that while U.S. law defines "income" for tax purposes, it does not define "earnings" for contract purposes. Mr. Tuttle thinks Mr. Blackstone committed fraud when he misrepresented the legal definition of "earnings" so that Mr. Blackstone received 10% of the bonuses!

You know that *fraud* especially as to *matters of fact or of law* usually does not constitute fraud, but you suspect this rule may have exceptions in Mr. Blackstone's case due to his training or his relationship with Mr. Tuttle.

Using the digest for Washington DC, and with reference to a case by the name of *Dixon*, please answer whether your client, Mr. Blackstone, is likely to be liable with regards to his misrepresentation.

Question 3: Your client is Will Blackstone. He has a law degree from the UK but is not a practicing lawyer. He is a literary agent who represents professional authors. His office is in Indianapolis, Indiana, which is located in the Seventh Circuit. His standard representation contract provides that he gets 10% of his clients' earnings.

One of his clients is Tommy Tuttle, a best-selling writer. Mr. Tuttle asked whether earnings meant base pay only or included signing and bonuses. Mr. Blackstone told Mr. Tuttle that U.S. law defines earnings to include all monies paid, including bonuses.

Based on this representation, Mr. Tuttle remitted 10% of his base pay and bonuses to Mr. Blackstone.

Mr. Tuttle recently learned, however, that while U.S. law defines "income" for tax purposes, it does not define "earnings" for contract purposes. Mr. Tuttle thinks Mr. Blackstone committed fraud when he misrepresented the legal definition of "earnings" so that Mr. Blackstone received 10% of the bonuses!

You know that *fraud* especially as to *matters of fact or of law* usually does not constitute fraud, but you suspect this rule may have exceptions in Mr. Blackstone's case due to the *representations* he made, and due to his training or his relationship with Mr. Tuttle.

Please answer whether your client, Mr. Blackstone, is likely to be liable for "fraud" with regard to his representations as to matters of fact as distinguished from law.

Use the Federal Digest fourth series with reference to a 1998 case from the Court of Appeals for the Seventh Circuit arising out of Indiana.

Question 4: You represent an attorney, Jennifer Jean, from Washington, D.C.

Jill was recently convicted of assault with a deadly object and vehicular assault arising out of an incident where she tried to run over her boss with a motorcycle. Based on the conviction, the board of bar examiners is considering disciplinary action against her. She might lose her license to practice law based on the criminal conviction. However, Jill claims that her actions can be explained by an addiction to the sleep medication Tylenol PM, which has recently been linked to all sorts of bizarre behaviors.

According to professional responsibility law related to *attorney and client* especially as regards *discipline* and *defenses* to charges of misconduct, will your client's drug addiction be a successful defense to a charge of misconduct? Please refer to the D.C. Digest with reference to a 1990 case from the United States Court of Appeals for the D.C. Circuit.

Question 5: You represent an attorney, Theodore Trust, from Los Angeles, California. Trust was recently sued by a former client for failing to file a timely appeal in his securities fraud case. The client also reported Trust to the California bar. The board of bar examiners is considering disciplinary action against him. He might lose his license to practice law.

However, Trust claims that he was unable to file the appeal because he was at a casino in Las Vegas at the slot machines. He admitted that he has a gambling addiction problem. He is seeking professional help for his gambling related illness.

According to professional responsibility law related to *attorney and client* especially as regards *discipline* and *defenses* to charges of misconduct, will your client's gambling addiction be a successful defense to a charge of misconduct? Please refer to the Californian Digest second series with reference to a 1981 case.

Question 6: Your client, Matt McDonnel and his wife divorced when their child, Brittney, was very young. Matt didn't see Britney much after that. He was just busy earning a living. At the time of the divorce, Matt entered into a separation agreement in which he agreed to pay $1,000 each month to his wife Jane until Brittney reached the age of 21.

Mr. McDonnel paid faithfully. However, he stopped paying last month. He saw a post on Britney's facebook last month where she was celebrating her 22 birthday! He had simply forgotten the year of her birth. Because of that mistake, Matt had overpaid by 12 months or a total of $12,000.

Matt came to your office to see if he can recover those *payments* from Jane due to his *mistake of fact.*

Using the District of Columbia digest, please answer the question with reference to a 1943 case from the Municipal Court of Appeals for the District of Columbia, located in volume 32 of the Atlantic Reporter, Second series, which is available in our library. Please do not use any online source for this assignment.

Question 7: Your client, Matt McDonnel and his wife divorced when their child, Britney, was very young. Matt didn't see Britney much after that. He was just busy earning a living. At the time of the divorce, Matt entered into a separation agreement in which he agreed to pay $1,000 each month to his wife Jane until Britney reached the age of 21.

Mr. McDonnel paid faithfully. However, he stopped paying last month. He saw a post on Britney's facebook last month where she was celebrating her 22 birthday! He had simply forgotten the year of her birth. Because of that mistake, Matt had overpaid by 12 months or a total of $12,000.

Matt came to your office to see if he can recover those *payments* from Jane due to his *mistake of fact.*

Using the California Digest, Second series, please answer the question with reference to a 1961 case from the California Appeals court. The case is located in volume 15 of the California Reporter, which is located in our library. Please do not use any online source for this assignment.

Question 8: Your client, Matt McDonnel and his wife divorced when their child, Britney, was very young. Matt didn't see Britney much after that. He was just busy earning a living. At the time of the divorce, Matt entered into a separation agreement in which he agreed to pay $1,000 each month to his wife Jane until Brandi reached the age of 21.

Mr. McDonnel paid faithfully. However, he stopped paying last month. He saw a post on Britney's facebook last month where she was celebrating her 22 birthday! He had simply forgotten the year of her birth. Because of that mistake, Matt had overpaid by 12 months or a total of $12,000.

He asked Jane for the money. However, Janet says she that she set up an automatic transfer with her bank. Each payment from Matt was transferred immediately into Britney's personal bank account. She says that Britney who is saving it to pay for her upcoming wedding. Jane assumed that was why Matt was still sending money, to pay for his daughter's wedding.

Matt came to your office to see if he can recover those *payments* from Jane or from Britney due to his *mistake of fact.*

Using the New York Digest, Third series, please answer the question with reference to a 1975 case from a County Court in New York. The case is located in volume 364 of the New York Supplement Reporter, Second series, which is located in our library. Please do not use any online source for this assignment.

[22]

Researching Cases: Electronic Research Exercise

Electronic Research Exercise Number 4 (R4)

Instructions

- This is your longest (by time) research assignment. Please plan ahead.
- Please type your answers. Answers should be single-spaced in Courier New Font size 8. Pages should be numbered.
- Your paper must have a header on the first page (not needed on subsequent pages) including the following: a title; your Professor's name; and your student ID number. Do not write your name; use your student ID number.
- Please e-mail your answers prior to class or hand them in at the beginning of class according to your professor's preference.
- If you cut and paste, you must use quotation marks!
- There are 25 total questions in this assignment. Please do not miss any.

The Assignment

There are many ways to find cases online. If you simply need to read a case, you can often find that case through a search engine.

Most cases are published online. The government publishes them online. Free websites, like findlaw.com, also aggregate cases.

Cases on free websites probably will not be annotated. They will not include helpful headnotes or links to other similar authorities.

In the past, understanding book research was of great benefit in navigating online research. However, free resources as well as commercial sources like Westlaw and Lexis now have simple interfaces. You can search easily.

In Westlaw and Lexis, of course, you can also do advanced searches. For example, you can search by jurisdiction or by subject matter.

For your assignment today, we will focus on the most basic way we research cases online.

Internet: Free Sources

Let's research based on the following facts:

> Remember our case about Bella Diball who got so upset about her prom dress. Bella lives in Trussville, Alabama.
>
> Bella and her boyfriend reunited after prom. Two months later, they decided to get married.
>
> Bella hired a local photographer to photograph their wedding. But he did a terrible job. Everyone agrees. Worst photos ever!
>
> Bella is so upset that her wedding photos, which should be a prized possession, look so terrible. She wants to sue the photographer. However, their contract was only for $500. She thinks the photographer should have to pay more, like, for her emotional distress.
>
> Once again, you face a question about whether damages for emotional distress can be recovered on this breach of contract.[1] Unlike the prom dress, this case does not involve the sale of goods. So it is

---

[1] Similarly, see https://web.archive.org/web/20180411002043/http://weddingindustrylaw.com/wedding-photographer-lawsuit/

not a commercial code case. It is a service contract. You also remember that contract law is often a common law issue.

Stop and think. What is the first step you should take?

Correct!

If you don't know a lot about an area of law, you should start by looking at secondary sources.

The simplest way to find basic secondary sources is to do an internet search. If you are more advanced, you might look for a state practice guide.

Let's try it. Open any search engine and look up:

Alabama contract damage emotional distress

For me, (because I am using google.com and not google.co.kr; how about you?) that search turned up the following law review article published by an author named Huffaker in a 2001 issue of the University of Alabama's Law Review. Let's check it out.

> [PDF] RECOVERY FOR INFLICTION OF EMOTIONAL DISTRESS: A ...
> https://www.law.ua.edu/pubs/lrarticles/Volume%2052/Issue%203/Huffaker.pdf ▾
> by W PAGE - Cited by 1 - Related articles
> of **emotional distress damages**, beginning largely with the **Alabama** Su- preme Court's ... Part I1 of this Comment, or in **contract** law, as explained in Part 111. In.

Reading the introduction, I can see that Section III of that article deals with emotional distress damages in the context of contracts.

Skipping ahead to Section III, on page 1017 of that law review (pdf page 15), I see the following:

> risk of physical harm. Early on, the Alabama Supreme Court recognized that when one party breaches a contract, the other party is entitled to damages "such as may fairly and reasonably be considered as arising naturally from such breach, or as may reasonably be supposed to have been in the contemplation of the parties at the inception of the contract as the possible result of a breach of it."[107] This recovery included, therefore, damages for emotional distress where such emotional distress arose naturally and proximately from the breach of contract.[108]

Wow, I really want to read the cases that are cited for those rules.

1. What case is cited to in footnote 107?

In reading that section, I can see that the author relied heavily on a case styled: *B&M Homes, Inc. v. Hogan*, 376 So. 2d 667 (Ala. 1979).

This case caption tells me that this case is located in Volume 376 of the Southern Reporter, Second Series, starting at page 667. The case was decided by the Supreme Court of Alabama in 1979.

The law review article says that case involved the sale of a new home. Does Bella's case involve the sale of a new home? No. It involves wedding photographs.

2. **How is Bella's case analogous (factually similar) to the *B&M Homes* case?**

We could, of course, look that case up on a free website or walk to a law library and read it in a book.

Instead, we are going to take advantage of modern technology and look it up in a commercial database like Westlaw or Lexis.

We are doing this for three reasons.

(1) First, we cannot use a secondary source as authority for a rule of law. Rules have to come from the laws of that jurisdiction.

(2) Second, we actually want to read the case.

(3) Even if the case is not perfect, it will link us to helpful secondary sources (like an ALR) or other primary sources (like cases or code sections).

WESTLAW

Please copy the volume, reporter, and page number of the *B&M Case*. That is all we will need to find the case on Westlaw or Lexis.

Copy and Paste the following into Westlaw: 376 So. 2d 667

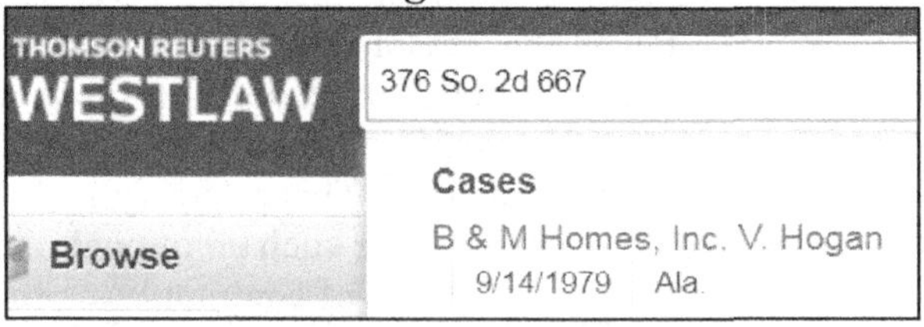

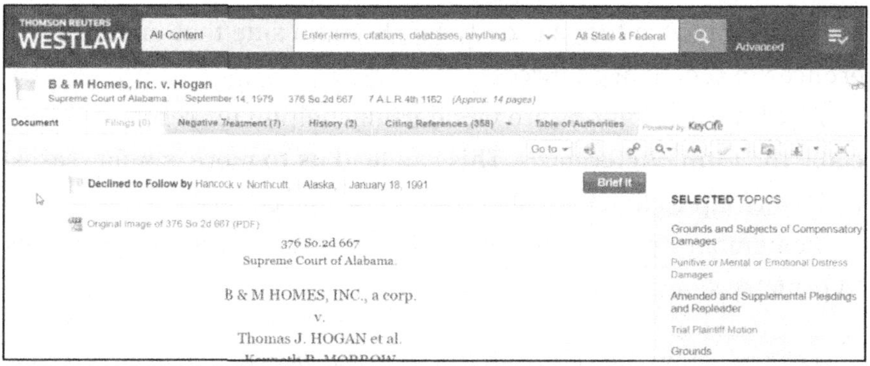

The first thing we see is a big YELLOW FLAG. This is part of Westlaw's Key Cite, a citator service that tells you if a case is still good law.

In this instance, a yellow flag is a warning that this case may have some negative treatment. Cases that came afterward may have distinguished it or criticized it. We would want to carefully consider the warning flag and evaluate whether this case is still good law for our legal point.

Looking across the top of the page, we find tabs that will allow us to read the original Filings; view any Negative Treatment; view the procedural History; browse through any Citing References.

We also see a tab for "Table of Authorities." That tab leads to a list of cases cited to by this court in this decision. Reading this table will give you great insight into whether the cases relied upon by this decision are still good law.

You also may see a big blue button that reads "Brief It." This gives you the Westlaw synopsis along with a list of headnotes. It also includes the Supreme Court's own "Syllabus" or summary of the decision.

Please don't be tempted to let a commercial source like Westlaw or Lexis Advance read and brief your cases for you in class!

Finally, on the right hand side of the screen we see options for printing or downloading.

We also have a tool bar on the right hand side that includes references to secondary sources.

All of these notations are wonderfully helpful for research, especially the Citing References. This can lead us to more, similar cases. Or it can help us find a helpful secondary source.

Remember, the flow of legal research is from secondary sources to primary sources and back and forth.

TIP: the flow of legal research is from secondary sources to primary sources

Let's read the *B&M Homes* case. The first thing you should read is the Synopsis. When you are doing research. A quick glance at the Synopsis will often help you eliminate cases that are not useful.

3. **According to the Synopsis, what did Judge Embry hold regarding damages for mental anguish?**

Next, we want to skim through the Headnotes. The Headnotes let us skip ahead to an important part of the case.

Please read the Headnotes for *B&M Homes*. Let's focus on Headnote 1. This is a helpful Headnote for our case. We can also see that 34 Cases have cited to this headnote. We may want to skim those cases!

> 1 **Damages** Breach of Contract or Warranty
> In Alabama, general rule is that mental anguish is not a recoverable element of damages arising from breach of contract.
>
> 34 Cases that cite this headnote

If you click on that Headnote Number (1), it will take you to the relevant portion of the text.

> 1 In Alabama the general rule is that mental anguish is not a recoverable element of damages arising from breach of contract. Sanford v. Western Life Insurance Co., 368 So.2d 260 (Ala.1979); Stead v. Blue Cross-Blue Shield of Alabama, 346 So.2d 1140

Clicking a Headnote Number in the main body of the decision will return you to the Headnotes at the top of the page.

4. **Reading the text following Headnote 1, what is the first exception to the general rule?**

Please note, the Alabama Supreme Court cites to authority from other states in support of that proposition. The Supreme Court is saying, *other states do the same thing—like in these cases.*

For example, let's look at a Michigan case.

5. **Please "Right Click" on the Michigan case, styled: *McConnell v. U.S. Express Co.* Open it in a New Tab if possible. If our case is about wedding photographs, and *B&M Homes* is about a home, what is the *McConnell* case about?**
6. **Between *McConnell* and *B&M Homes*, which is factually more like our case? Why?**

Let's go back to *B&M Homes*. So far, we can use *B&M Homes* as authority for rules. That case references the rules about whether emotional distress damages are available for breach of contract.

Sometimes students ask, should I cite to *B&M Homes* or should I go back, read, and cite to the decisions that *B&M Homes* used.

Either way is fine.

When citing a court to a rule, typically we want to find a case that many courts have cited to. Or we want to find the original case that courts cite to. Or we want to find a recent case from the highest court.

But before we use *B&M Homes* as authority for a rule, we better check that Yellow Flag to see if *B&M Homes* is still good law.

If we click the Yellow Flag, we can see whether *B&M Homes* is still good authority.

Under "Negative Treatment," We note that there is minimal negative treatment. And that negative treatment comes mainly from outside jurisdictions and lower courts. However, the 11th Circuit decision (#3 below) is a bit concerning. The federal court must have been interpreting state law in a diversity jurisdiction case.

B&M is "distinguished by" the 11th Circuit. The "Depth" indicates that there is some discussion of our case. Also the discussion concerns items exactly like our Headnotes!

We better read that case.

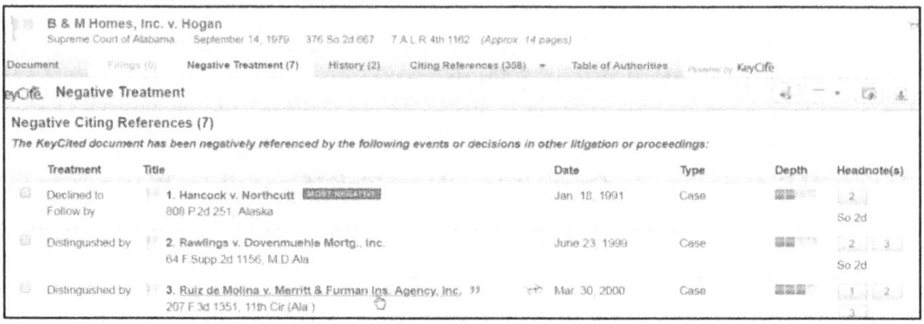

B & M Homes, Inc. v. Hogan
Supreme Court of Alabama September 14, 1979 376 So.2d 667 7 A.L.R.4th 1162 (Approx. 14 pages)

Document | Filings (0) | Negative Treatment (7) | History (2) | Citing References (358) | Table of Authorities | Powered by KeyCite

KeyCite. Negative Treatment

Negative Citing References (7)

The KeyCited document has been negatively referenced by the following events or decisions in other litigation or proceedings:

Treatment	Title	Date	Type	Depth	Headnote(s)
Declined to Follow by	1. Hancock v. Northcutt MOST NEGATIVE 808 P.2d 251, Alaska	Jan. 18, 1991	Case		2 So 2d
Distinguished by	2. Rawlings v. Dovenmuehle Mortg., Inc. 64 F.Supp.2d 1156, M.D.Ala.	June 23, 1999	Case		2 3 So 2d
Distinguished by	3. Ruiz de Molina v. Merritt & Furman Ins. Agency, Inc. 207 F.3d 1351, 11th Cir.(Ala.)	Mar. 30, 2000	Case		1 2 3

7. **If our case is about wedding photographs, and *B&M Homes* is about a home, what is the *Ruiz de Molina* case about?**
8. **Looking at the 11th Circuit's distinguishing of *B&M Homes*, is *B&M Homes* still good law? Was the 11th Circuit critical of the *B&M Homes* decision?**

Returning to *B&M Homes*, if it is still good law, we can cite to it as authority for a rule or for a sub-rule.

Here is a *summary* of the rules one can take from *B&M Homes*: (1) in general, no emotional distress damages for breach of contract; (2) but there are two exceptions including reasonable foreseeability and zone of danger; and (3) a plaintiff does not have to prove physical injury.

In addition to rules, we can also use *B&M Homes* as a factual analogy—to show how a rule was applied to a factually similar case. In Questions 2 & 6 above, you considered whether and in what way *B&M Homes* is "factually similar" to our case. You also considered whether the facts of *McConnell* are more similar.

In each case, *B&M Homes* and *McConnell* are positive analogies—the outcomes of those cases are the same that our client wants.

The outcome of *Ruiz de Molina* is the opposite of what our client wants. Therefore, it is a negative analogy. If it was closely factually similar, you would need to "distinguish" that case from ours.

As we find, read, and synthesize cases, we begin to form a predictive function in our minds.

In cases with "these types of facts" the elements are met, meaning a court grants relief to the plaintiff.

Are the facts in our case in the same class or category?

9. **Based on the three cases so far, what do you think? Is a court likely to hold in favor of Bella? Please answer using a full sentence(s).**

However, based on these three cases alone, we may not be ready to make a prediction.

B&M Homes cites to many similar cases, like *McConnell.*

We would want to read all of those cases.

In addition, we would want to check the "Citing References" to see if any similar cases in the future, cited back to *B&M Homes.*

Remember the 34 Cases that Cited to Headnote 1? We could read those cases. We might even search them for the word "wedding" or "photographer."

We can also look at Secondary Sources that cited to *B&M Homes.* Those Secondary Sources might contain cases that are even more factually similar.

Let's switch to Lexis. We can do the same thing in Lexis.

Lexis

Copy and Paste the following into Westlaw: 376 So. 2d 667

That brings up our familiar case:

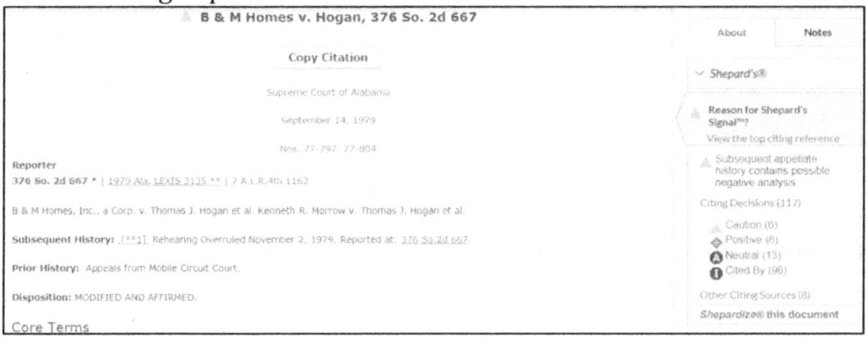
B & M Homes v. Hogan, 376 So. 2d 667

Copy Citation

Supreme Court of Alabama

September 14, 1979

Nos. 77-797, 77-804

Reporter

376 So. 2d 667 * | 1979 Ala. LEXIS 3135 ** | 7 A.L.R.4th 1162

B & M Homes, Inc., a Corp. v. Thomas J. Hogan et al. Kenneth R. Morrow v. Thomas J. Hogan et al.

Subsequent History: [**1] Rehearing Overruled November 2, 1979, Reported at: 376 So.2d 667.

Prior History: Appeals from Mobile Circuit Court.

Disposition: MODIFIED AND AFFIRMED.

Core Terms

About | Notes

Shepard's®

Reason for Shepard's Signal™?

View the top citing reference

Subsequent appellate history contains possible negative analysis

Citing Decisions (117)

Caution (6)

Positive (8)

Neutral (13)

Cited By (96)

Other Citing Sources (8)

Shepardize® this document

First, we note that it has a YELLOW TRIANGLE. This is a warning that there is some negative treatment.

Lexis gives a "Case Summary" at the start of the case. Again, please don't use these to brief your cases for your substantive law classes. Do the hard work on your own first, then maybe use these to check your work.

Lexis also provides Headnotes.

Let's focus on Headnote 1.

> HN1 **Types of Damages, Compensatory Damages**
>
> In Alabama, the general rule is that mental anguish is not a recoverable element of damages arising from breach of contract. Yet where the contractual duty or obligation is so coupled with matters of mental concern or solicitude, or with the feelings of the party to whom the duty is owed, that a breach of that duty will necessarily or reasonably result in mental anguish or suffering, it is just that damages therefor be taken into consideration and awarded. Another exception is where the breach of the contract is tortious, or attended with personal injury, damages for mental anguish may be awarded. More like this Headnote
>
> Shepardize - Narrow by this Headnote (3) 2

We can see that this Headnote is written using plain language. Thanks, Lexis!

As with Westlaw, there are helpful research tools built-in to the Headnote. Here we can search for "More like this Headnote." We can also "Shepardize—Narrow by this Headnote (3)."

That means there are 3 sources that cite to this Case for a similar proposition. The yellow triangle means 2 of the 3 sources are slightly negative.

10. **Following the Shepardize Link, what Alabama Supreme Court case distinguishes *B&M Homes*?**
11. **Skimming that case where it discusses *B&M Homes*, does it have any impact on your analysis of our case? Why or why not?**

Shepards is a citator service, like Westlaw's Key Cite. You may notice it is not spelled like "Shepherd" as in the shepherds who came to visit Jesus on his birthday. Rather, it is named after a person named "Shepard" who invented the citator service.

Shepards is the most famous citator service. Sometimes an attorney will ask you, "Did you Shepardize it?" (Watch out, though, because Lexis owns the trademark. =)

She means, did you check to make sure your case is still good law.

Shepards is useful for that.

Shepards is also a brilliant research tool.

There is also a Shepards link on the right hand side of the case. Let's click on that now. Then click on the link for "Other Citing Sources."

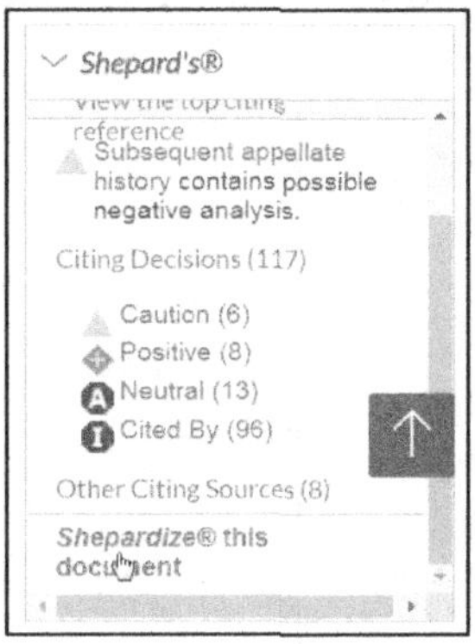

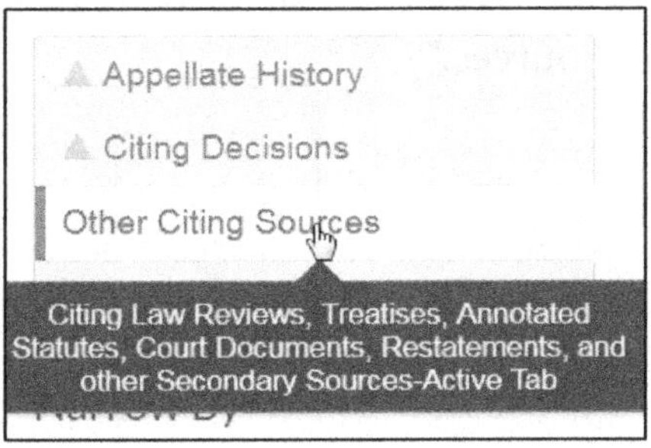

Hey! There is the article by Huffaker.

And . . . precious little else.

Well, sometimes Lexis has more sources than Westlaw. Sometimes Westlaw has more than Lexis. If you have access to both, why not check both!

Back to Westlaw

Let's go back to Westlaw.

If you logged out, go to the History tab in the top right.

You can find the case we were recently looking at.

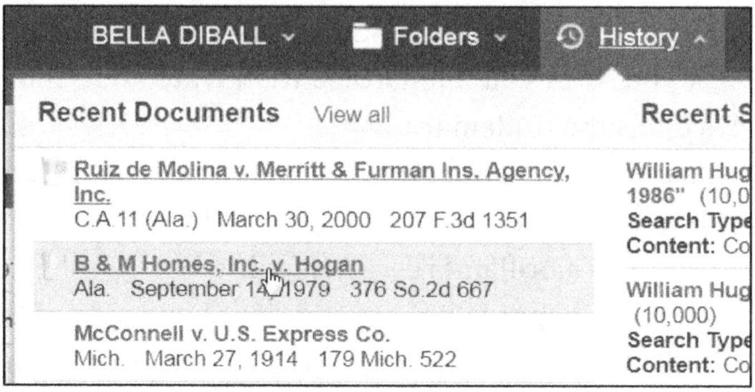

Now, let's go to the "Citing References" tab and look at "Secondary Sources."

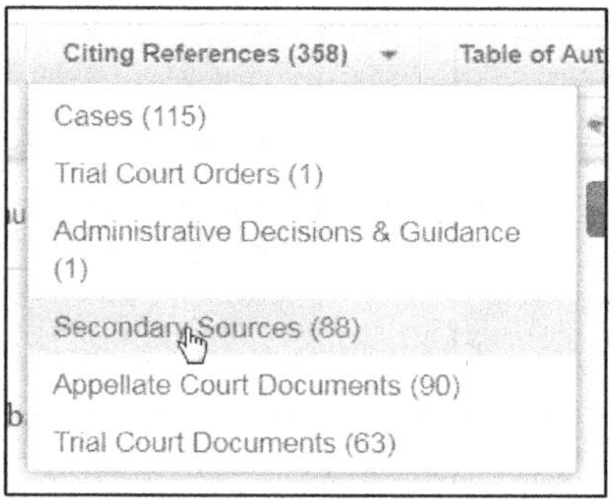

Now, I would love to find a good ALR annotation on point. But these ALR are about construction law. Probably not specific enough for our case.

Let's use the Narrow function. First, select "All Results." Then, let's search All Results for the word wedding.

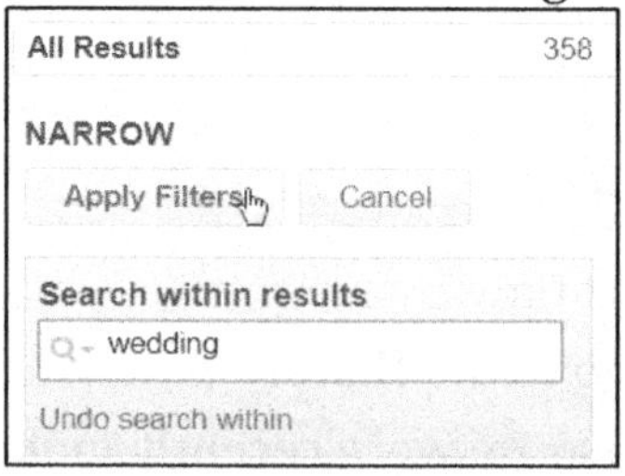

If this was a real research assignment, I'd advise you to skim all those sources, looking for similar cases, maybe about weddings. I did the hard work for you.

In that Narrowed search, there is a secondary source entitled: "Modern Law of Contracts § 18:13, "Reason to know" cases-Foreseeability of damages."

Please skim that source looking or a Louisiana case concerning a wedding. (Use a CTRL+F search on a Windows machine or its equivalent on your Apple or other device.)

12. Please give a citation to that case.

13. If *B&M Homes* is about houses and our case is about photographs, what is the Louisiana case about?

14. Is the holding of that case positive or negative for your client?

Please click on the link to the Louisiana case (in the footnote) and look at the case in Westlaw.

Check the "Citing References" for "Secondary Sources."

Boom! We just found the mother-lode. All these secondary sources are golden.

15. What is the name of the ALR 4th series annotation?

We want to find analogous (factually similar) cases from Alabama. The Table of Cases to that ALR annotation has many Alabama cases!

However, unlike rules, analogous case authorities can come from outside jurisdictions. Especially if they're very factually similar like the Louisiana case.

The index to the ALR has entries for "Photographs" as well as an entry for "Weddings."

Photographers photographs, and film developing §§ 6[a], 7[b], 11
Physical injuries §§ 5[e], 6[a], 10[a], 12
Physicians §§ 5[b], 7[a], 8

Go to Section 11. In that section, you find a case styled: t, in *Grather v Tipery Studios, Inc.*

16. Describe the holding from that case? And what jurisdiction is it from?

17. Is that case positive or negative for your client?

SEARCHING CASES BY TOPIC AND JURISDICTION

In Westlaw and Lexis, you can search by topics.

You can also limit your searches to a particular jurisdiction, like Alabama.

BACK TO LEXIS

In Lexis, let's select the Tab for "Practice Areas."

Under this Tab, let's select "Contracts"

Let's run a very specific search:

wedding & ("emotional distress" s/ "breach of contract")

18. Please describe this search string in one sentence. What exactly are we searching for?

The search results default to the Category: Statutes.

We have to manually go and Select Category: Cases. Or select Secondary Materials.

Let's select Secondary Materials.

19. What is the top result in Secondary Materials?

Interesting.

Let's do the same thing for "Cases."

But this time, we want to use the "Filters" on the left side of the screen to limit our search to Alabama:

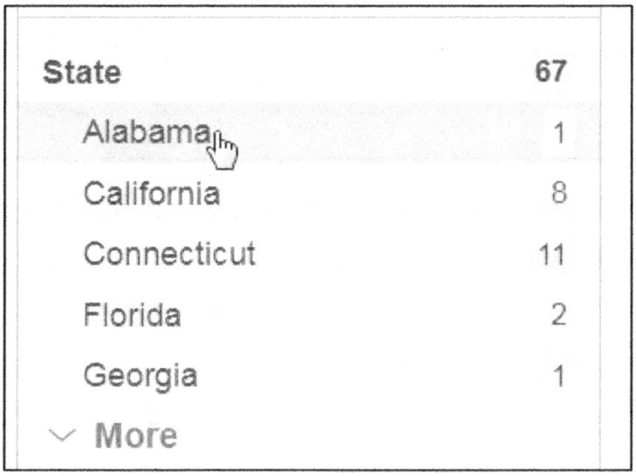

20. In that one Alabama case, did the cause of action involve a wedding? Under Section II Part C of the court's decision, were damages for mental anguish recoverable in that case?

We might be better off looking at other cases found by our search. But this illustrates the difficulty of a keyword search. Even when you know the topic very well, and know what terms should be in your search, it can be difficult to lay your finger directly on the right case.

Whereas, finding a secondary source, like an ALR that is on point, may immediately lead to good cases.

Let's try one more time.

Go to the Lexis home page.

Instead of "Search: Everything," click on that one. Then, let's limit our search to Alabama only.

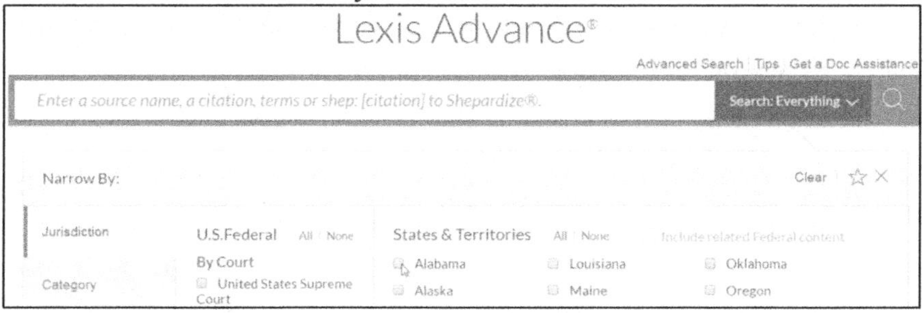

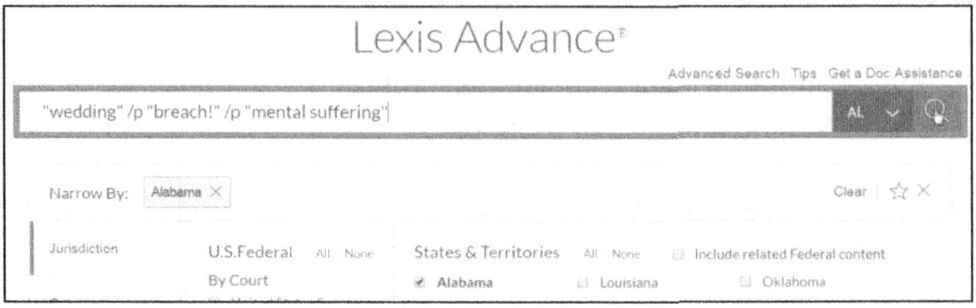

21. Run a search as pictured above. First, describe this search string in one sentence.

Remember, the search defaults to Statutes. There may not be any. That is okay.

Let's Select Category: Cases.

22. Please give the citation to the top (only?) case.

23. If our case is about wedding photos and *B&M Homes* is about a newly built house, what is this new case about?

24. Is the holding positive or negative for your client?

You've done a great job. Now, it's time to put all your research together.

25. Do you think your client Bella Diball is likely to recover against the wedding photographer? Please answer in a short IRAC paragraph. Please give the relevant rules. Please also reference the facts and case names (by first party name) of all of the positive analogous cases!

[23]

Case Analogies: A Single Analogous Case

Introduction

As explained in the preceding chapter, we use cases in one of two ways: as authority for a rule or to show how a rule was applied in a factually similar situation.

Reading a case to find authority for a rule is fairly straightforward. A case precedent might define an element of a rule. It might add something new to our understanding of a rule. Sometimes, we're simply looking for the best language to cut and paste into our legal brief. (If that's the case, the best advice is to pull rules from positive case analogies—where the outcome of the case matches the outcome your client wants.)

Sometimes a rule is ambiguous or an element has not yet been defined. Those questions of first impression can be quite fun and challenging.

Usually, we are applying known law to a particular set of facts. We need to know what a court is likely to do. Simply stated: do our facts match the elements.

To build this section of our legal proof, we use analogous logic.

We have to compare our case with a factually similar, case precedent (that we may have found while reading the annotated code or browsing the Internet).

In comparing our case to a factually similar case, we generally look at three things:

1. Holding
2. Facts
3. Reasoning and other factors

After comparing these items, we can determine if a case precedent is useful in building our analogous argument.

1. Holding

It may sound counterintuitive, but the first thing to look at is the holding.

If the holding similar to what our client wants, we call it an "analogous case" by which we mean a "positive" analogy. If a lawyer asks if you found an analogous case, in general, he's asking if you found a positive analogy.

If the holding is different than the outcome your client wants, it is a "negative" analogy.

If you find only negative analogies, be careful. It is difficult to predict or to persuade based on negative analogies alone.

Regardless, the way we handle a case precedent largely depends on whether the holding is positive for our client or negative.

2. Facts

A useful case analogy is one in which the legally relevant facts are similar.

As you read a case, consider making a list of the material facts. (If you are doing legal research, a good way to sort cases quickly is to read the case summary or the statement of facts. A quick read should be sufficient to determine whether that case will be useful as an analogous case.)

Defining the "relevant facts" with precision—not too narrow or too broad—is a skill that comes with practice. You are learning this every day in your substantive law classes as your professors challenge you to list the relevant facts of a case and to handle fact hypotheticals.

As we read factually similar cases in the context of a legal problem, we typically sort the cases at a broad level *first by element*. For example, if our client has a battery claim, we might ask whether the case we are reading can be used to prove that our client's facts fit the element of intent or one of the other elements of battery.

Under each element, we typically sort cases by *positive and negative analogies*.

We analyze each individual case, and we synthesize groups of cases.

For an individual case, we ask whether the material, legally relevant facts similar or dissimilar. If they are similar, then we can predict or argue for a similar result.

If you find a case that has *less* desirable facts and yet is a positive case analogy, that is good news for your client. If a court found that the elements were met by less favorable facts, a court should hold in your client's favor.

We also try to synthesize cases. As we read cases, we keep a running tally in our minds of how the case fits with other cases. We look for commonalities or differences. We try to create a predictive function—a statement as to the types of facts the courts are looking for when considering a particular element.

Unfortunately, fact analogies are some of the weakest forms of logic. Parties on opposite sides may rely on the same case! A lawyer making a positive analogy to the case may admit that some facts are different, while arguing that the relevant facts are the same. Whereas, opposing counsel, drawing a negative analogy, will argue that although some facts are similar, the relevant facts are different.

Welcome to the law!

3. Reasoning and other points

Finally, when analyzing a factually similar case, a lawyer ought to consider the court's reasoning. Should the same reasoning apply in the client's case?

There may be factual similarities, but the reasoning might lead to a different outcome. For example, the stated public policy goals may not match. Or, the reason for the rule might not cover your client's particular factual circumstances.

For instance, a law that limits professional speech in a counseling setting might not be Constitutional if applied to the classroom, where freedom of speech and opinion are valued.

In addition, you might consider the following points when evaluating the usefulness of a case analogy:

a. Jurisdiction

Cases from your jurisdiction might be binding if they have very similar facts. Otherwise, they may still be extremely persuasive. Cases from neighboring jurisdictions may be more persuasive than jurisdictions that are far away.

b. Level of the court

Cases from higher courts may be more persuasive.

For instance, a Supreme Court case may be more persuasive than an appellate court case which may, in turn, be more persuasive than a trial court decision.

c. Date of decision

It may sound strange, but a valid way to distinguish a negative case is to argue, "Your honor, that case is so old!"

The actual argument should sound a bit more nuanced like, that decision reflects the policies and concerns of a bygone era.

d. Rules of ethics

Lawyers are officers of the court. Hence, lawyers have an ethical duty to report cases that are "directly adverse." As previously discussed, this would include cases from higher courts in your direct line of appeal.

Whether they an authority is "directly adverse" would depend on whether the court applied the rule to a factually similar case. If the case analogy is directly, factually "on point," and it is negative for your client, then you *must* disclose it. If there are relevant factual distinctions, then you *may* disclose it.

Hiding cases is usually not a good persuasive strategy anyway and may diminish your personal credibility. Believe it or not, your most persuasive feature is not your brain. It is your good reputation. You must be scrupulously honest.

Sample Case: Facts

Before we begin reading a case or a group of cases, let's consider the following facts:

> A client approached your law office in Knoxville, Tennessee. Your client is Hole Foods, Inc. It is a trendy grocery store recently purchased by Blamazon.com.
>
> Hole Foods has an entire section of prepared foods, where people can come in and pick out dinner. It looks a bit like a buffet. Patrons scoop food into recycled paper boxes. They then pay for their food by weight. It is a popular lunch and dinner option.
>
> Hole Foods has a large craft beer selection. Customers can also purchase "growlers" to take away draft beer. Growlers contain about 2 liters of draft beer.
>
> In addition, Hole Foods has a room called "The Stoop." After customers go through the checkout lanes, they can go to The Stoop and eat their food. The Stoop has tables and chairs. It also has a bar area where Hole Foods holds special events like wine tastings. The bar area is closed except during special events.

The Stoop has a cafeteria vibe. There is no wait staff. Customers clean their own tables and take care of themselves.

Hole Foods says it is being sued under the Tennessee Dram Shop Law.

Last month, according to the cashier, two men brought a growler of beer and two boxes of food to her cash register.

The younger man, named Doug Thompson, attempted to pay the for the items. The cashier asked for his ID.

Mr. Thompson looked shocked. The cashier said she could not sell him beer if he did not have ID.

Mr. Thompson said, "Oh I am not 21 yet. Actually, the beer is his." He pointed to his friend, Mr. Brent Lane.

The cashier checked Mr. Lane's ID. He was over the age of 21.

Brent Lane then paid for all the items including the growler and the two boxes of food.

Mr. Lane and Mr. Thompson went to The Stoop.

Unbeknownst to Hole Food employees, Mr. Lane shared beer from the growler with Mr. Thompson.

Mr. Thompson became intoxicated. He drove his car and hit a pedestrian named Adam Moyers causing serious physical injuries.

Adam is suing Hole Foods Inc. alleging that his injuries were the direct result a minor, Doug Thompson, being sold alcohol.

Single Case Analogy

Let's recall, the Tennessee Dram Shop Law, which we read in a previous chapter:

> 57-10-101. Proximate cause.-The general assembly hereby finds and declares that the consumption of any alcoholic beverage or beer rather than the furnishing of any alcoholic beverage or beer is the proximate cause of injuries inflicted upon another by an intoxicated person.
>
> 57-10-102. Standard of proof.-Notwithstanding the provisions of § 57-10-101, Notwithstanding the provisions of § 57-10-101, no

> judge or jury may pronounce a judgment awarding damages to or on behalf of any party who has suffered personal injury or death against any person who has sold any alcoholic beverage or beer, unless such jury of twelve (12) persons has first ascertained beyond a reasonable doubt that the sale by such person of the alcoholic beverage or beer was the proximate cause of the personal injury or death sustained and that such person:
>
> (1) Sold the alcoholic beverage or beer to a person known to be under the age of twenty-one (21) years and such person caused the personal injury or death as the direct result of the consumption of the alcoholic beverage or beer so sold; or
>
> (2) Sold the alcoholic beverage or beer to a visibly intoxicated person and such person caused the personal injury or death as the direct result of the consumption of the alcoholic beverage or beer so sold.

We outlined section 57-10-102:

1. Where a sale of alcohol is the proximate cause of injury or death,
2. Beyond a reasonable doubt,
3. Any person who sold alcohol or beer is liable if
   A. The sale was,
   B. To a person known to be under the age of twenty-one OR to a visibly intoxicated person, AND
   A. Such person caused the personal injury or death as the direct result of the consumption of the alcoholic beverage or beer so sold.

Let's read a case together that interprets the Tennessee Dram Shop Law. When you read it, consider whether you might use part of the case as authority for a rule or as a factual case analogy.

Worley v. Weigles, Inc.
Supreme Court of Tennessee (1996)

This decision comes from our jurisdiction's highest court in 1996. Not recent..

REID, Justice. This case presents for review the liability of a seller of alcoholic beverages to a person under 21 years of age. [FN1 For the purpose of this opinion, no distinction is made between a "minor" and a "person under 21 years of age."] The trial court granted summary judgment of no liability to the seller. The Court of Appeals reversed on the finding that the case presents issues for the jury. This Court finds that, pursuant to public policy expressly declared by the legislature regarding liability for the sale of intoxicating liquors, the seller in this case is not liable for the injuries alleged, as a matter of law.

We should be looking for a public policy rationale

For purposes of summary judgment, the facts are not in dispute. At about 2:50 a.m. on September 8, 1991, the plaintiffs' child, Phillip Worley, sustained serious and permanent personal injuries when the vehicle in which he was riding as a guest passenger and which was being operated by Anthony Kaiser, crashed into a utility pole while traveling at a high rate of speed.

On the prior evening, Worley, Kaiser, Scott Goosie, and several of their friends, all of whom were under 21 years of age, gathered at the residence of one of the group whose parents were away from home. During the evening, Goosie and Worley were dispatched to a store owned by the defendant, Weigel's, Inc., to purchase beer. Goosie, who was 20 years of age at the time, purchased a substantial quantity of beer. He purchased the beer without showing or being asked by the clerk to show any evidence of his age. Goosie did not drink any beer during the evening. However, Kaiser became intoxicated from drinking beer purchased by Goosie. While en route from the party, with Worley as a passenger, Kaiser, because of his intoxication, lost control of his vehicle and the collision resulted.

How are these facts similar to the facts in our case?

Worley's parents, individually and as his conservators, sued the defendant and alleged as a cause of action the violation of the provisions of Tenn.Code Ann. §§ 57-4-203(b)(1) and 57-5-301(c) (Supp.1995). [criminalizing sale, furnishing, or gift of alcohol to a minor and the state anti-loitering statue]

. . .

These paragraphs deal with procedural history

The trial court granted the defendant's motion for summary judgment. That court held that Tenn.Code Ann. § 57-10-101, in a clear statement designed to protect the sellers of alcoholic beverages, provides that the consumption of alcoholic beverages, rather than the sale, is the proximate cause of injuries inflicted by an intoxicated person. The court further held that under Tenn.Code Ann. § 57-10-102, one who sells alcoholic beverages to a minor may be liable if the seller had actual or constructive knowledge that the purchaser was under 21 years of age, but then only if the injury is caused by the purchaser's consumption of the beverage.

The Court of Appeals agreed with the trial court's decision that the imposition of liability does not require actual knowledge that the purchaser was under 21, but reversed the summary judgment, finding that Tenn.Code Ann. §

57-10-102 does not limit the seller's liability to injuries caused by the purchaser's consumption of the alcoholic beverages and, further, that the seller in this case is estopped from denying that Worley's injuries were caused by the purchaser Goosie. Those same issues are before this Court for decision.

These sound like similar issues to our case

. . .

III

The first issue is whether a seller may be held liable for injuries caused by an intoxicated minor who consumed alcoholic beverages furnished by another minor who purchased the beverages from the seller. The defendant contends that the statutes prohibit recovery unless the buyer consumes the beverage and, as a direct result of that consumption, causes injury. The plaintiffs contend that liability extends to injuries caused by other minors where it was reasonably foreseeable that the other minors would consume the alcoholic drink. Their position is that, even though Tenn.Code Ann. § 57-10-101 limits proximate causation generally, Tenn.Code Ann. § 57-10-102 preserves its usual application in the two particular situations set forth in the statute, sales to minors and sales to intoxicated persons.

Sounds like an issue statement; sounds like the issue in our case

Here is the key point of contention. The parties offer two possible interpretations of the statute. Which will the court adopt?

In *Brookins v. The Round Table, Inc.*, 624 S.W.2d 547 (Tenn.1981), the Court summarized the development of the law at that time:

Here is the old common law rule

> At common law, an individual who sold or furnished alcohol to another generally was held not to be liable for damages resulting from the other's intoxication, even if

> those damages were foreseeable, in part because the other's acceptance and use of the intoxicants was considered an independent intervening cause, cutting off any liability. Today, even in the absence of statutes prohibiting the sale of intoxicating beverages to a minor or to an intoxicated person, courts generally recognize that the furnishing of intoxicants may be the proximate cause of an injury resulting from intoxication, the negligence consisting of the creation of a situation or condition which involves unreasonable risk because of the foreseeable action of another.

Id. at 549 (citations omitted). Reversing the lower court's grant of summary judgment, the *Brookins* court stated, "[W]hether the sale of intoxicants is the proximate cause of subsequent injuries is essentially a question of foreseeability...." *Id. Brookins* noted the purpose of the legislation prohibiting the sale of alcohol to minors:

> These broad prohibitions are intended not only to protect minors from the folly of their own actions, but are for the protection of members of the general public as well. They are directed to minors as a class in recognition of their susceptibilities and the intensification of dangers inherent in the consumption of alcoholic beverages, when consumed by a person lacking in maturity and responsibility.

Here is a policy statement that might be helpful later

Id. at 550. Under the *Brookins* decision, the plaintiffs' cause of action in the present case would survive summary judgment, and the issue for the jury to decide would be whether the injury sustained by Worley was reasonably foreseeable.

The statute overrides the common law

However, Title 57, Chapter 10, of the Tennessee Code, entitled "Alcohol-Related Injuries", replaced the rule stated in *Brookins*. Section 57-10-101 (1989) provides:

> The general assembly hereby finds and declares that the consumption of any alcoholic beverage or beer rather than the furnishing of any alcoholic beverage or beer is the proximate cause of injuries inflicted upon another by an intoxicated person.

Section 57-10-102 provides: [statute omitted]

With the enactment of these statutes, the legislature made a definite distinction between the basis for civil liability and the basis for criminal liability incident to the sale of alcoholic beverages. These statutes, rather than the duties imposed by criminal statutes, [footnote omitted] determine the civil liability of the seller. These statutes declare that the "consumption" rather than the "furnishing of" intoxicating beverages is deemed the "proximate cause of injuries inflicted" by the intoxicated person, except that a sale may be deemed to be the proximate cause when the sale is to a person known to be a minor and whose consumption causes the injury or to a person who is "obviously intoxicated" and whose consumption caused the injury. Since the purchaser in this case did not consume the beverage purchased, the accident was not caused by the purchaser's consumption of the beverage. Therefore, there is no liability on the seller.

Interesting language here

The court summarizes (or outlines) the statute! This entire paragraph is super helpful.

This language seems important. I might cut and paste it.

The second issue also precludes recovery and requires the grant of summary judgment. That issue is the meaning of the phrase "known to be under the age of twenty-one (21) years." The trial court found that Section 57-10-102(1) does not require actual knowledge, and that, where reasonable inquiry is not made as to the age of the buyer, the seller will be deemed to have constructive knowledge that the buyer is a minor. The Court of Appeals agreed. Nevertheless, that construction is not permitted by the plain language of the statute. Under the statute, an action will not lie against a seller of intoxicating beverages unless it is proved beyond a reasonable doubt that the seller knew that the purchaser was a minor and sold intoxicating beverages to him or her anyway.

The Supreme Court defines "knowledge" under the dram shop law

"Generally, statutes in derogation of the common law are to be strictly construed and confined to their express terms...." *Ezell v. Cockrell*, 902 S.W.2d 394, 399 (Tenn.1995). However, "[t]he most basic principle of statutory construction is to ascertain and give effect to the legislative intent without unduly restricting or expanding a statute's coverage beyond its intended scope." *Owens v. State*, 908 S.W.2d 923, 926 (Tenn.1995); *State v. Sliger*, 846 S.W.2d 262, 263 (Tenn.1993). "When the words of a statute are plain and unambiguous, the assumption is 'that the legislature intended what it wrote and meant what it said.' The pertinent language must be [applied] 'without any forced or subtle construction extending its import.' " *McClain v. Henry I. Siegel Co.*, 834

Good language for statutory construction

S.W.2d 295, 296 (Tenn.1992) (citations omitted). These statutes are models of clarity. Construction or interpretation of their plain language would be an exercise in obfuscation.

Great dicta. Cut & paste

Even if the meaning of the statutes was not clear, the legislative history demonstrates a legislative intent to protect sellers from liability in the situation presented in this case. The legislative history reveals that the bill enacting the two statutes was promoted by the Tennessee Hotel/Motel Association to insulate the sellers of intoxicating beverages from suits for injuries caused by their patrons. The Senate sponsor stated during the discussion of the proposed legislation:

Legislative history rationale

Reason for the rule

> I guess I feel like a person should be responsible for his own actions and no other people.... What the bill does now was say that in 2 exceptions, that except in the cases of serving to a minor or serving to an obviously intoxicated person, that the establishment serving alcoholic beverages should not be held liable. Many, many cases have come to us this year whereby the establishments, restaurants, or lounges cannot obtain insurance at any cost.

With regard to the issue of intent, the following explanation was given:

> If this bill passes as it has been written, you have involved the intent in the law of sale to minors. I have to know he is a minor. I have to intend that he had it as a minor otherwise, you are not going to be able to recover.

The legislative intent was that the seller's penalty for selling to minors would be sanctions other than civil liability. The sponsor stated further:

> On the minor situation, I think that the providers of alcoholic beverages have an absolute deterrent to sell to minors because they can lose their license and be put out of business if they sell to a minor.

The bill was debated extensively. The cost to society of protecting sellers of intoxicating beverages was discussed. In opposition to the proposed legislation, the legislature was presented with a case similar to the present one, a mother of three small children sustained severe brain damage as the result of injuries caused by an intoxicated driver. The testimony before the legislature showed that the woman would not have recovered damages from the seller had the proposed statute been in effect, and the victim, therefore, would have become a ward of the state.

Nevertheless, the legislation was enacted, and the clear conclusion is that the legislature intended that civil liability for the sale of alcoholic beverages to a minor may not be imposed on the seller unless the seller knew that the purchaser was a minor, and the minor who purchased the beverage also consumed it and thereby directly caused the accident. This record does not support these conditions necessary for the imposition of liability upon the seller of the alcoholic beverage.

Legislative intent language, very helpful

. . .

IV

The judgment of the Court of Appeals is *reversed,* and the trial court's order granting summary judgment is *reinstated.*

Judgment: holding is in our client's favor. This is a "positive" case analogy.

Costs are adjudged against the plaintiffs.

. . .

Exercise

After reading *Worley v. Weigel's Inc.* consider the following questions:

1. Which elements from the statute might be at issue in our client, Hole Foods', case? Which elements are not at issue?

2. How can you use this case as authority for the general rule? What sub-rules for each element can you pull from this case? Are there any other rules you might want to use from this case including public policy or general legal principles? Please make an organized list.

3. How can you use this case as an analogy? How is it factually similar? How might the reasoning and policy be similar? Please make an organized list (matching factual similarities to elements from the statute).

[24]

CASE ANALOGIES: MULTIPLE ANALOGOUS CASES

SYNTHESIZING MULTIPLE CASES

It is one thing to deal with an individual case. It is another thing altogether to deal with multiple analogous cases.

When a lawyer talks about synthesizing cases, she might mean the inductive process whereby we read multiple cases to divine the common law rule.

Usually, however, when a lawyer asks about case synthesis, she means: how is a group of cases factually similar.

Remember, we use analogous cases to build our legal proof. We must argue that our client's facts are in the same class or category as the legal elements of a rule of law. Therefore, we look to court rulings in factually similar cases.

If there are many factually similar cases, we use inductive reasoning to synthesize them, meaning we take factually diverse cases and find a strain of commonality.

The goal is to come up with a predictive function—a statement that helps us understand the class or category of an element of a rule of law. For example, "in *these* types of factual circumstances, as to *this* element the courts reach *this* outcome for the following reasons."

The trick is to define "these types of factual circumstances." The process of synthesis used in this context, describes combining factually similar cases. Therefore, you might ask yourself, how are the cases I'm reading similar in a *factually material way*? Which facts are material and why? For instance, how do those facts relate to the reason for the rule?

It is important to remember that you aren't creating a new "rule." For instance, in the exercise below, the rule comes from the Tennessee Dram Shop Law and any sub-rules the courts have adopted for each element.

Finally, recall the organizational structure mentioned in the previous chapter.

As we read factually similar cases in the context of our client's legal problem, we typically sort the case *first by element*. Under each element, we *sort cases by positive and negative analogies*. This means we might synthesize the positive cases. Then we might synthesize the negative cases. Other times, you can synthesize both positive and negative cases into one glorious, illustrative predictive function. Try to do that in the exercise below.

Case synthesis is difficult. It's a skill acquired by practice. Therefore, let's practice on some additional dram shop cases.

Case Synthesis Exercise

Using the Hole Foods Inc. fact pattern from the previous chapter, please read the following four cases: *LaRue*, *Temlock*, *Montgomery*, and *Widner*. (You already read *Worley*.)

1. **Please glean any rules from the cases.**
2. **Make a chart of factual similarities.**
3. **Please write a one sentence, factual synthesis of all factually analogous cases.**

LaRue v. 1817 Lake, Inc. d/b/a Bonkers

Court of Appeals of Tennessee (1997)

McMURRAY, Judge. This case arises from a motorcycle accident in which Randy LaRue, the 20-year old son of the plaintiffs, was killed. Plaintiffs sued 1817 Lake, Inc. d/b/a Bonkers, a Knoxville restaurant and bar, and Howard Tannenbaum, president of 1817 Lake Inc., alleging that the defendants negligently and unlawfully served Randy and his companion, defendant Danny Brewer, alcoholic beverages on the evening of the accident. Plaintiffs also sued Robert Archer, the bartender who allegedly provided LaRue and Brewer with the drinks, and Ricky Chambers, the doorman on duty at Bonkers that night. The remaining defendant, Danny G. Brewer was the operator of the motorcycle at the time of the accident which resulted in Randall Charles LaRue's death.

The case proceeded to trial before a jury. At the close of plaintiffs' proof, however, the trial court directed a verdict in favor of all the defendants and dismissed the complaint. This appeal resulted. We affirm the court's ruling as to the "dram shop" defendants and reverse the directed verdict in favor of Danny Brewer, the driver of the motorcycle.

On October 26, 1992, Randy LaRue and Danny Brewer played golf in the morning and early afternoon. Brewer testified that they bought a 12-pack of beer on the way and while playing, each of them drank four or five. They played from about 10:00 a.m. until 2:00 in the afternoon. On the way back they went to a liquor store and bought a bottle of cheap wine called Cisco, and split it while "driving around." Brewer testified that they ended up at LaRue's house between 4:15 and 5:00 p.m. and ate dinner there.

While at the LaRue house, they spoke with Pam Vandergriff, who was cleaning the house. She testified that neither one of them appeared to be drunk or under the influence of alcohol and that "they just seemed to be just normal guys." She did not see either of them drink any beer while they were there. Brewer testified that he had a cup of beer at the LaRue house.

After leaving LaRue's house, they made two brief stops, one at a friend's house and another at Brewer's house. At Brewer's house, they decided to take Brewer's Suzuki motorcycle to Bonkers. Bonkers is a restaurant and bar on that portion of Cumberland Avenue, in close proximity to the University of Tennessee campus, known as "the strip." Responding to the question of whether he was under the influence of an intoxicant before they got to Bonkers, Brewer replied, "I had a slight buzz, but I was not intoxicated drunk, no."

They arrived at Bonkers before its regular opening hour and were allowed to enter. Brewer testified that the doorman, Chambers, let them in, but both Chambers and the bartender, Archer, testified that it was Archer who opened the door for them. It is undisputed that no one asked either Randy LaRue or Brewer for age identification nor did anyone stamp their hands with a designation of either under or over 21 years of age, which was Bonkers' normal policy.

The witnesses' stories diverge considerably at this point. Brewer testified that he and Randy sat down at the bar, and Archer served them a pitcher of beer. Brewer testified that to the best of his knowledge, Archer gave them the drinks they had that night, because Archer was a friend of Randy LaRue. Brewer did not pay for any drinks, and he said that he did not see Randy pay for any either, although he couldn't be completely sure whether he did or not. At one point in his testimony, Brewer said he thought that they drank between one and three pitchers, and probably one apiece, and at another point he said he thought he had drunk 10 or 12 beers at Bonkers.

Archer testified that after they were admitted, they requested to be served, and Archer refused because they were not "of age." Randy LaRue then told Archer not to worry because Brewer had a fake I.D., and Archer replied that it didn't matter. Archer testified that later he noticed that the two were sitting with some friends that had bought a pitcher, and they had glasses and were drinking from the pitcher.

Archer stated that although he knew both LaRue and Brewer were under 21, he did nothing about them sharing drinks from the pitcher. Archer testified that he thought they were drunk when they got there, and no more drunk when they left. However, plaintiffs introduced Archer's signed statement to police investigator Tom Pressley, in which Archer stated, "I don't know what they had before they came in here, but I don't think they were drunk."

LaRue and Brewer were at Bonkers for a little over an hour. Brewer testified that as they were leaving, Archer gave him a Crown Royal and coke, saying, "here's one for the road, guys." Brewer stated that he "slammed" the drink just before leaving.

LaRue briefly conversed with Chambers as he was leaving and while Brewer, who had already exited, was sitting on his motorcycle. Chambers testified that he was very concerned that Brewer was drunk, because his eyes were red and glassy and "he was acting wild." He stated that he expressed concern to LaRue about getting on the motorcycle with Brewer, and tried to persuade him not to do so and offered to find him another ride. Chambers testified that Randy LaRue did not appear drunk at the time, and that he couldn't tell that anything was wrong with him. LaRue's last words to Chambers were, "Rick, if I didn't think he were capable of driving it, I wouldn't get on it."

Both Archer and Chambers testified that they witnessed the two leaving, and that they were headed east, toward downtown and the accident site with Brewer driving. Brewer testified that before the accident occurred they headed west, and stopped at a friend's house on Concord Street to pick up a video game.

The accident occurred on the Main Avenue ramp in downtown Knoxville, between 9:15 and 9:30 p.m., almost immediately after the two left Bonkers. The motorcycle struck the right side of a guardrail as they were exiting the ramp. No other vehicles were involved. Randy LaRue was thrown between 30 and 40 feet from the motorcycle, sustained a massive head injury and never regained consciousness.

First on the scene was Mr. Jim Henderson, an employee of the Knox County Sheriff's Department who was then off duty and traveling with his wife. He stopped his car and assisted Brewer, who had sustained a serious leg injury but was conscious. Henderson asked Brewer what happened and he said "that they had came off the hill at Main Street going too fast and he had lost control." Ms. Tricia Ammons, a paramedic, testified that Brewer told her at the scene that he "was driving a little too fast and he lost control and wrecked."

At the time of the accident, Brewer's blood alcohol level was determined to be 0.21, and LaRue's was measured at 0.10. Brewer later pled guilty to a charge of criminally negligent homicide.

I.

The first issue we will address is the propriety of the trial court's action in directing a verdict in favor of the "dram shop" defendants, i.e., all those defendants that were alleged to be negligent in providing alcohol to LaRue and Brewer. As the parties recognize, our analysis is governed by T.C.A. §§ 57–10–101 and 102, which state: [statutes omitted]

It seems quite clear that for T.C.A. § 57–10–102 to apply, the plaintiffs must prove beyond a reasonable doubt that the defendants "sold " an alcoholic beverage to LaRue and Brewer. The statute in each and every instance requires a sale before liability can be imposed. There is no direct evidence nor evidence in the record from which an inference can reasonably be drawn, that there was a sale to either Brewer or LaRue by the "dram shop" defendants. Plaintiffs argue, however, that the statute should not be construed as to require a "sale" of alcohol to a minor or obviously intoxicated person. They argue that, because of public policy against furnishing alcohol to minors, a showing beyond a reasonable doubt that a defendant "furnished" alcohol to a person under 21 should be enough to allow a jury to decide whether the furnishing was the proximate cause of an accident. We most respectfully disagree. We should first note that it is within the province of the General Assembly to establish and proclaim public policy. The Supreme Court in Watson v. Cleveland Chair Co., 789 S.W.2d 538 (Tenn.1989), made the following observations:

A definitive statement on the authority of the courts to determine public policy can be found in Nashville Ry. and Light Co. v. Lawson, 144 Tenn. 78, 91, 229 S.W. 741 (1921), citing from License Tax Cases, 72 U.S. 462, 5 Wall. 462, 18 L.Ed. 497:

> "This Court can know nothing of public policy except from the constitution and the laws, and the course of administration and decision. It has no legislative powers. It cannot amend or modify any legislative acts. It cannot examine questions as expedient or inexpedient, or as politic or impolitic. Considerations of that sort must, in general, be addressed to the legislature. Questions of policy determined there are concluded here."

Watson, supra at page 540. See also Smith v. Gore, 728 S.W.2d 738 and the cases cited therein.

The General Assembly has unambiguously declared the public policy with regard to the furnishing of alcohol to persons under the age of 21 as it relates to "dram shops." We are not at liberty to hold otherwise. Accordingly, in the absence of evidence of a sale, the trial court was correct in directing a verdict in favor of the "dram shop" defendants.

[Omitting section analyzing Plaintiff's contributory negligence in causing his own injuries by riding with a drunk person.]

. . . Here, it is reasonable to conclude that more probable than not both parties were negligent. Sufficient doubt exists, however, to require the case to be submitted to the jury.

Accordingly, we reverse the action of the trial court in directing a verdict against the plaintiffs and in favor of the defendant, Brewer. The trial court is affirmed in all other respects.

In our discretion costs of this appeal are assessed equally between the plaintiffs and the defendant, Brewer. We remand the case to the trial court for a new trial as to the defendant, Brewer.

GODDARD, Presiding Judge, concurring. I concur in Judge McMurray's reversal of the Trial Court's dismissal of the case against the operator of the motorcycle, Mr. Brewer, for the reasons stated therein, and in his affirmance of the dismissal as to the "dram shop" Defendants. I base my concurrence as to the latter upon T.C.A. 57–10–101, which provides that consuming rather than furnishing alcoholic beverages is the proximate cause of injuries inflicted by an intoxicated person.

In reaching this conclusion I note that no constitutional attack is leveled as to the statute and, further, that the import of T.C.A. 57–10–102 is not entirely clear. My reading of both Code Sections, however, persuades me that T.C.A. 57–10–102 is intended as an exception to 57–10–101 and allows recovery if the requirements contained therein are met. While it seems anomalous to me that the Legislature would insulate an alcoholic dispensing establishment from liability when the spirits are given away to those under 21 or intoxicated, as opposed to being sold, I conclude that under the clear language of T.C.A. 57–10–101 the acts of the "dram shop" Defendants, who furnished but did not sell the intoxicating beverage, are not the proximate cause of the death of Mr. LaRue, which is necessary to cast them in judgment.

SUSANO, Judge, concurring. I concur completely in Judge McMurray's holding that the dram shop defendants were entitled to a directed verdict. I also agree with his reasoning in support of that holding. As to the defendant Brewer, I agree that, based upon the plaintiffs' proof, a jury could reasonably find that any negligence on the part of the deceased was less than the negligence of Brewer. Therefore, I agree that the plaintiffs' claim against Brewer must be remanded for a new trial. My concurrence is limited to these statements.

###

Temlock v. McGinnis

Court of Appeals of Tennessee (2006, unpublished)

D. MICHAEL SWINEY, J. Alec J. Temlock ("Plaintiff") sued Robert M. McGinnis ("McGinnis") and Pub Ventures of S.C., Inc., d/b/a Barley's Taproom & Pizzeria ("Barley's") for injuries Plaintiff received when he was hit by a vehicle driven by McGinnis. Barley's filed a motion for summary judgment arguing, in part, that at no time on the evening of the accident did it sell alcoholic beverages to McGinnis and, therefore, it could not be held liable for the accident and Plaintiff's injuries. The Trial Court granted Barley's motion for summary judgment. Plaintiff appeals. We vacate the grant of summary judgment to Barley's.

Background

On December 15, 2000, at approximately 1:15 a.m., Plaintiff was walking across private property when a vehicle driven by McGinnis left the roadway, crossed over the sidewalk on to the private property, and struck and injured Plaintiff. From the record before us, McGinnis earlier had consumed alcoholic beverages, specifically beer, at Barley's prior to operating the vehicle. When tested by police at the accident scene, McGinnis registered a Breathalyzer blood alcohol level of .20. McGinnis was arrested at the scene and charged with driving under the influence and vehicular assault. McGinnis later pled guilty to vehicular assault, and his plea was accepted by the Criminal Court for Knox County.

Plaintiff sued McGinnis and Barley's. Barley's filed a motion for summary judgment claiming only that there is no evidence it sold alcoholic beverages to McGinnis on the night in question because McGinnis did not pay for the beer he ordered and drank. Plaintiff opposed Barley's motion for summary judgment, in part, by filing McGinnis' affidavit, which stated, as pertinent to this appeal:

> 7. While at Barley's Taproom as a customer, I continued to drink beer. I may have had something to eat there but do not specifically

> remember. I ordered beer by the glass from the Barley's Taproom wait staff, as did others at my table. The wait staff at Barley's Taproom served the beer to me and my companions as it was ordered.
>
> 8. Taylor S. Griswold and I stayed at Barley's Taproom and continued to drink beer until we decided to leave. I do not know how many beers I drank at Barley's Taproom.
>
> 9. The waiters and waitresses at Barley's Taproom served me beer during the entire time I was at Barley's Taproom. I did not drink beer at any other place that evening other than the original beers I drank at Taylor S. Griswold's house.

The Trial Court heard argument and granted Barley's motion for summary judgment by order entered September 27, 2005. The Trial Court pursuant to Tenn. R. Civ. P. 54.02 directed the entry of this judgment be a final judgment. Plaintiff appeals to this Court.

Discussion

Although not stated exactly as such, Plaintiff raises one issue on appeal: whether the Trial Court erred in granting summary judgment to Barley's.

[omitting portions of legal standard for summary judgment]

> The standards governing the assessment of evidence in the summary judgment context are also well established. Courts must view the evidence in the light most favorable to the nonmoving party and must also draw all reasonable inferences in the nonmoving party's favor. See Robinson v. Omer, 952 S.W.2d at 426; Byrd v. Hall, 847 S.W.2d at 210-11. Courts should grant a summary judgment only when both the facts and the inferences to be drawn from the facts permit a reasonable person to reach only one conclusion. See McCall v. Wilder, 913 S.W.2d 150, 153 (Tenn.1995); Carvell v. Bottoms, 900 S.W.2d 23, 26 (Tenn.1995).

Staples v. CBL & Assocs., Inc., 15 S.W.3d 83, 89 (Tenn.2000).

The Trial Court's grant of summary judgment to Barley's does not specifically state that the Trial Court found that no sale to McGinnis had occurred. However, from the record before us, the briefs on appeal, and the parties' arguments during oral argument before this Court, it is clear that the issue of whether summary judgment was proper revolves around the question of whether, under Tenn.Code Ann. § 57-10-102, Barley's sold beer to McGinnis on the night of the accident.

Two statutes pertaining to alcohol-related injuries are relevant to this appeal, Tenn.Code Ann. § 57-10-101 and Tenn.Code Ann. § 57-10-102. Tenn.Code Ann. § 57-10-101 provides: [statutes omitted]

Our Supreme Court discussed Tenn.Code Ann. §§ 57-10-101 and 57-10-102 in Biscan v. Brown, 160 S.W.3d 462 (Tenn.2004). The Biscan Opinion stated:

> The effect of [Tenn.Code Ann. § 57-10-101] is to make it impossible for one who has been injured by an intoxicated person to state a claim for negligence against the person or entity who furnished the alcoholic beverage or beer because the statute removes, as a matter of law, the required element of legal causation. See, e.g., Turner v. Jordan, 957 S.W.2d 815, 818 (Tenn.1997) (a claim for negligence requires a duty of care owed by the defendant to the plaintiff; a breach of that duty; an injury or loss; causation in fact; and legal, or proximate, causation.) In other words, there can be no cause of action resting on the allegation that one person "furnished" alcohol to another because it is impossible to prove proximate cause. The statute does not merely provide immunity from suit where one has furnished alcohol to another; rather, the statute constitutes the legislative determination that persons who furnish alcohol are not at fault for injuries inflicted by an intoxicated person.
>
> The second part of the statute carves out an exception to the first part. It provides that a seller of alcohol may be liable to a third party for injuries if the seller sold alcohol to a minor or if the seller sold alcohol to an obviously intoxicated person and the sale was a proximate cause of the injuries suffered by the third party:
>
> * * *
>
> The clear language of the statute admits of only one conclusion: that the legislature intended to shield persons ... who "furnish" alcohol in a social setting.

> * * *
>
> Moreover, as the Court of Appeals discussed, the legislative history of sections 101 and 102 reveals that the statute was intended to codify the common-law rule that an individual who furnishes alcohol to another is not liable for any damages resulting from the other's intoxication, even if those damages are foreseeable. See, e.g., Cecil, 575 S.W.2d at 271. Thus, although the legislative history reflects much debate and concern over the extent to which sellers of alcoholic beverages and beers should be covered, the starting point was that the mere furnishing of alcohol, whether gratuitously or for commercial gain, is not a basis for liability. See Worley v. Weigel's, 919 S.W.2d at 593-94.

Biscan, 160 S.W.3d at 472-73.

McGinnis' affidavit shows: (1) that he was a customer at Barley's on the night of the accident; (2) that he directly ordered beer by the glass from Barley's wait staff; (3) that Barley's wait staff brought to McGinnis the beer he ordered and served it directly to him; (4) and that McGinnis while still at Barley's consumed the beer that he had ordered. Barley's does not argue that it intended no sale of this beer or that it was giving beer away that night. Barley's instead argues that the individual it sold the beer to was McGinnis' friend, Taylor Griswold, who paid for the beer.

Barley's argues on appeal that the facts of this case are similar to the facts of Worley v. Weigel's, Inc., wherein our Supreme Court held: "Since the purchaser in this case did not consume the beverage purchased, the accident was not caused by the purchaser's consumption of the beverage. Therefore, there is no liability on the seller." Worley v. Weigel's, Inc., 919 S.W.2d 589, 593 (Tenn.1996). In Worley, two young men both under the age of 21 entered a store owned by the defendant where one of the young men purchased "a substantial quantity of beer." Id. at 591. A third young man also under the age of 21 consumed the beer, became intoxicated, and lost control of his vehicle resulting in a collision that caused injuries to a passenger. Id. Barley's argues, in part, that it "sold the beer to Taylor Griswold in return for payment by credit card," and that "McGinnis did not pay for or purchase any beer at Barley's on the night in question...," and, therefore, Barley's has no liability for the accident in question.

Worley, however, clearly is distinguishable from the case at hand. In Worley, the third young man who drank the beer, became intoxicated, and lost control of his vehicle was not in defendant's store when his friends purchased the beer. Id. Clearly the young man in Worley did not directly order the beer from the Weigel's, Inc., did not have the beer delivered directly into his hands by Weigel's, Inc., and did not consume the beer while in the Weigel's store. In the case now on appeal, McGinnis was a customer at Barley's on the night in question, McGinnis directly ordered beer by the glass from Barley's wait staff, Barley's wait staff brought the beer to McGinnis and served it directly to him, and McGinnis while still in Barley's drank each beer that he had ordered and which had been delivered to him.

Our Legislature clearly intended to shield sellers from liability in situations such as in Worley where the intoxicated person was not even in the seller's establishment when the sale of the alcoholic beverages occurred, did not order the beer from the seller, did not have the seller deliver the beer directly to him, and did not consume the beer while in the seller's place of business. In such a situation, the seller has no control over who consumes the alcoholic beverage after the product leaves the store premises. The facts in Worley are very different from those in the instant case. In the case now on appeal, McGinnis not only was present when the sale occurred, but he was the one who ordered the beer from Barley's wait staff, the beer was delivered directly to him by Barley's wait staff with the expectation of payment in return, and McGinnis consumed the beer while in Barley's.

As our Supreme Court stated in Stewart v. State, an appellate court's "primary goal in interpreting statutes is 'to ascertain and give effect to the intention and purpose of the legislature.' " Stewart v. State, 33 S.W.3d 785, 791 (Tenn.2000) (quoting Gleaves v. Checker Cab Transit Corp., 15 S.W.3d 799, 802 (Tenn.2000)).

Whether McGinnis was the individual who paid for the beer that he ordered, that was served directly to him, and that he consumed on site, or whether one of his friends paid or even whether McGinnis walked out without paying is not dispositive of the question of whether a "sale" occurred pursuant to Tenn.Code Ann. § 57-10-102(2) making this statute applicable. In making this determination, all relevant circumstances must be considered. McGinnis was in Barley's, an establishment in the business of selling beer. McGinnis ordered beer directly from Barley's wait staff, and Barley's wait staff served the beer ordered by McGinnis directly to McGinnis with the expectation by Barley's that it would be paid for the beer as Barley's has never contended it was giving away beer. McGinnis drank this beer while on Barley's premises. We hold these facts are sufficient to constitute a sale to McGinnis for purposes of Tenn.Code Ann. § 57-10-102. Under the facts of this case, we hold Barley's sold McGinnis the beer under Tenn.Code Ann. § 57-10-102, regardless of who actually ended up paying for it or even if Barley's customers skipped out on the beer tab altogether and no one paid for it.

It was the clear intent and purpose of our Legislature that a fact situation such as the one now before us constitutes a sale under the provisions of Tenn.Code Ann. § 57-10-102. We hold that when a customer enters an establishment that sells alcoholic beverages such as beer, places his own alcohol order, has the alcohol he ordered delivered directly to him by the seller with the seller's expectation of payment in return, and the customer who ordered the alcohol consumes that alcohol on the seller's premises, there is a sale to that customer under Tenn.Code Ann. § 57-10-102. To hold otherwise would mean that a business could adopt a policy that in serving any group of more than one individual, only one person in the group is to be allowed to "pay" for the alcohol ordered and consumed by all other members in that party even though those other individuals directly ordered the alcohol from the seller's wait staff, had the alcohol delivered by the seller's wait staff directly to them, and they consumed the alcohol on the seller's premises, and, the seller then would have no potential liability under Tenn.Code. Ann. § 57-10-102 except as to the one person who paid. Such a decision would be directly contrary to the clear intent and purpose of the Legislature to hold such a seller liable if it sells "alcohol to a minor or if the seller sold alcohol to an obviously intoxicated person and the sale was the proximate cause of the injuries suffered by the third party...." Biscan, 160 S.W.3d at 472. Our holding is required by the clear intent and purpose of the Legislature in enacting Tenn.Code Ann. § 57-10-102, and is limited to the application of that statute.

As Barley's did sell beer to McGinnis on the night in question, it neither affirmatively negated an essential element of Plaintiff's claim nor conclusively established an affirmative defense. We, therefore, vacate the grant of summary judgment to Barley's.

Conclusion

The judgment of the Trial Court is vacated as to the grant of summary judgment to Barley's, and this cause is remanded to the Trial Court. The costs on appeal are assessed against the Appellee . . . .

###

Montgomery v. Kali Orexi, LLC
d/b/a Gondolier Italian Restaurant and Pizza

Court of Appeals of Tennessee (2008, Unpublished opinion)

CHARLES D. SUSANO, JR., J. In this wrongful death action, Edwina Montgomery ("the Plaintiff"), individually and as the surviving spouse of Thomas M. Montgomery ("the Deceased"), brought suit under the Tennessee Dram Shop Act ("the Dram Shop Act" or "the Act"), Tenn.Code Ann. §§ 57–10–101 and 102 (2002). The Plaintiff also sued for negligence and negligence per se. The Plaintiff sued Kali Orexi, LLC, which operates under the trade name of Gondolier Italian Restaurant and Pizza ("Gondolier"). Gondolier moved for summary judgment, which was granted as to all theories of recovery.

We affirm the summary judgment on what appears to be an issue of first impression. We hold that Tenn.Code Ann. §§ 57–10–101 and 102 (2002) apply to third parties and do not authorize an action against a seller of an "alcoholic beverage or beer" by or on behalf of the supplied, or "first" party. Since the Dram Shop Act does not address first parties, its enactment leaves the law as to first parties as it existed before the Act's enactment. In addition, under the circumstances of this case, the trial court correctly held that the injuries to the Deceased were not foreseeable; thus, Gondolier owed the Deceased no duty. Furthermore, even if a duty were owed, it was not breached. The question whether the actions of the Deceased and a taxi driver, who was paid by Gondolier to take the intoxicated Deceased home, were intervening and superseding causes that relieve Gondolier of liability are not addressed since we hold that the Plaintiff had no cause of action under the Dram Shop Act or for common law negligence. Accordingly, we affirm.

I.

Viewing the evidence, and all reasonable inferences to be drawn from it, in the light most favorable to the nonmoving party, i.e., the Plaintiff, we state the facts that are pertinent to this appeal by quoting the Plaintiff, as follows:

> On June 24, 2006, [the Deceased] was a customer at [Gondolier] in Gatlinburg, Tennessee. While at [Gondolier], [the Deceased] was served alcoholic beverages and became extremely intoxicated.
>
> Gondolier staff later summoned Ken Kirkland, a local taxi cab driver, to take the Deceased home from the restaurant.
>
> Upon first contact with [the Deceased], Mr. Kirkland observed that [the Deceased] was intoxicated. Mr. Kirkland testified that [the Deceased] exhibited physical symptoms of intoxication, such as "slurred speech, unable to stand, very wobbly when he moved." Mr. Kirkland described [the Deceased] as being "extremely intoxicated."

* * *

Shortly after departing from Gondolier, [the Deceased] informed Mr. Kirkland that he did not want to go home, and that he wanted Mr. Kirkland to take him back to the Gondolier. As Mr. Kirkland continued to drive towards the area [where the Deceased] resided, [the Deceased] grabbed the steering wheel of the cab, causing the cab to veer into the other lane of the roadway. Mr. Kirkland testified that in response he "slapped his hand away" and "hit the brakes and moved over to the side of the road."

After a brief discussion [in which Mr. Kirkland warned the Deceased not to grab the steering wheel again], Mr. Kirkland resumed driving towards the area in which [the Deceased] resided. Shortly thereafter, [the Deceased] again stated that he did not want to go to his house, and wanted to return to the Gondolier. At which time, [the Deceased] grabbed at the cab's steering wheel a second time. Mr. Kirkland testified that at that time he pushed [the Deceased] back towards the passenger seat and pulled the cab over onto the side of the road and turned off the vehicle's engine.

Mr. Kirkland exited the cab and went to the passenger side to remove [the Deceased] from the vehicle.

* * *

As he was driving away, Mr. Kirkland placed a telephone call to 911, and informed the operator that he had put a "very drunk" man out of his cab and left him on the side of the road. The Sevier County Sheriff's Department responded to the 911 call, but was unable to locate [the Deceased] at the location described by Mr. Kirkland.

On June 26, 2006, [the Deceased's] body was located by the Sevier County Sheriff's Department in a river underneath a bridge on Highway 321 in Sevier County....

Autopsy test results revealed that [the Deceased] was heavily intoxicated at the time of his death. [The Deceased's] blood alcohol content was measured at .37%. The attending pathologist listed the cause of death as blunt force trauma injuries sustained by [the Deceased] when he fell from a bridge.

II.

The issues presented are as follows:

Whether a cause of action under Tenn.Code Ann. § 57–10–102 against a seller of an "alcoholic beverage or beer" is available to the Deceased or his representative, who is not a third party, but was himself the consumer of the alcohol.

Whether the enactment of Tenn.Code Ann. §§ 57–10–101 and 102 changed the common law with respect to liability of furnishers of alcohol or beer to an intoxicated person who injures himself.

Whether the Trial Court was correct in holding as a matter of law that the Deceased's injuries were so unforeseeable that no legal duty arose on the part of Gondolier.

Whether the Trial Court was correct in holding as a matter of law that if Gondolier had a duty, it fulfilled it.

Whether the Trial Court was correct in holding as a matter of law that the actions of the Deceased and Mr. Kirkland constitute intervening superseding acts that relieved Gondolier of liability.

. . .

IV.

A.

The first issue we address is whether a person who purchases an "alcoholic beverage or beer" and is injured or dies as a result of the consumption may sue the supplier of the alcohol under the Dram Shop Act. This inquiry calls upon us to interpret the language of Tenn.Code Ann. §§ 57–10–101 and 102, which comprise the entirety of the Dram Shop Act.

The Plaintiff contends that Tenn.Code Ann. § 57–10–102 ("section 102") permits what she calls "first party causes of action." She says that under section 102 "any party" who has suffered personal injury or death may bring a cause of action against a commercial seller of an "alcoholic beverage or beer" in circumstances in which the alcoholic beverage or beer was sold to an obviously intoxicated person or a minor.

Gondolier contends that Tenn.Code Ann. § 57–10–101 ("section 101") states a general rule, i.e., that it is the consumption of the beverage and not the furnishing of it that is the proximate cause of injuries to third parties by intoxicated persons, and that section 102 states two narrow exceptions to the general rule of non-liability to third parties set out in section 101. These exceptions address circumstances in which a purveyor of the beverage sells it to 1) a person known to be a minor or 2) an "obviously intoxicated" person. According to Gondolier, on the other hand, section 102 applies only in circumstances in which a third party is injured by the intoxicated person.

[Dram Shop Statute Omitted]

Interpreting sections 101 and 102, the Supreme Court has stated:

> When the words of a statute are plain and unambiguous, the assumption is "that the legislature intended what it wrote and meant what it said." The pertinent language must be [applied] "without any forced or subtle construction extending its import."

Worley, 919 S.W.2d at 593 (quoting McClain v. Henry I. Siegel Co., 834 S.W.2d 295, 296 (Tenn.1992) (citations omitted)).

The Worley Court went on to note:

> These statutes are models of clarity. Construction or interpretation of their plain language would be an exercise in obfuscation.

Id. Section 101 states a general rule, and section 102 states two narrow exceptions to the general rule. In Biscan v. Brown, a 2005 case interpreting sections 101 and 102, the Supreme Court noted that the specific exceptions in section 102 "must be confined to their terms and cannot be read to somehow limit the broad rule stated in section 101." Biscan v. Brown, 160 S.W.3d 462, 473 (Tenn.2005). Quoting Burns v. City of Nashville, the Supreme Court added, " 'Where a general rule has been established by statute, with exceptions, the court will not curtail the former, not add to the latter by implication.' " Id.

(quoting Burns v. City of Nashville, 132 Tenn. 429, 435, 178 S.W. 1053, 1054 (1915)).

The general rule stated at section 101 applies in circumstances in which a third party is injured. The statute is silent about a circumstance in which an intoxicated person (i.e., a first party) is injured. The Plaintiff asks this court, however, to interpret the generic language, "any person," in section 102 to bring intoxicated persons within the coverage of the statute.

We decline to read section 102 in isolation from section 101. Rather, we look to the statutory scheme as a whole. Faust v. Metro. Gov't of Nashville, 206 S.W.3d 475, 490 (Tenn.Ct.App.2006). As this Court has said:

> The rule relative to "pari materia " construction applies ... with equal force to separate provisions within a single statute. The different parts of a statute reflect light upon each other, and statutory provisions are regarded as in pari materia where they are parts of the same act. Hence, a statute should be construed in its entirety, and as a whole. All parts of the act should be considered and construed together. It is not permissible to rest a construction upon any one part alone, or upon isolated words, phrases, clauses, or sentences, or to give undue effect thereto. The legislative intention, as collected from an examination of the whole as well as the separate parts of a statute, is not to be defeated by the use of particular terms.

Id. (citations omitted). In this case, reading section 101 and 102 in pari materia, it is clear to us that the isolated phrase "any person" in section 102 should not be read so as to defeat the legislative intent that is stated as the general rule in section 101. We decline to construe section 102 in such a way as to add to the overall ambit of the Dram Shop Act.

The Supreme Court has previously reviewed the history of sections 101 and 102 and concluded that the statute was "intended to codify the common-law rule that an individual who furnishes alcohol to another is not liable for any damages resulting from the other's intoxication, even if those damages are foreseeable." Biscan,

160 S.W.3d at 473 (citing Cecil v. Hardin, 575 S.W.2d 268, 271 (Tenn.1978)).

While recognizing the Supreme Court's pronouncement in Biscan and other cases, the Plaintiff, nevertheless, argues that some states allow first-party actions, and points out cases in Texas and Florida. The Florida statute does not include the third-party language ("injuries inflicted upon another by an intoxicated person") of section 101, however. See Fla. Stat. § 768.125 (2003) (liability "for injury or damage caused by or resulting from the intoxication of such minor or person"). The same is true of the Texas statute. See Tex. Alco. Bev.Code Ann. § 2.02(b)(1) (1993) (refers to person receiving alcohol who "was obviously intoxicated to the extent that he presented a clear danger to himself and others") (emphasis added). The Florida and Texas cases, based on statutes with wording different from our own, are of no help to the Plaintiff.

Our job in interpreting statutory provisions is to determine and give effect to the legislature's intent. Kyle v. Williams, 98 S.W.3d 661, 664 (Tenn.2003). By its clear language section 101 provides that the consumption of an alcoholic beverage or beer, and not the furnishing of it, "is the proximate cause of injuries inflicted upon another by an intoxicated person." (Emphasis added.) The two exceptions to the general rule of non-liability of furnishers of alcohol must be read narrowly and within the parameters set forth in section 101.

Since the general rule stated in section 101 deals with circumstances in which a third party is injured by an intoxicated person, the exceptions to the general rule likewise were intended to apply in circumstances in which a third party is injured by an intoxicated person—either when a sale was knowingly made to a minor who injures another or when a sale is made to "an obviously intoxicated person" who injures another. On this issue of first impression we hold that Tenn.Code Ann. §§ 57–10–101 and 102 apply only to third parties and do not permit an action against a seller of an "alcoholic beverage or beer" by or on behalf of the supplied party, i.e., a first party. We thus affirm the trial court's grant of summary judgment as to the

Plaintiff's suit predicated upon an alleged violation of the Dram Shop Act.

B.

We now turn our attention to the Plaintiff's suit for damages based upon the common law.

The General Assembly has plenary power within constitutional limits to change the common law by statute. See Southern Ry. Co. v. Sanders, 193 Tenn. 409, 415, 246 S.W.2d 65, 67 (1952). The "[r]ules of the common law are not repealed by implication, and if a statute does not include and cover such a case, it leaves the law as it was before its enactment." Monk v. Ramsey, 223 Tenn. 247, 252, 443 S.W.2d 653, 655 (1969) (citation omitted).

The Plaintiff argues that the common law foreseeability inquiry set forth in Brookins v. The Round Table, Inc., 624 S.W.2d 547 (Tenn.1981), has been superseded by the Dram Shop Act. In Brookins, the Supreme Court stated, "[W]hether the sale of intoxicants is the proximate cause of subsequent injuries is essentially a question of foreseeability...." 624 S.W.2d at 549 (adopting Mitchell v. Ketner, 54 Tenn.App. 656, 666, 393 S.W.2d 755, 759 (1964)). In Worley, the High Court explicitly stated: "Title 57, Chapter 10, of the Tennessee Code entitled 'Alcohol–Related Injuries' [Tenn.Code Ann. §§ 57–10–101 and 102 (2002)] replaced the rule stated in Brookins." Worley, 919 S.W.2d at 592. The portion of the holding in Brookins that was replaced was the rule as to proximate cause in third-party actions. Section 101 provides that it is the consumption of the beverage, not the furnishing of it, that is the proximate cause of any injury to a third party, thus rejecting the notion that proximate cause is an inquiry of foreseeability under the Act.

In this opinion, we have held that the Dram Shop Act does not apply to first parties, such as the Plaintiff's decedent in this case. Since the statute does not cover first party actions against furnishers of an alcoholic beverage or beer, it leaves the law concerning first-party actions as it existed before the Act's enactment. As we have previously noted, the common law is not repealed by implication. Our holding regarding the common law is further bolstered by appellate decisions since the enactment of the Dram Shop Act. For example, in Cook v. Spinnaker's of Rivergate, Inc., 878 S.W.2d 934 (Tenn.1994), which was a post-Dram Shop Act decision of the Supreme Court, the Court analyzed a case in which a minor sued a restaurant that had served her alcohol shortly before she drove and was injured in a one car accident. Id. at 936. There was no mention of, citation to, or discussion of the Dram Shop Act.

We conclude and hold that the enactment of the Dram Shop Act did not affect the common law rules applicable to first-party actions against a furnisher of an alcoholic beverage or beer.

C.

We hold that the trial court correctly applied common law principles to the Plaintiff's cause of action for negligence. That court noted as follows: "The Court also finds that the [Deceased's] injuries were not reasonably foreseeable and, as such, no duty arose on the part of Gondolier to protect against them." To establish a negligence claim at trial a plaintiff must show the following elements: (1) a duty of care owed by the defendant to the plaintiff; (2) conduct by the defendant falling below the applicable standard of care that amounts to a breach of that duty; (3) an injury or loss; (4) causation in fact; and (5) proximate, or legal causation. See White v. Lawrence, 975 S.W.2d 525, 529 (Tenn.1998) (citations omitted); McCall v. Wilder, 913 S.W.2d 150, 153 (Tenn.1995) (citations omitted).

At early common law there was no cause of action for first-party claims. For example in a 1940 case, the Supreme Court said:

> It was not a tort at common law to either sell or give intoxicating liquor to a strong and able-bodied man, and it can be said safely that it is not anywhere laid down in the books that such act was even held at common law to be culpable negligence that would impose legal liability for damages upon the vendor or donor of such liquor.

Tarwater v. Atlantic Co., 176 Tenn. 510, 144 S.W.2d 746 (1940) (quoting Cruse v. Aden, 127 Ill. 231, 233, 20 N.E. 73, 74 (1889)). Refusal to impose liability on the furnisher of an alcoholic beverage or beer was found on two bases. One was that the person who voluntarily became intoxicated was the proximate cause of the injury. Id. at 176 Tenn. at 513, 144 S.W.2d at 748. The second basis was that the intoxicated person's acceptance of the alcohol was an independent intervening cause that cut off liability. Tarwater, 176 Tenn. at 511–12, 144 S.W.2d at 747.

This bright-line approach began to change with the decision in Mitchell v. Ketner, 54 Tenn.App. 656, 393 S.W.2d 755 (Tenn.Ct.App.1964). In Mitchell, this court stated that it was "unwilling to hold that, no matter what the circumstances, the act of the purchaser and not the sale constitute the proximate cause of injury to third persons or that consumption of the intoxicant is always an independent, intervening act which breaks the chain of causation." 54 Tenn.App. at 665, 393 S.W.2d at 759 (citation omitted). Some years later, in Brookins, the Supreme Court adopted the analysis of Mitchell, quoting that decision and concluding that whether the sale of intoxicants is the proximate cause of subsequent injuries is essentially a question of foreseeability. Brookins, 624 S.W.2d at 549. In 1986, the legislature expressed its concern that the courts had moved away from the traditional common law approach; as a consequence, it passed the Dram Shop Act.

Our review of the case law leads us to conclude that no Tennessee case has altered the common law rule in relation to first-party claims by adults who are injured while intoxicated and seek to recover damages directly from the furnisher of the beverage. Indeed, in the same year the Dram Shop Act was passed, this court considered a case in which a "grossly intoxicated" 27–year–old plaintiff was injured in a single-car accident after drinking at the defendant's bar. Jordan v. The Krystal Co., 1986 WL 11218, at *1 (Tenn.Ct.App. W.S., filed October 7, 1986). This court affirmed the trial court's dismissal of the case for failure to state a claim for which relief can be granted, noting that "one cannot recover damages when he actively contributes to his own intoxication, which is the proximate cause of his injury." Id. at *3.4

We recognize that if a person drives while intoxicated there is a foreseeable risk that accidents, injuries and deaths may result. See West v. East Tenn. Pioneer Oil Co., 172 S.W.3d 545, 552 (Tenn.2005) (common knowledge that drunk driving directly results in accidents, injuries, and deaths). In this case, however, the Deceased did not drive. Rather, a Gondolier staff person called a taxi, assisted the Deceased into the taxi and paid for the Deceased's trip home. She also moved the Deceased's car, which was not parked on Gondolier's premises, so that it would not be towed. These facts are undisputed.

The Plaintiff refers this court to McClenahan v. Cooley, 806 S.W.2d 767 (Tenn.1991). The Plaintiff quotes McClenahan, as stating that "[t]he foreseeability requirement is not so strict as to require the tortfeasor to foresee the exact manner in which the injury takes place...." Id. at 775. The Plaintiff omits an important qualification to the rule stated, however. The complete sentence reads, "The foreseeability requirement is not so strict as to require the tortfeasor to foresee the exact manner in which the injury takes place, provided it is determined that the tortfeasor could foresee, or through the exercise of reasonable diligence should have foreseen, the general manner in which the injury or loss occurred." Id.

Questions regarding foreseeability are ordinarily questions of fact for a jury. However, even this question may be decided at the summary judgment stage if the evidence is uncontroverted and if the facts and the inferences reasonably drawn from them permit reasonable persons to reach only one conclusion. See McCall, 913 S.W.2d at 153; Carvell v. Bottoms, 900 S.W.2d 23, 26 (Tenn.1995); Staples, 15 S.W.3d at 89. This is such a case.

Based on the facts, and considering the inferences to be drawn from the facts favorable to the Plaintiff, we hold that a reasonable person can reach only one conclusion and it is that Gondolier could not have foreseen the general manner in which the Deceased's injuries occurred; nor through the exercise of reasonable care should Gondolier have foreseen that once the Deceased was safely in a taxi to be driven home, he would grab the steering wheel of the taxi turning it into the oncoming lane, be warned, repeat the same conduct, and be put out of the taxi onto the roadside by the taxi driver, following which he would fall off a bridge to his death.

We affirm the trial court's holding that the Deceased's injuries were not reasonably foreseeable and, as such, no duty arose on the part of Gondolier to protect against them. Giggers v. Memphis Housing Auth., 277 S.W.3d 359, 365–66 (Tenn.2009); Satterfield v. Breeding Insulation Co., 266 S.W.3d 347, 366 (Tenn.2008). Given the undisputed facts, Gondolier negated an element of the Plaintiff's prima facie case for negligence, i.e., that the defendant owed a duty to the Deceased. Summary judgment was thus properly granted on the basis that Gondolier did not owe the Deceased a duty.

D.

When a risk of injury is not generally foreseeable, no duty arises. If no duty arises, there can be no breach of duty. The trial court held that even if there had been a duty, however, Gondolier fulfilled that duty as a matter of law. We agree.

The Plaintiff analyzes the issue of breach of duty with reference to the Dram Shop Act. The Plaintiff asserts that Gondolier had a duty not to serve alcohol to an obviously intoxicated person, but the only law the Plaintiff cites is section 102 of the Dram Shop Act.5 Since we have held that sections 101 and 102 are not applicable to a first-party action such as the one the Plaintiff has brought, this analysis is inapposite. Going beyond the Act, we hold that the Plaintiff's position is at odds with the common law.

"At common law, an individual who sold or furnished alcohol to another generally was held not to be liable for damages resulting from the other's intoxication, even if those damages were foreseeable...." Brookins, 624 S.W.2d at 549 (citations omitted). For example, the Supreme Court has specifically declined to impose a duty on a commercial business to physically control an intoxicated driver by preventing him or her from leaving the premises. East Tenn. Pioneer Oil Co., 172 S.W.3d at 552 ("[W]e do not hold that convenience store employees have a duty to physically restrain or otherwise prevent intoxicated persons from driving."); Biscan, 160 S.W.3d at 482 ("Reasonable care [of adult social host] under the circumstances may not have included physically restraining his guests").

In Collins, this court noted that the reasoning of Biscan "is consistent with the general principle that a defendant's duty to control the conduct of another depends in part on the defendant having the means and ability to control the third party." Collins v. Arnold, No. M2004-02513-COA-R3-CV, 2007 WL 4146025, at *11 (Tenn.Ct.App. M.S., filed November 20, 2007) (citing Biscan, 160 S.W.3d at 481; Puckett v. Roberson, 183 S.W.3d 643, 652 (Tenn.Ct.App.2005)). In this case Gondolier controlled the Deceased's conduct to the extent of seeing that he did not pose a danger by driving while intoxicated. But just as in the cases where the courts have found no duty to control an intoxicated person who chooses to drive, so Gondolier had no means and no ability to control the Deceased once he left the restaurant in a taxi.

The Plaintiff argues that the seller is not relieved of its duty to an intoxicated patron by calling a taxi or otherwise removing the individual from the premises. However, "[t]he general duty of care does not include an affirmative duty to act for the protection of another...." Biscan, 160 S.W.3d at 478. In the circumstances of this case, if Gondolier can be said to have any duty to the Deceased, which we assert it did not, it did not breach it as a matter of law. The facts and the inferences from the facts in this case are such that a reasonable person can reach only one conclusion: by calling a cab, seeing the Deceased safely into it as a passenger and paying the Deceased's fare, Gondolier fulfilled any duty it might have. Gondolier negated a second necessary element (breach of duty) of the Plaintiff's common law claim of negligence. Summary judgment was thus appropriate.

E.

In the Judgment, the trial court also found that "the actions of the [Deceased] and Mr. Kirkland constitute intervening [superseding] acts in this case." We have held that the Plaintiff has no cause of action under Tenn.Code Ann. §§ 57–10–101 and 102 (2002) and that she cannot proceed under a common law theory of negligence. Thus, whether intervening actions by the Deceased and/or Mr. Kirkland were superseding causes that relieved Gondolier of liability need not be decided.

V.

The judgment of the trial court is affirmed. Costs on appeal are taxed to the appellant, Edwina Montgomery. This case is remanded to the trial court for further proceedings, consistent with this opinion. [all footnotes omitted]

###

Widner v. Chattanooga Entertainment, Inc. d/b/a Electric Cowboy

Court of Appeals of Tennessee (2014, Unpublished opinion)

D. MICHAEL SWINEY, J. Heather Widner, Administratrix of the Estate of Glenn Edward Smith ("Plaintiff") sued Chattanooga Entertainment, Inc. d/b/a Electric Cowboy ("Electric Cowboy") and Ashley Langworthy with regard to the tragic death of Glenn Edward Smith ("Deceased"). Electric Cowboy filed a motion for summary judgment. After a hearing, the Trial Court granted Electric Cowboy summary judgment finding and holding, inter alia, that on the relevant night there had been no sale of alcoholic beverages pursuant to Tenn.Code Ann. § 57–10–102 by Electric Cowboy to Ashley Langworthy. Plaintiff appeals to this Court raising issues regarding whether the Trial Court erred in granting Electric Cowboy summary judgment and whether the Trial Court erred in refusing to allow Plaintiff additional time for discovery. We find and hold, as did the Trial Court, that no sale of alcoholic beverages by Electric Cowboy to Ashley Langworthy occurred on the relevant night, and that the Trial Court did not abuse its discretion in refusing to allow further discovery. We, therefore, affirm.

Background

In the early morning hours of March 20, 2011, 71 year old Deceased was killed when a vehicle driven by Ashley Langworthy crashed into Deceased's home. Ms. Langworthy was intoxicated at the time of the crash, and had consumed alcohol earlier that evening at Electric Cowboy. Plaintiff sued Ms. Langworthy and Electric Cowboy. Plaintiff settled her claims against Ms. Langworthy, and the Trial Court entered an order of dismissal of Plaintiff's claims against Ms. Langworthy with prejudice on October 11, 2012. Ms. Langworthy is not involved in this appeal.

Electric Cowboy filed a motion for summary judgment supported by, among other things, the affidavit of Ms. Langworthy, the affidavit of Emily Isaacs, and the testimony of Ms. Langworthy and Officer David Smith taken during Ms. Langworthy's criminal trial. In her affidavit, Ms. Langworthy states, in pertinent part:

> 2. On March 19, 2011, I drove to Chili's Restaurant in Johnson City, Tennessee where I ate dinner and drank two margaritas. I then drove from Chili's to a liquor store. However, I did not purchase anything at the liquor store. I then went into a Kroger's grocery store in Johnson City, Tennessee and I purchased a container of wine coolers called "Smirnoff Ice Coolers". I then drove to the parking lot of a strip shopping center where the Electric Cowboy nightclub is located.
>
> 3. I waited in the parking lot with a friend of mine for three other friends to travel from Greeneville, Tennessee to meet us at the Electric Cowboy. While I sat in the parking lot with my friend, I drank two of the Smirnoff Ice Coolers.

4. I then learned by a text message that the three people that we were waiting for to meet us at the Electric Cowboy had already arrived and were inside the Electric Cowboy.

5. When my friend and I walked into the Electric Cowboy we found our three friends standing at a private table to the left of the bar. When my friend and I arrived at the private table one of the men in the group of three friends who had already arrived purchased a round of tequila shots for each of us to drink. I did not order the tequila shot and I did not pay for the tequila shot. I then drank the tequila shot.

6. My friend and I socialized with the three other friends who met us at the Electric Cowboy. At that time, one of the men went to the bar and ordered another round of tequila shots. That friend also paid for the shots at the bar. I did not ask for, I did not order and I did not pay for the second round of tequila shots. When he returned to the private table with a second round of tequila shots, I drank one of the shots.

7. My friends and I danced and socialized for awhile after the second round of shots. At some point, a man I did not know went to the bar and ordered a third shot of tequila. That man also paid for the shot at the bar. I did not ask for, I did not order and I did not pay for the third round of tequila shots. When he returned to the private table where I was, I drank the shot of tequila.

8. We stayed at the Electric Cowboy for a period of time and then my friend and the three other friends that we had met at the Electric Cowboy left. We left before closing time.

9. My friends and I decided to go to Perkins Restaurant. We each drove our respective vehicles from the Electric Cowboy north on Roan Street to Perkins Restaurant. The three male friends that had met us at the Electric Cowboy followed me in their vehicle.

10. My friends and I decided to go to Perkins Restaurant. We each drove our respective vehicles from the Electric Cowboy north on Roan Street to Perkins Restaurant. The three male friends that had met us at the Electric Cowboy followed me in their vehicle. [sic]

11. When we all arrived at the Perkins Restaurant on Roan Street we parked in the parking lot. After some discussion in the parking lot, the three male friends decided they needed to go ahead and drive back to Greeneville, Tennessee. While my friend was talking to the male friends, I decided to leave. I have no memory other than backing out of the parking space as to what happened after that moment in time.

> 12. Although I ordered and consumed the two margaritas at Chili's Restaurant, and I selected, purchased and consumed the two Smirnoff Ice Coolers, I did not place any alcohol order at the Electric Cowboy, nor was the alcohol that I consumed at the Electric Cowboy delivered directly to me by anyone employed at the Electric Cowboy.

In her affidavit, Ms. Isaacs states that she is the friend who accompanied Ms. Langworthy on the night in question to Chili's Restaurant, to a liquor store, to Kroger's grocery store, to Electric Cowboy, and to Perkins Restaurant. Ms. Isaacs's affidavit confirms the details provided in Ms. Langworthy's affidavit and adds the following pertinent information:

> 2. On March 20, 20111, I drove to Chili's Restaurant in Johnson City, Tennessee where I met Ashley Langworthy for dinner. We both drank two margaritas. We purchased the first round, but some gentlemen from the bar purchased our second round. We then drove separately from Chili's to a liquor store. I believe that I purchased a few miniature bottles of liquor from this store, but I have no memory of Ms. Langworthy purchasing liquor at this location. We then drove separately to Kroger's grocery store in Johnson City, Tennessee and we each purchased a container of six wine coolers called "Smirnoff Ice Coolers". We then drove separately to the parking lot of a strip shopping center where the Electric Cowboy nightclub is located.
>
> 3. We waited in the parking lot in Ms. Langworthy's vehicle for three other friends to travel from Greeneville, Tennessee to meet us at the Electric Cowboy. While we sat in the parking lot waiting on the rest of our group, we each drank two of the Smirnoff Ice Coolers from our respective six-packs.
>
> * * *
>
> 5. When Ms. Langworthy and I walked into the Electric Cowboy we found our three friends standing at a private table to the left of the bar. Shortly after our arrival, one of the men in the group of three friends who had already arrived had purchased a round of tequila shots for each of us to drink. Ms. Langworthy did not order the tequila shot, she did not pay for the tequila shot, and no employee of the Electric Cowboy delivered the shot of tequila to her. The entire group then drank the tequila shots.

6. Ms. Langworthy and I socialized with the three other men who met us at the Electric Cowboy for approximately one hour. At that time, one of the men went to the bar and ordered another round of tequila shots. That friend also ordered, paid for and received the shots at the bar. Ms. Langworthy did not order the second tequila shot, she did not pay for the second tequila shot, and no employee of the Electric Cowboy delivered the shot to her. The friend who purchased the second round of shots brought them back to the group's table. The entire group then drank the tequila shots.

7. Ms. Langworthy and I then socialized with the three other men who met us at the Electric Cowboy for approximately one hour. At that time, one of the men went to the bar and ordered another round of tequila shots. That friend also ordered, paid for and received the third round of shots at the bar. He then brought the third round of shots back to our table. Ms. Langworthy did not order the third tequila shot, she did not pay for the third tequila shot, and no employee of the Electric Cowboy delivered the third shot to her. The entire group then drank the tequila shots.

8. My friends and I then went to the dance floor and danced for some period of time. At that point, another male that I did not know began dancing with Ms. Langworthy. After dancing for a while we went back to the private table and the male that had joined us on the dance floor followed us to the table. After we talked for a while he then went to the bar by himself and ordered a mixed drink for Ms. Langworthy. This man ordered, paid for and received the drink at the bar. Ms. Langworthy did not order the drink, she did not pay for the drink, and no employee of the Electric Cowboy delivered the drink to her. Ms. Langworthy stayed at our table while this gentleman got her drink. I observed Ms. Langworthy consume some of this drink, but I believe that it was at least half full when we left shortly thereafter.

9. We stayed at the Electric Cowboy for a period of time and then our group of five decided to leave. We left before closing time.

10. Throughout the course of the evening I had the opportunity to observe Ms. Langworthy's behavior. She did not appear intoxicated at any point while we were at the Electric Cowboy. Additionally, I made it a point to watch her walking to her vehicle. She did not weave or stumble in any manner as she approached her vehicle.

11. Ms. Langworthy drove her vehicle from the Electric Cowboy north on Roan Street to Perkins Restaurant. I drove my vehicle following her to the Perkins Restaurant. The three male friends that

> had met us at the Electric Cowboy followed me in their vehicle, with Mr. Burks driving.
>
> 12. When we all arrived at the Perkins Restaurant on Roan Street we parked in the parking lot side-by-side with our windows rolled down for conversation. After some discussion in the parking lot, the three male friends decided they needed to go ahead and drive back to Greeneville, Tennessee. At some point we observed Ms. Langworthy suddenly back her vehicle out of the parking lot and leave. I have no knowledge of why she decided to leave at that time.
>
> 13. I was with Ms. Langworthy for the entire evening before the accident until she left Perkin's parking lot. Ms. Langworthy did not place any alcohol order at the Electric Cowboy, nor was the alcohol that she consumed at the Electric Cowboy delivered directly to her by anyone employed at the Electric Cowboy. I am sure that she did not purchase anything while at the Electric Cowboy because she and I both left our wallets and money in our vehicles before entering the club.

Ms. Langworthy incurred criminal charges arising out of the accident that caused Deceased's death. Officer David Smith testified during Ms. Langworthy's criminal trial that he was called to the scene of the accident around 3:20 a.m. Officer Smith arrived at the scene within five to ten minutes of receiving the call. Ms. Langworthy's vehicle had been driven into Deceased's apartment, and Deceased was pinned underneath the vehicle when Officer Smith arrived on the scene. Ms. Langworthy had to be extricated from her vehicle. Officer Smith testified that Ms. Langworthy's blood was drawn at the hospital and showed that her BAC was .18. Based upon skid marks at the scene, Officer Smith determined that just prior to the crash Ms. Langworthy was traveling in the range of 83 to 94 miles per hour. He stated that Ms. Langworthy's vehicle "left approximately about 185 feet of skid marks, so the vehicle was at 100 percent braking." Officer Smith explained that Ms. Langworthy had struck a tree, gone airborne, and crashed into a corner of the brick apartment building landing inside the apartment. Deceased was 71 years old at the time of his death and had raised six children.

Ms. Langworthy testified during her criminal trial that she was a twenty-five year old college graduate. Ms. Langworthy testified that on the night in question, she drank two margaritas, two Smirnoff Ice Coolers, and three shots of tequila. She testified that she did not pay for the tequila shots. She stated: "That was the friends we had met there who bought them for everybody." Ms. Langworthy testified that she and her friend ate dinner at Chili's between 10:00 and 11:00 p.m. and left Electric Cowboy before it closed, around 2:30 or 2:45 a.m. Ms. Langworthy testified that she does not remember leaving Perkins and stated that her next memory is:

> waking up in my truck with bricks, and everything after that is very in and out. I don't have, it's very patchy. I don't remember being in the hospital. I don't remember being pulled out of my truck. I don't remember being taken to jail. I didn't even know what had happened.

The Trial Court held a hearing on Electric Cowboy's motion for summary judgment, and then entered an order on December 19, 2012, which stated, in pertinent part:

> It appearing to this Court that the plaintiff did not file a response to the defendant's Motion for Summary Judgment in compliance with Rule 56 of the Tennessee Rules of Civil Procedure, but it appearing to this Court that the plaintiff filed a Motion to Quash a Notice of Hearing concerning the Motion for Summary Judgment indicating that the plaintiff wished to conduct further discovery in the case, but did not state with adequate or reasonable specificity what discovery was needed in order to respond to the defendant's Motion for Summary Judgment and further considering that the liability alleged against Chattanooga Entertainment, Inc. d/b/a Electric Cowboy is limited to all [sic] alleged violation of the Tennessee Dram Shop Act, and considering the statements of counsel, it is hereby
>
> ORDERED, ADJUDGED and DECREED that the plaintiff shall file a response complying with the provisions of Rule 56 of the Tennessee Rules of Civil Procedure defining with particularity the discovery needed in order to determine where the plaintiff can establish a genuine issue of material fact in response to this defendant's Motion for Summary Judgment on or before December 17, 2012.

On December 18, 2012 Plaintiff filed a response to the motion for summary judgment and a motion seeking additional time to depose Ms. Langworthy and a representative of Top Shelf. In this motion, Plaintiff stated:

> 2. That since the date of the aforesaid hearing, attorney for Plaintiff has interviewed former Defendant, Ashley Langworthy, at Ms. Langworthy's present location, the Johnson City, Tennessee jail. During this interview Ms. Langworthy gave details of her state of intoxication and her blacking out while at Electric Cowboy on the evening in question. She also spoke of her belief that she exhibited intoxication while at Electric Cowboy on the evening in question, as well information [sic] that at least nine shots of tequila were purchased by a male companion (the first sale being five shots and the second sale being four shots) and how this sale took place at the bar, just a few feet from where she sat.
>
> 3. That Ms. Langworthy further provided information that she had never drunk as much alcohol in her whole life as she did on the evening in question and was concerned about how she walked and acted while in the Defendant's establishment.

The Trial Court held another hearing on Electric Cowboy's Motion for Summary Judgment and on Plaintiff's motion to permit further discovery, and entered its order on December 21, 2012 finding and holding, inter alia:

> Defendant's previously filed Statement of Undisputed Material Facts included the following:
>
> 1. Ashley Langworthy did not order an alcoholic beverages from the wait staff at the defendant bar.
>
> 2. The wait staff did not directly serve alcoholic beverages to Ashley Langworthy.
>
> 3. Ashley Langworthy did consume alcoholic beverages on defendant's premises.
>
> 4. Ashley Langworthy did not pay for any of those alcoholic beverages.

The issue before the Court is whether, under T.C.A. § 57–10–102, defendant "sold" alcoholic beverages to Ashley Langworthy. Both parties have cited the Court to the case of Temlock v. McGinnis 2006 Tenn.App. Lexus [sic] 481, July 20, 2006. This appears to be the most recent and definitive case on the issue before the Court. The Temlock court found that monetary payment alone is not dispositive of whether a sale took place. The Court indicated that "all relevant circumstances must be considered." Thus, this Court's inquiry to the plaintiff was whether discovery would reveal any such relevant circumstances.

In its December 18, 2012 response, there is no indication that the discovery requested by the plaintiff would alter the fact that Ms. Langworthy did not order from the wait staff, was not served by the wait staff, and did not pay for the beverages consumed by her. The requested deposition of a trainer from Top Shelf would appear to have no bearing on any elements of whether a sale took place.

Upon the undisputed facts before the Court and there being no indication that further discovery would uncover relevant circumstances or material disputed facts for the Court to consider, this Court finds as a matter of law that a sale cannot be proven. Defendant's Motion for Summary Judgment is granted.

Plaintiff filed an appeal to this Court. A Statement of the Evidence was filed and approved by the Trial Court. The Statement of the Evidence provides, in pertinent part, that during the hearing on the motion for summary judgment and the motion to permit further discovery:

> The trial court then questioned the plaintiff's counsel concerning the defendant's position. The plaintiff's counsel agreed that the facts contained in the Defendant's Statement of Undisputed Material Facts were, indeed, undisputed due to the fact that counsel for the plaintiff had met with Ashley Langworthy in her jail cell prior to the hearing on December 19, 2012. During that meeting, Ashley Landworthy [sic] confirmed to the plaintiff's counsel the accuracy of the facts contained in the Defendant's Statement of Undisputed Material Facts.
>
> Although the plaintiff's counsel agreed that the facts were undisputed and agreed that Timlock v. McGinnis, 2006 Tenn.App. LEXIS 481, 2006 WL 2032518 July 26, 2006, [sic]

> represented the case law applicable to the issue raised by the defendant's Motion for Summary Judgment, the plaintiff should be entitled to take the deposition of Ashley Langworthy and a representative from Top Shelf in order to create "new law" that if a patron comes to a bar and orders two or more drinks, pays for the drinks, and then disperses those drinks to other patrons, then the bar should be liable if a patron who receives a dispersed drink from another patron becomes intoxicated and is involved in a motor vehicle accident.

Discussion

We restate the issues on appeal as: 1) whether the Trial Court erred in granting summary judgment to Electric Cowboy; and, 2) whether the Trial Court erred in refusing to allow Plaintiff to depose Ms. Langworthy and a representative of Top Shelf prior to ruling on the motion for summary judgment. Electric Cowboy raises an issue regarding whether Plaintiff's motion to amend the complaint, which was never heard by the Trial Court, would have been futile.

We first consider whether the Trial Court erred in granting summary judgment to Electric Cowboy.

[omitting summary judgment rules]

The issue of whether summary judgment was proper revolves around the question of whether, under Tenn.Code Ann. § 57–10–102, Electric Cowboy sold alcoholic beverages to Ms. Langworthy on the night of the accident.

Two statutes pertaining to alcohol-related injuries are relevant to this appeal, Tenn.Code Ann. § 57–10–101 and Tenn.Code Ann. § 57–10–102. Tenn.Code Ann. § 57–10–101 provides: [statutes omitted]

Our Supreme Court discussed Tenn.Code Ann. §§ 57–10–101 and 57–10–102 in Biscan v. Brown, 160 S.W.3d 462 (Tenn.2005). The Biscan Opinion stated:

> The effect of [Tenn.Code Ann. § 57–10–101] is to make it impossible for one who has been injured by an intoxicated person to state a claim for negligence against the person or entity who furnished the alcoholic beverage or beer because the statute removes, as a matter of law, the required element of legal

> causation. See, e.g., Turner v. Jordan, 957 S.W.2d 815, 818 (Tenn.1997) (a claim for negligence requires a duty of care owed by the defendant to the plaintiff; a breach of that duty; an injury or loss; causation in fact; and legal, or proximate, causation.) In other words, there can be no cause of action resting on the allegation that one person "furnished" alcohol to another because it is impossible to prove proximate cause. The statute does not merely provide immunity from suit where one has furnished alcohol to another; rather, the statute constitutes the legislative determination that persons who furnish alcohol are not at fault for injuries inflicted by an intoxicated person.
>
> The second part of the statute carves out an exception to the first part. It provides that a seller of alcohol may be liable to a third party for injuries if the seller sold alcohol to a minor or if the seller sold alcohol to an obviously intoxicated person and the sale was a proximate cause of the injuries suffered by the third party:
>
> * * *
>
> The clear language of the statute admits of only one conclusion: that the legislature intended to shield persons ... who "furnish" alcohol in a social setting.
>
> * * *
>
> Moreover, as the Court of Appeals discussed, the legislative history of sections 101 and 102 reveals that the statute was intended to codify the common-law rule that an individual who furnishes alcohol to another is not liable for any damages resulting from the other's intoxication, even if those damages are foreseeable. See, e.g., Cecil, 575 S.W.2d at 271. Thus, although the legislative history reflects much debate and concern over the extent to which sellers of alcoholic beverages and beers should be covered, the starting point was that the mere furnishing of alcohol, whether gratuitously or for commercial gain, is not a basis for liability. See Worley v. Weigels, 919 S.W.2d at 593–94.

Biscan, 160 S.W.3d at 472–73 (footnote omitted).

In Temlock v. McGinnis, this Court interpreted and applied Tenn.Code Ann. §§ 57–10–101 and 57–10–102, and stated that "all relevant circumstances must be considered," when making a determination regarding whether a sale of alcoholic beverages had occurred. Temlock v. McGinnis, E2005-02646-COA-R3-CV, 2006 Tenn.App. LEXIS 481, at *13, 2006 WL 2032518 (Tenn.Ct.App. July 20, 2006). In Temlock, we held that

> when a customer enters an establishment that sells alcoholic beverages such as beer, places his own alcohol order, has the alcohol he ordered delivered directly to him by the seller with the seller's expectation of payment in return, and the customer who ordered the alcohol consumes that alcohol on the seller's premises, there is a sale to that customer under Tenn.Code Ann. § 57-10-102.

Id. at 14-15.

In Temlock we held that a sale of alcoholic beverages did occur because Mr. McGinnis ordered the beer he consumed from Barley's wait staff, Barley's wait staff delivered the beer directly to Mr. McGinnis with the expectation of payment in return, and Mr. McGinnis consumed the beer on Barley's premises. Id. at * 14.

The facts in the case now before us are distinguishable from the facts in Temlock. Electric Cowboy filed a properly supported motion for summary judgment showing that there were no genuine disputed issues of material fact that Ms. Langworthy did not order any alcoholic beverages from the wait staff at Electric Cowboy, that Ms. Langworthy was not served any alcoholic beverages by any wait staff at Electric Cowboy, and that Ms. Langworthy did not pay for any alcoholic beverages at Electric Cowboy. Given all of the relevant undisputed circumstances in this case, the fact that Ms. Langworthy consumed alcoholic beverages while at Electric Cowboy is insufficient by itself to show that a sale of alcoholic beverages by Electric Cowboy to Ms. Langworthy occurred on the night of the accident.

As found by the Trial Court, there are no genuine disputed issues of material fact and Electric Cowboy was entitled to judgment as a matter of law as there was no sale of alcoholic beverages by Electric Cowboy to Ms. Langworthy. As such, we find no error in the Trial Court's grant of summary judgment to Electric Cowboy.

[omitting analysis of discovery issue and motion to amend]

We find no error by the Trial Court. We, therefore, affirm the Trial Court's December 21, 2012 order granting summary judgment to Electric Cowboy.

Conclusion

The judgment of the Trial Court is affirmed, and this cause is remanded to the Trial Court for collection of the costs below. The costs on appeal are assessed against the appellant.

[All footnotes omitted]

Additional Questions

1. **The *Temlock* case concerns an adult, therefore it cannot be used as an analogous case. True or false?**
2. **What is the difference between a "published" case like *LaRue* and an unpublished case like *Temlock*?**
3. **Can the *Worley* case be used for a rule or as a factually analogous case or both?**
4. **Can the *Montgomery* case be used for a rule or as a factually analogous case or both?**
5. **Two decisions were written by Appellate Court Judge Swiney (*Temlock* and *Widner*). Were you surprised at the different conclusions reached by the same judge in those two cases?**
6. **The *Montgomery* decision was by an Appellate Court. Appellate Court cases are presided over by three judges. In that case, all three judges wrote opinions. There was a main opinion and two concurring opinions. How is that possible, or what effect does that have? (Was this, strictly speaking, a "plurality opinion"?)**

IRAC Paragraph

At the instruction of your professor, consider drafting a one-page IRAC paragraph based on the Hole Foods Inc. fact pattern.

[25]

Case Analogies: Writing Exercise 5 [W5]

Introduction

Based on the previous chapter, let's synthesize a group of cases and write an IRAC paragraph on your own. Your paper should be in the form of a one page, one paragraph IRAC writing assignment.

You should summarize the rule from the statute and any helpful rules from cases. You might also use a case(s) as a factually analogous case. You must attempt to synthesize factually similar cases. That synthesis should be used to support your analogous legal reasoning.

Remember, sometimes a case can give you a good rule and be a factually similar case.

The Problem

You might recall the "KIA Kickass" hypothetical from earlier.

Word has gotten out around the office that you are a trademark genius.

Your supervising attorney asks you to look into a new case.

A client, Jack Whitey, wants to apply to register a trademark as indicated below on the Principal Register for goods identified as:

"Toiletries, exfoliation, and shaving supplies including but not limited to razors, both electric and analog, razor blades, shaving cream and powders, exfoliants and other shaving paraphernalia."

The mark consists of the words "BEARD BOMBER" in typed drawing form and the design below. Color is not a claimed part of the mark:

You supervising attorney is concerned that the mark might violate Trademark Act Section 2(a), 15 U.S.C. § 1052(a), on the grounds that the applied-for marks would be "offensive, disparaging and scandalous" to Muslims.

Articles like "The Beard in Islam" at www.islam.tc/beard seem to indicate how important beards are for Muslims. Your supervising attorney is concerned that the mark seems to emphasize a Muslim-looking bomb-cartoon man using a suicide bomb as a means of getting rid of his beard. He says the act of removing a Muslim's beard is offensive as well as referring to Islam, which is a religion of peace, by an image of a bomb is likewise offensive.

Is your supervising attorney being overly sensitive?

How do you *predict* whether an Examining Attorney at the Patent and Trademark Office might rule that the mark is "disparaging"? (Not "scandalous"; focus on "disparaging.")

THE STATUTE

15 U.S.C. § 1052(a), reads as follows:

> No trademark by which the goods of the applicant may be distinguished from the goods of others shall be refused registration on the principal register on account of its nature unless it—
>
> (a) Consists of or comprises immoral, deceptive, or scandalous matter; or matter which may disparage or falsely suggest a connection with persons, living or dead, institutions, beliefs, or national symbols, or bring them into contempt, or disrepute . . . .[23]

THE CASES

In re Reemtsma Cigarettenfabriken G.M.B.H.

Patent Office Trademark Trial and Appeal Board

Patent and Trademark Office (P.T.O.) (1959)

An application has been filed to register "SENUSSI" for cigarettes. Ownership of German Reg. No. 235,739 dated September 27, 1919 is asserted.

Registration has been refused on the ground that "SENUSSI", as applied to cigarettes, is scandalous within the purview of Section 2(a) of the Act of 1946.

Applicant has appealed.

"SENUSSI" is the name of a Moslem sect whose followers and adherents are in many lands. The tenets of this religious sect forbid the use of cigarettes. (See: Encyclopedia Brittanica, 1953 Edition, Volume 20, Page 333).

The application of the name of any religious order or sect to a product whose use is forbidden to the followers or adherents of such sect or order is an affront to such persons and tends to disparage

---

[23] This statute was later held unconstitutional by the U.S. Supreme Court. Don't worry about that for now. This is an exercise in legal reasoning based on a closed universe.

their beliefs. The use of "SENUSSI" on cigarettes, therefore, would be scandalous within the purview of Section 2(a) of the Act of 1946 and is not entitled to registration.

Decision of the Board

The Examiner of Trademarks properly refused registration; and his refusal to register is affirmed.

###

In re In Over Our Heads, Inc.

Trademark Trial and Appeal Board

Patent and Trademark Office (P.T.O.) (1990)

In Over Our Heads, Inc. (applicant) seeks to register MOONIES and design (shown below) for "dolls."

Registration was refused pursuant to Section 2(a) of the Lanham Trademark Act 15 U.S.C. Section 1052(a) on the basis that the mark comprises scandalous matter which disparages The Unification Church founded by the Reverend Sun Myung Moon. The Examining Attorney notes that the two "o"s in applicant's mark are caricatures of naked buttocks and that applicant's mark is used in connection with dolls (pictured below) which drop their pants when a collapsible bulb is squeezed, thus exposing their buttocks.

When the refusal was made final, applicant appealed to this Board. Applicant and the Examining Attorney filed briefs and were present at the oral hearing held on July 17, 1990.

We note at the outset that the Examining Attorney has not contended that the term "Moonies" (or "moonies") is per se scandalous or disparaging. If it was, then presumably the same Examining Attorney would not have passed to publication the mark MOONIES in block letters used by another applicant for clothing. Rather, the Examining Attorney contends that applicant's mark is "lacking in taste and is an affront to an organized religious sect" because the second and third letters in applicant's mark form the "caricature of naked buttocks" and because the mark is used on dolls whose pants can be dropped, thus exposing their buttocks. (Examining Attorney's brief pages 5-6).

As previously noted, there are dictionary definitions of record which show that the term "Moonie(s)" refers, in one sense, to a member of The Unification Church. However, there are also dictionary listings of record showing that the term "moon" means to expose one's buttocks. Moreover, we note that the term "moony" or "mooney" is defined as "of or relating to the moon .. [or] shaped like the moon." Webster's Third New International Dictionary Unabridged (1976). We believe that applicant's mark MOONIES--with its naked buttocks design and spelled without emphasizing the letter "m"--would, when used on a doll, most likely be perceived as indicating that the doll "moons," and would not be perceived as referencing members of The Unification Church.

We recognize that this is a close case, and in making our determination that applicant's mark is not scandalous or disparaging, we are not free of doubt. However, the guidelines for determining whether a mark is scandalous or disparaging are "somewhat vague" and the "determination [of whether] a mark is scandalous [or disparaging] is necessarily a highly subjective one." In re Hershey, 6 USPQ2d 1470, 1471 (TTAB 1988). Because the guidelines are somewhat vague and because the determination is so highly subjective, we are inclined to resolve doubts on the issue of whether a mark is scandalous or disparaging in favor of applicant and pass the mark for publication with the knowledge that if a group does find the mark to be scandalous or disparaging, an opposition proceeding can be brought and a more complete record can be established. Cf. In re Gourmet Bakers, Inc., 173 USPQ 565 (TTAB 1972) ("It has been recognized by this and other tribunals that there is no easy applicable objective test to determine whether or not a particular mark, as applied to specific goods, is merely descriptive or merely suggestive. The distinction between marks which are 'merely descriptive' and marks which are 'suggestive' is so nebulous that more often than not it is determined largely on a subjective basis with any doubt on the matter being resolved on applicant's behalf on the theory that any person who believes that he would be damaged by the registration will have an opportunity under Section 13 to oppose the registration of the mark and to present evidence, usually not present in the ex parte application, to that effect.")

Decision: The refusal to register is reversed.

[Footnotes omitted]

###

In re Hines

Trademark Trial and Appeal Board

Patent and Trademark Office (P.T.O.) (1994)

Request for Reconsideration:

The Board, in a decision dated June 10, 1994, affirmed the refusal to register on the ground that the applied-for mark shown below

is disparaging as contemplated under Section 2(a) of the Trademark Act.

Applicant timely filed a request for reconsideration. Applicant essentially argues that the Office did not sustain its burden of proof, and that what evidence there is of record raises doubts as to whether applicant's mark is disparaging of Buddhism or Buddhists. Accordingly, applicant urges that the mark be published for opposition. Alternatively, applicant requests that the case be remanded to the Examining Attorney to consider newly-obtained evidence showing that persons in the Buddhist community do not consider applicant's mark to be disparaging, and to consider other registrations of marks featuring the name or depiction of religious figures.

Upon further reflection, the Board is persuaded that the applied-for mark should be passed to publication. Of particular significance to the Board in reconsidering the original decision in this appeal is a recent decision of the United States Court of Appeals for the Federal Circuit, the Board's primary reviewing court. The Federal Circuit vacated the Board's decision that BLACK TAIL for adult entertainment magazines is scandalous under Section 2(a) of the Act. In re Mavety Media Group Ltd., --- USPQ2d ----, Appeal No. 93-1464, Ser. No. 74/066,893 (Fed.Cir. August 23, 1994). The case was remanded to the Board for "further proceedings," one option being for the Board to "simply pass the mark for publication to permit interested members of the public to demonstrate through an opposition proceeding that a substantial composite of the general public would consider the mark scandalous."

The Court in In re Mavety Media Group Ltd. pointed to the non-vulgar definitions of "tail" and concluded that the Board, "[a]rmed with only personal opinions and dictionary sources," erred in "concluding that in the context of the adult entertainment magazine, the substantial composite of the general public would necessarily attach to the mark BLACK TAIL the vulgar meaning of 'tail' as a female sexual partner, rather than the admittedly non-vulgar meaning of 'tail' as rear end." The Court also noted "the view of our predecessor court that the § 1052(a) prohibition against scandalous marks is not 'an attempt to legislate morality, but, rather, a judgment by the Congress that such marks not occupy the time, services, and use of funds of the federal government.' " [citation omitted]. The Court went on to therefore commend the practice adopted by the Board in another case to resolve the issue whether a mark comprises scandalous matter under § 1052(a) "in favor of [the] applicant and pass the mark for publication with the knowledge that if a group does find the mark to be scandalous ..., an opposition proceeding can be brought and a more complete record can be established." In re In Over Our Heads Inc., 16 USPQ2d at 1654-55.

In the original decision in the present appeal, the Board acknowledged that the determination here of whether a mark is disparaging is necessarily a highly subjective one, "perhaps being all the more subjective due to the relative obscurity of Buddhism in this country."

The Court in In re Mavety Media Group Ltd. made the following point:

> [E]ven if the members of this panel personally find the mark BLACK TAIL disgustingly scandalous, the legal conclusion that a trademark comprises scandalous matter must derive from the perspective of the substantial composite. To be sure, appellate judges are a part of the composite of the general public, but they represent only a tiny fraction of the whole, which necessarily encompasses a wondrous diversity of thought. Although constantly at odds, progressive views and conservative or traditional thinking participate alike in the formation of the composite of the general public. While we recognize the inherent difficulty in fashioning a single objective measure like a substantial composite of the general public from the myriad of subjective viewpoints, we are duty bound to apply the standard set forth by our predecessor court.

Although the Court in In re Mavety Media Group Ltd. was discussing the public reaction to a scandalous mark, and the present case involves a mark that may disparage a religion or religious figure, the principles expressed by the Court still apply. Thus, when the original decision in this appeal is reexamined with the benefit of the Court's most recent views on these types of cases, it is imperative that the Board be careful to avoid interposing its own judgment for that of Buddhists.

Accordingly, reconsideration of the present record, in light of the Court's recent decision, raises concerns not unlike the Court's concerns expressed in In re Mavety Media Group Ltd. Lest the Board be similarly characterized here as being "armed with only personal opinions and [encyclopedia] sources," we now are persuaded to publish the mark for opposition.

Applicant's request for reconsideration is granted. The Board's decision dated June 10, 1994 is vacated. The refusal to register is reversed and the mark will be passed to publication.

CONCURRING OPINION

For the reasons set forth in my dissenting opinion of June 10, 1994 (31 USPQ2d 1685), I concur with the decision to pass the mark for publication.

###

In re Lebanese Arak Corporation

Trademark Trial and Appeal Board

Patent and Trademark Office (P.T.O.) (2010)

Lebanese Arak Corporation, a California corporation, has appealed from the final refusal of the trademark examining attorney to register KHORAN in standard characters as a trademark for "alcoholic beverages, namely wines." The application was filed on December 27, 2006, and is based on use in commerce, with a claim of July 1, 2000 as the date of first use and first use in commerce. By examiner's amendment, the following translation statement was entered into the record: The English translation of the word KHORAN in the mark is ALTAR.

Registration has been refused pursuant to Section 2(a) of the Trademark Act, 15 U.S.C. § 1052(a), on the ground that applicant's mark is disparaging. In particular, it is the examining attorney's position that applicant's mark, KHORAN, is the phonetic equivalent of "Koran"; that the Koran is the sacred text of Islam; that the Koran forbids consumption of alcoholic beverages, including wine; and therefore that the use of KHORAN for wine is disparaging to the beliefs of Muslims. Before considering the refusal in more detail, it is useful to review the structure and development of Section 2(a) of the Act, for it has influenced the development of the case law on marks implicating religious or ethnic sensibilities.

Section 2(a) contains three parts separated by semi-colons, but encompasses five grounds for possible refusal of registration. The first part prohibits registration of "immoral, deceptive, or scandalous matter." Deceptiveness, however, is a separate ground for refusal, involving a different test from that for determining whether a proposed mark is immoral or scandalous, two terms that are typically discussed as though basically synonymous. See In re McGinley, 660 F.2d 481, 211 USPQ 668 n.6 (CCPA 1981). The second part of Section 2(a) bars registration of a proposed mark that falsely suggests a non-existent connection, as well as registration of matter which "may disparage ... persons, living or dead, institutions, beliefs, or national symbols, or bring them into contempt, or disrepute." Again, this part involves two separate grounds for refusal - false suggestion of a connection and disparagement - and two distinct tests.

The structure of Section 2(a), with various refusals and, therefore, different tests, interwoven into its various parts, is the result of its legislative development. In the Trademark Act of 1905, Section 5(a) was a simple bar against registration of marks comprising "immoral or scandalous matter." Section 5 of the Act of 1905 became Section 2 of The Trademark Act of 1946, and that act inserted deceptiveness into the existing provision, added a semi-colon, and appended what is currently the second part of Section 2(a). The third part was added by still later amendment.

It is likely a result of the chronological development of Section 2(a) that the first reported case dealing with a mark involving religious sensibilities was decided under the "immoral or scandalous matter" provision, because the disparagement provision did not then exist. See In re Riverbank Canning Company, 95 F.2d 327, 37 USPQ 268 (CCPA 1938) (MADONNA for wine held "scandalous"). Further, the existence of the Riverbank Canning decision influenced a later case before the Board. See In re Sociedade Agricola E. Comerical Dos Vinhos Messias, S.A.R.L., 159 USPQ 275 (TTAB 1968) (MESSIAS held unregistrable for wine and brandy). The Board specifically noted in that case that the examiner had made the Section 2(a) refusal relying on the Riverbank Canning case, which may explain the assertion of a scandalousness refusal rather than a disparagement refusal, and the Board, too, stated its reliance on the earlier CCPA case.

Notwithstanding that Riverbank Canning and various subsequent Board decisions involving religious sensibilities discussed scandalousness as the ground for refusal, likely because of the historical development of Section 2(a), all such decisions clearly contemplated the beliefs of particular groups of individuals as critical. See Riverbank Canning, 37 USPQ at 270:"The Virgin Mary stands as the highest example of the purity of womanhood, and the entire Christian world pays homage to her as such. Her representation in great paintings and sculpture arouses the religious sentiments of all Christians."See also, In re Reemtsma Cigarettenfabriken G.m.b.H., 122 USPQ 339 (TTAB 1959), in which the applicant sought to register SENUSSI for cigarettes. Because Senussi is the name of a Muslim sect and the tenets of this sect forbid the use of cigarettes, the Board affirmed the refusal of registration. The Board stated that "[t]he application of the name of any religious order or sect to a product whose use is forbidden to the followers or adherents of such sect or order is an affront to such persons and tends to disparage their beliefs."Accord, In re Waughtel, 138 USPQ 594 (TTAB 1963), which reversed a refusal to register AMISH (and the design of a man in Amish clothing) for cigars because "the use of the mark for cigars and the like is not an affront to the followers or adherents of said sect and does not, in any way, tend to disparage their religious or moral beliefs." Further, in In re Hines, 31 USPQ2d 1685, 1687 (TTAB 1994), the Board noted that older reported cases involving Section 2(a) refusals, although they were made on the Section 2(a) ground of being scandalous, concerned a perceived offense to religious sensibilities.[

With the Federal Circuit's decision in In re Mavety Media Group, 33 F.3d 1367, 1371, 31 USPQ2d 1923, 1925 (Fed. Cir. 1994), it has become clear that the proper ground for refusing marks which would offend the sensibilities of an ethnic or religious group is that the matter is disparaging to the members of that group, rather than that the matter is offensive or scandalous. In Mavety, the Federal Circuit held a mark may be found scandalous only if it is offensive to a substantial composite of the general public. However, because many ethnic and religious groups constitute small minorities of the entire U.S. population, marks that are offensive only to members of such groups could never be refused under the "scandalous" ground of refusal under Section 2(a). The focus of the Board in Reemtsma, Waughtel, the Hines affirmance, and other cases, on whether the application of a mark to a product would tend to disparage the beliefs of the followers of a particular religion, is an explicit acknowledgement that the proper focus, when religious beliefs or tenets are involved, is on the group of persons that adhere to those beliefs or tenets. As a leading commentator has put it:

> [The disparagement bar] differs from the scandalousness provision, foremost because there is a particular object of disparagement, i.e., a person, group, set of beliefs, institution or symbol, and the statutory bar depends on the perspective of the object of disparagement. In contrast, the scandalousness provision protects the public as a whole and the effect of the trademark is judged from the perspective of the general public.

1 Jerome Gilson et al., Trademark Protection and Practice §3.04[6][a][i][B], at 3-122 (December 2003).

The Mavety decision did not purport to extend the Section 2(a) scandalousness analysis to cases involving religious or ethnic sensibilities. Thus, whatever inconsistency or uncertainty may have resulted from Riverbank Canning and subsequent Board decisions, the ground for a refusal involving a perceived offense to religious or ethnic sensibilities is now clearly the ground of disparagement.

The determination whether a proposed mark is disparaging requires application of the following two-part test:

> 1) what is the likely meaning of the matter in question, taking into account not only dictionary definitions, but also the relationship of the matter to the other elements in the mark, the nature of the goods or services, and the manner in which the mark is used in the marketplace in connection with the goods or services; and
>
> 2) if that meaning is found to refer to identifiable persons, institutions, beliefs or national symbols, whether that meaning may be disparaging to a substantial composite of the referenced group.

In re Heeb Media LLC, 89 USPQ2d 1071, 1074 (TTAB 2008) [string citation omitted]

There is no real dispute that the Office has met the burden of proving the second part of the test. Specifically, the examining attorney has submitted a significant amount of evidence showing that the Koran is "the sacred text of Islam, considered by Muslims to contain the revelations of God to Muhammad," and that Islamic authorities view alcohol as a prohibited substance. Applicant does not dispute that this is the case. Applicant's only argument, with respect to this prong of the test, is that "whether the mark comprises of [sic] disparaging matter is to be ascertained from the standpoint of not necessarily a majority, but a substantial composite of the general public." Brief, p. 6. However, the test quoted by applicant, for which it cites In re Mavety Media Group, 33 F.3d at 1371, 31 USPQ2d at 1925 (and which case, in turn, cites In re McGinley, 660 F.2d at 485, 211 USPQ at 673 (CCPA 1981)), refers to the determination of whether a mark is scandalous, not disparaging. As previously discussed, whether a proposed mark is disparaging must be determined from the standpoint of a substantial composite of the referenced group. In re Heeb Media LLC, 89 USPQ2d at 1074.

The evidence submitted by the examining attorney in the case at hand, which shows that drinking alcohol is considered unacceptable by Muslims, is sufficient to show that the use of the name of the sacred text of Islam for a substance prohibited by that religion, indeed, a substance prohibited by that very text, would be disparaging to followers of Islam and their beliefs.

It is in connection with the first prong of the test, i.e., the likely meaning of the matter in question, that the real disagreement exists between applicant and the examining attorney, and between the majority and the dissent. The examining attorney, as noted, takes the position that applicant's mark, KHORAN, is the phonetic equivalent of Koran, while applicant asserts that it is a different word, namely, an Armenian term with the English translation of "altar."

The evidence of record shows that the word "Koran" comes from Arabic. As a transliterated word, the spelling in English varies. One article states that "Quran is spelled as Qur'aan, Koran and commonly as Quran." www.articlesbase.com. The American Heritage Dictionary, supra, lists "Qur'an" as a variant form, and states that the text is also called "Alcoran." The examining attorney has made of record numerous submissions in which the Koran is referred to by variant spellings. Among these submissions are several personal postings, in the form of comments or blogs, as well as web articles, in which Koran is spelled "Khoran." See, for example:

> There is no true alliance with the Islamic governments because the Khoran forbids it. ...Read this book and you will be compelled to also read parts of the Khoran to see why our government's policies are leading us into a terrible trap. Publisher's notes on book Princes of Islam, website headed "Welcome to C.T.U. Bookstore," (Conservative Theological University), http://97.66.25.67/bookstore/store.php

> It is forbidden for muslims [sic] to hurt or kill anyone, according to the Khoran. http://messageboard.rediff.com, (letter posted on a message board)

> He says the surgeons are fine, but the nurses and those involved in aftercare view painkillers like they do drugs or alcohol—against the laws of the Khoran. Live Journal, http://zainybrain.livejournal.com (journal entry by Wendy Wheeler about her dinner with "Jungle Bob")

> In Prager's view, allowing Ellison to be sworn in on the Khoran "will embolden Islamic extremists and make new ones...."“Will

> Samson, On a Journey of Discovery Toward God, Society and Sustainability," Nov. 28, 2008, http:// willzhead.typepad.com

> I cringe [sic] anytime I found a Holy Bible in the drawer of my hotel rooms. Why not the Khoran, the Taoism of Buddha, the Torah? Comment by gingersoul, Dec. 11, 2006 on article "Religion finds firm footing in some offices," SoulCast, http://soulcast.com

> But this points much more at the human aspect of interpreting what is in the Khoran. Post by Sparky on FaithFreedom.org website

We do not suggest that these uses by individuals show that "Khoran" is an accepted spelling of "Koran." However, the fact that there are recognized variations in the transliterated spelling of this word, and that some people believe that "Khoran" is an accepted spelling, show that people viewing the mark KHORAN are likely to understand it as a variation or misspelling of "Koran." See In re Carlson, 91 USPQ2d 1198, 1201 (TTAB 2009) ("We do not mean to suggest that listings in blogs or even a slang dictionary show that 'houzing' is an accepted alternate spelling of 'housing' or that this spelling is in common and widespread use. But these uses indicate either that 'housing' may be misspelled as 'houzing' or that the writers who deliberately use this spelling view 'houzing' as a misspelling or alternate spelling that readers will immediately understand as 'housing.'").

A mere misspelling of a word does not serve to avoid a finding that it is disparaging. In In re Hines, supra, the Board did not even discuss the fact that the mark BUDDA BEACHWEAR and design was a misspelling of Buddha; there was no suggestion that the misspelling of Buddha avoided the finding that the mark referred to Buddha. See also, In re Carlson, 91 USPQ2d at 1200, and cases cited therein ("In general, a mere misspelling of a word is not sufficient to change a merely descriptive term into an inherently distinctive trademark"). The question is whether KHORAN would be perceived as the word Koran, or whether it would be understood as a totally different word, i.e., the Armenian word for "altar" or, as the dissent suggests, a term of unknown meaning.

We find that KHORAN gives the commercial impression that it is the word Koran, and that the public (other than Armenian speakers) in general, and Muslim Americans in particular, would regard the mark as referring to the holy text of Islam. First, KHORAN can be pronounced identically to the word "Koran." Although we note applicant's argument that the letter "H" in its mark is not silent, but has a distinct sound in combination with the letter "K", it has long been held that there is no correct pronunciation of a trademark that is not a recognized English word. Whether or not KHORAN may be pronounced by an Armenian speaker as applicant asserts, many Americans, including Muslim Americans, would pronounce it as "Koran." This pronunciation would be particularly troubling if KHORAN wine were advertised on the radio, where consumers would not even be aware that applicant's mark contains an "H." Second, because "Koran" has various accepted spellings, people are likely to regard KHORAN as another variant spelling, even if not an "official" one. Third, there is evidence that people do use "Khoran" as a spelling for "Koran." Fourth, there is no evidence that people other than those who speak and understand Armenian are likely to recognize "Khoran" as the Armenian word for "altar." In particular, there is no evidence that Muslim Americans would be aware of the Armenian meaning of the word.

In determining the first prong of the disparagement test, the dissent states that one must look to the meaning of applicant's mark from the standpoint of the general public, rather than that of Muslim Americans. For the reasons discussed above, in this case whether we consider how the mark would be perceived by Muslim Americans or the public in general, the result would be the same. However, we cannot agree with the dissent that we must consider the mark only from the standpoint of the public at large. We can envision situations in which, for example, a term or symbol would be clearly understood by members of a religious group as being significant in their worship, but would not be known or understood by the public at large. We cannot conclude that the prohibition against registration of disparaging marks would ignore such situations. The Reemtsma case is an example of this; it is unlikely that, at the time registration for the mark SENUSSI was sought, the public in general was aware that Senussi was the name of a Muslim sect.

This is not to say that a term that otherwise might be considered disparaging could not also have such a well-known alternative meaning that, as used in connection with particular goods or services, that alternative meaning would be found to be the applicable one. For example, in In re Over Our Heads Inc., 16 USPQ2d 1653 (TTAB 1990), the Board found that the mark MOONIES and design (with naked buttocks substituted for the letters "O") used for a doll that moons would be perceived as indicating that the doll moons, rather than as a reference to members of The Unification Church. Here, however, the Armenian meaning of KHORAN would not be known to the vast majority of Americans and, as discussed, they would view KHORAN as the equivalent of Koran.

[omitting a portion of the discussion concerning the dissent]

As for the dissent's comment that there is no apparent intent by applicant to disparage Muslims or Islam, such intent is not necessary in order to find that the mark does, in fact, disparage them or their beliefs. See In re Heeb Media LLC, 89 USPQ2d at 1077:"The fact that applicant has good intentions with its use of the term does 19 Ser No. 77072261 not obviate the fact that a substantial composite of the referenced group find the term objectionable."

Accordingly, we conclude that Muslims would find the mark KHORAN used for wine as disparaging to themselves, their religion and their beliefs.

We have considered applicant's arguments based on the fact that, on reconsideration, the Board in In re Hines reversed the refusal of registration of BUDDA BEACHWEAR and the design of a Buddha and vacated its earlier decision affirming such refusal(see discussion at footnotes 4 and 5). The Board did so in that case because there was no evidence in the record that Buddhists would find the mark disparaging, and in light of the Federal Circuit's decision in the Mavety case, the Board's concern was to avoid interposing its own judgment for that of Buddhists. This was sufficient to raise doubt as to whether the mark was disparaging, and in accordance with Board policy, the Board resolved that doubt in favor of publication of the mark for opposition.

In the present case, however, we have a very different situation. The record is replete with evidence that alcohol, including wine, is prohibited by the tenets of Islam. Therefore, the Board is not in a position in which it is interposing its own judgment for that of Muslims. Because we have no doubt both that KHORAN would be recognized as the name of the holy text of Islam, and that the use of this term for wine would be disparaging to the religion and beliefs of Muslim Americans, the Mavety principle of resolving doubt in favor of publication does not come into play. In re MBNA Am. Bank, 340 F.3d 1328, 67 USPQ2d 1778 (Fed. Cir. 2003)

Decision: The refusal of registration is affirmed.

[all footnotes omitted]

DISSENTING OPINION

We respectfully dissent from the decision of the majority that the examining attorney has sustained the burden of demonstrating that the mark KHORAN, used for wine, is disparaging to Muslims. In particular, we believe the majority has misapplied the disparagement test and we disagree with their determination as to what is the likely meaning of KHORAN.

At the outset, we note that the Board has acknowledged previously that decisions as to whether a mark is scandalous or disparaging can be difficult ones and, at least with respect to ex parte cases, it is preferable to resolve doubts in favor of the applicant:

> [T]he guidelines for determining whether a mark is scandalous or disparaging are 'somewhat vague' and the 'determination [of

> whether] a mark is scandalous [or disparaging] is necessarily a highly subjective one.'In re Hershey, 6 USPQ2d 1470, 1471 (TTAB 1988). Because the guidelines are somewhat vague and because the determination is so highly subjective, we are inclined to resolve doubts on the issue of whether a mark is scandalous or disparaging in favor of applicant and pass the mark for publication with the knowledge that if a group does find the mark to be scandalous or disparaging, an opposition proceeding can be brought and a more complete record can be established....

In re Over Our Heads Inc., 16 USPQ2d 1653 (TTAB 1990)(Board resolved doubt regarding the scandalous nature of the mark MOONIES in favor of publication). In In re Mavety Media Group Ltd., 33 F.3d 1367, 1374, 31 USPQ2d 1923, 1928 (Fed. Cir. 1994), the Court of Appeals for the Federal Circuit, our primary reviewing court, expressly approved of the Board's approach in In re Over Our Heads Inc. to resolve doubt in applicant's favor with the knowledge that any person who believes he would be damaged by registration of the mark may bring an opposition or cancellation proceeding. We have significant doubt in this case as to whether, based on the current record, applicant's mark is disparaging of Muslims and we think the better course is to allow the mark to be published for opposition.

The majority has properly set forth the two prongs of the disparagement test; however, we strongly disagree with the majority's application of the first prong of the test. Specifically, we dispute the majority's contention that the determination of "what is the likely meaning of the matter in question" should be made from the perspective of the disparaged group. Rather, we believe the Board must look to the general population of the United States and how they will understand applicant's mark when it is being used in connection with the identified goods or services, in this case wine. It is only after we determine the likely meaning of applicant's mark that we consider the second prong which is from the standpoint of the purported disparaged group, i.e., "whether that meaning may be disparaging to a substantial composite of the referenced group."In its decision, the majority appears to have conflated the two prongs and made both determinations from the standpoint of the purported disparaged group, in this case Muslims. We believe this approach is incorrect inasmuch as the test, as enunciated by the majority itself and used by the Board for many years, does not support such an interpretation. Moreover, by considering only the purported disparaged group in determining the likely meaning of a mark would essentially be "loading the deck" for purposes of any disparagement test and will lead to cases where a proposed mark will be found disparaging despite the fact that most Americans attribute a different and inoffensive meaning to that mark.

The majority's interpretation is also a significant departure from our application of the disparagement test. We are unaware of any other cases where the Board has limited the analysis of the likely meaning of a mark by deciding how only the alleged disparaged group would understand the mark. To the contrary, our determination of the likely meaning of an applicant's mark appears to have always been from the standpoint of the general public encountering the mark in connection with the identified goods or services. For example, in In re Over Our Heads Inc., 16 USPQ2d 1653 (TTAB 1990) (involving the mark MOONIES, with the two "O" letters forming a caricature of a naked buttocks), the Board noted that the term "Moonie(s)" is a reference to a member of The Unification Church, but also took into consideration several other possible meanings of the term, including the act of exposing one's buttocks. Ultimately, the Board decided "[w]e believe that applicant's mark MOONIES — with its naked buttocks design and spelled without emphasizing the letter "m" — would, when used on a doll, most likely be perceived as indicating that the doll "moons," and would not be perceived as referencing members of The Unification Church."16 USPQ2d at 1654. Noticeably absent in this decision is any consideration of how members of the alleged disparaged group themselves would perceive the mark. Clearly, had the Board considered the likely meaning of the mark only from the standpoint of members of The Unification Church, the outcome in that case would likely have been different.

In addition to our dispute with the majority's application of the first prong of the disparagement test, we further disagree with the majority because we believe that most persons encountering applicant's mark on wine will not attribute any specific meaning to the mark. Rather, we find it more likely that the general public will perceive the mark as designating the source of the goods, rather than see the mark as a misspelling of the word "Koran."

We have considered all of the evidence submitted during prosecution of the application, including the submissions showing the Koran being referred to by different spellings. Among these are several references in comments or blogs, in which Koran is spelled "Khoran." At the same time, we note that the spelling "Khoran" is not identified in any of the dictionary evidence of record as one of the usual or accepted spellings for Koran. Rather, the evidence merely indicates that "Khoran" has been used by several persons, possibly as a misspelling of Koran. And, as to the examining attorney's argument that applicant's mark is the phonetic equivalent of "Koran," we have often stated that there is no correct pronunciation of a trademark when the term is not a recognizable English word. See In re Belgrade Shoe, 411 F.2d 1352, 162 USPQ 227 (CCPA 1969) and Interlego AG v. Abrams/Gentile Entm't Inc., 63 USPQ2d 1862 (TTAB 2002). Here, applicant's mark begins with the uncommon consonant combination "Kh," which may increase any possible confusion as to the pronunciation. Nevertheless, it is quite reasonable to assume that applicant's mark will, at least for some, be pronounced the same as or similar to "Koran."

Also of relevance, there is evidence of record supporting applicant's contention that the term "Khoran" means "altar" in Armenian. This evidence includes:

The Armenian Orthodox Church publishes its official periodical, KHORAN (Altar), in Armenian, Greek and English. www.armenianprelacy.com

The Armenian Church...A Badark Glossary... Khoran Altar www.armenianchurch.net

The Armenian word for the altar is Khoran, which means the tent or tabernacle where the Ark of the Covenant was placed, symbolizing the presence of God... www.hyeetch.nareg.com

Again, in making the determination as to the likely meaning of applicant's mark, we believe the Board should consider how the general public, not just the alleged disparaged group, will perceive the mark. Furthermore, the likely meaning of the mark is not considered in a vacuum, but in the context of the identified goods, in this case, wine, as well as the way the mark is used in the marketplace. See Heeb Media LLC, 89 USPQ2d at 1074 (the "likely meaning" of an applicant's mark is determined by "taking into account the nature of the goods and services and the manner in which it is used in the marketplace"). In this regard, the only real evidence of the mark being used in connection with wine is applicant's specimen of use. Although applicant's particular method of use of its mark is only relevant to the extent that it shows one of many possible uses of the mark on or in connection with wine, we note that there is nothing in the way applicant uses its mark (as show in the specimen of use) which would suggest any connection to Islam or its holy text.

There is no dispute that Islamic authorities view alcoholic beverages, such as wine, as prohibited based on the Koran and the record is replete with evidence establishing this. To the extent that the mark should be considered in the wine marketplace, we find this prohibition on alcoholic beverages as a factor that may decrease the likelihood that anyone from the general public, at least those familiar with the prohibition, would understand applicant's mark as a reference to the Koran. It would be counterintuitive for such persons to associate applicant's mark with the holy text prohibiting the goods being sold under the mark. We must also bear in mind that the evidence showing the spelling "Khoran" to identify the Koran, was in the context of religion. Thus, that evidence was presumably limited to those who are more likely predisposed to perceiving that term as a reference to the Koran. Put differently, the examining attorney's evidence shows "Khoran" being used by a few individuals to reference the Koran, but it is unclear how well-recognized this spelling would be out of the context of religion because it is not a widely-accepted spelling for the Islamic holy text.

Considering the evidence of record, we believe that when applicant's KHORAN mark is heard or seen in connection with wine, it is more likely that the general public will not attach any particular meaning to the mark. Accordingly, we do not believe that the first part of the disparagement test has been satisfied by the Office and we would reverse the refusal of registration on that basis.

Inasmuch as we would find that the office has not satisfied the first prong of the disparagement test, we see no need to discuss the second part of the test, namely, if the meaning of applicant's mark is also a reference to Muslims and, if so, would it be considered disparaging to a substantial composite of Muslims. We would be remiss if we did not further point out that this case essentially involves an applicant seeking to register a mark that has a plausible and innocuous meaning, as provided by applicant and accepted by the first examining attorney, i.e., the mark is the transliteration of the Armenian term for "altar." However, registration is being refused because the Office believes that the mark is likely to be understood as a misspelling of "Koran," which is also a transliteration and, when used on wine, the mark is disparaging to Muslims. There is no dispute that the term "Koran", by itself and as defined, has no disparaging meaning or connotation. Moreover, there is absolutely no evidence in the record showing that applicant or anyone else has ever used the term "Koran" in a disparaging manner in connection with wine (or otherwise). This case is somewhat novel because the Office contends that applicant's mark takes on a disparaging connotation when used in connection with wine. This is unlike other disparagement cases where, at the very least, the marks themselves arguably conveyed a negative connotation and were therefore considered to be disparaging. And, in previous cases with very similar factual scenarios to the matter before us, the asserted refusal was based under Section

2(a)'s prohibition against marks containing "scandalous matter," rather than the separate and distinct prohibition against "disparaging" marks.[see FN14 below] This is not a distinction without a difference because, as the majority points out, the tests for determination are clearly different, including whether the mark is scandalous based on the perceptions of a substantial composite of the general population or whether the mark is disparaging to a substantial composite of the referenced group. Compare, e.g., Mavety, 31 USPQ2d at 1926 (scandalous), with In re Squaw Valley Dev. Co., 80 USPQ2d 1264, 1267 (TTAB 2006) (disparaging).

In any event, we believe that there is significant doubt as to whether or not the general public is even likely to equate applicant's mark, when considered in the context of wine, with the Islamic holy text. We would rather choose to resolve this doubt by allowing the mark to be published for opposition, bearing in mind that any decision in an ex parte appeal is without prejudice to any opposition or cancellation which may be filed where the parties will have an opportunity to fully develop an evidentiary record and argue the issue.

[omitting all footnotes, save footnote 14]

. . .

Footnote 14

A review of prior Section 2(a) decisions reveals that those cases with facts most analogous to the matter before us involved the "scandalous matter" ground for refusal rather than "disparagement"; in particular, we looked at several cases that dealt with marks with religious terms that by themselves were not objectionable, but were refused registration based on a perceived offense to religious sensibilities due to the nature of the identified goods. See, e.g., In re Riverbank Canning Co., 95 F.2d 327, 37 USPQ 268, 270 (CCPA 1938)(MADONNA for wine held "scandalous"); In re Reemtsma Cigarettenfabriken G.m.b.H., 122 USPQ 339 (TTAB 1959)(SENUSSI for cigarettes held "scandalous" ("Senussi" being the name of a Muslim sect whose adherents are forbidden the use of cigarettes)); and In re Sociedade Agricola E. Comerical Dos Vinhos Messias, S.A.R.L., 159

USPQ 275 (TTAB 1968)(MESSIAS for wine and brandy held scandalous). This line of cases may be distinguished from other cases, such as our decision in In re Hines where it was the mark itself that was essentially at issue. In re Hines, 31 USPQ2d 1685 (TTAB 1994), opinion vacated on reconsideration, 32 USPQ USPQ2d 1376 (TTAB 1994). In that initial decision (since vacated for other reasons), we affirmed the disparagement refusal essentially because the mark's "depiction of the religious founder [Buddha] in tree-emblazoned casual wear, strictly for commercial purposes, is disparaging." Id. at 1688.We are not saying a rule has been established that dictates when either a "scandalous" or "disparaging" refusal is appropriate, but merely pointing out that what appear to be the most analogous cases, while older, they involved a scandalous refusal.

The majority, on the other hand, discusses many of the same cases and comes to the conclusion that "the ground for refusal involving a perceived offense to religious or ethnic sensibilities is now clearly the ground of disparagement." We remain unconvinced that the case law leads to such a rule or that a rule is even necessary.

[26]

RESEARCHING WITH CITATORS

INTRODUCTION

By now, you are familiar with the four sources of primary law: (1) federal and state constitutions, (2) statutes, (3) cases, and (4) administrative regulations (next chapter).

You have learned how to locate these sources using their citations. For example, you may never be able to forge that *McBoyle v. United States* is located on page 25 of volume 283 of the United States Reporter.

McBoyle v. United States, 283 U.S. 25 (1931), is called a "citation."

For example, a judge might ask, "Can you 'cite' to legal authority that supports your statement of the rule?"

The judge means, "Where does that rule come from?"

The judge would expect you to provide a legal citation to a case, like *McBoyle v. United States*, 283 U.S. 25 (1931). Or you might cite a judge to the statute that provides the rule, like the National Motor Vehicle Theft Act, 18 U.S.C. § 308 (1919). The NMVTA used to be located in section 308 of Title 18 of the United States Code.

Judges will expect you to be able to build a legal proof using IRAC. They will also expect you to be able to prove each step with citations to legal authority.

Judges do the same thing when they write decisions. Each step of the decision is supported by citations to legal authorities, including statutes, cases, and secondary sources.

You may have noticed these citations when reading your casebook. American lawyers typically don't use footnotes. Legal citations are provided immediately, in the body of the text. These internal citations can be annoying at first, but you soon learn to ignore them.

Meanwhile, judges expect that the legal sources you cite are "good law"—that is, they haven't been reversed on appeal or overturned by a later decision.

Citator services are designed to tell lawyers, at a glance, whether a legal authority is still good law.

Citators are primarily used for cases, though they may also be used to check statutes and regulations as well. A citator can tell you whether a case is still good law.

Moreover, if you check the Table of Authorities for a case, a citator service will even tell you whether the authorities cited within that case are good law.

Citators serve a number of other purposes. They can give you the direct history of a case on appeal.

A citator is also helpful for research purposes. A citator can tell you every primary and every secondary legal authority that has "cited" to your case.

For example, if you are looking at a case from 1950, the citator will tell you every case that cited to your case up till present day.

Of those cases, it will tell you which cases contain positive discussions and which contain negative discussions.

SHEPARDS & KEY CITE

The most well-known citator is Shepards. It is available on Lexis Advance. The trademark is owned by Lexis.

Lawyers may say, "Did you Shepardize that case?" They mean, "Did you check to make sure the case is still good law?"

Westlaw also offers a citator service called Key Cite.

Electronic Research Exercise Number 5 (R5)

Instructions

- Please type your answers. Answers should be single-spaced in Courier New Font size 8. Pages should be numbered.
- Your paper must have a header on the first page (not needed on subsequent pages) including the following: a title; your Professor's name; and your student ID number. Do not write your name; use your student ID number.
- Please e-mail your answers prior to class or hand them in at the beginning of class according to your professor's preference.
- If you cut and paste, you must use quotation marks!
- There are 12 total questions in this assignment. Please do not miss any.

Lexis

Log on to your own personal Lexis account. Let's research based on the following facts:

> Your client is Youngho Hwang. Like many of our clients, he lives in Trussville, Alabama. Mr. Hwang's 15-year-old daughter was injured. She was playing on an old swing-set in the neighbor's yard. The neighbor's children are now in college. The swing-set has sat neglected for many years. It looks very rusty and old.
>
> While Mr. Hwang's daughter, Elia, was playing on the swing-set, the plastic seat broke. She fell and broke her arm.
>
> Elia did not have permission to be on the neighbor's property, which would usually mean she was a trespasser. Ordinarily, the neighbor would owe no duty toward her. However, there is a legal doctrine called "attractive nuisance." This doctrine makes a landowner liable for dangers that "attract" a child.
>
> Let's research this doctrine to find out whether it can apply to a 15-year-old child.

Let's pretend based on your preliminary, secondary source research you located the following case citation: *Central of G. R. Co. v. Robins*, 95 So. 367 (Ala. 1923).

Use that citation to find that case on Lexis Advance.

Note that it has a bright, red stop sign next to the case name.

A panel on the right hand of the screen gives you more information about the subsequent case history.

Shepard's is saying that 37 cases have cited to the *Central of G. R. Co.* case. It also characterizes those citations as Warnings or Questioned or Caution.

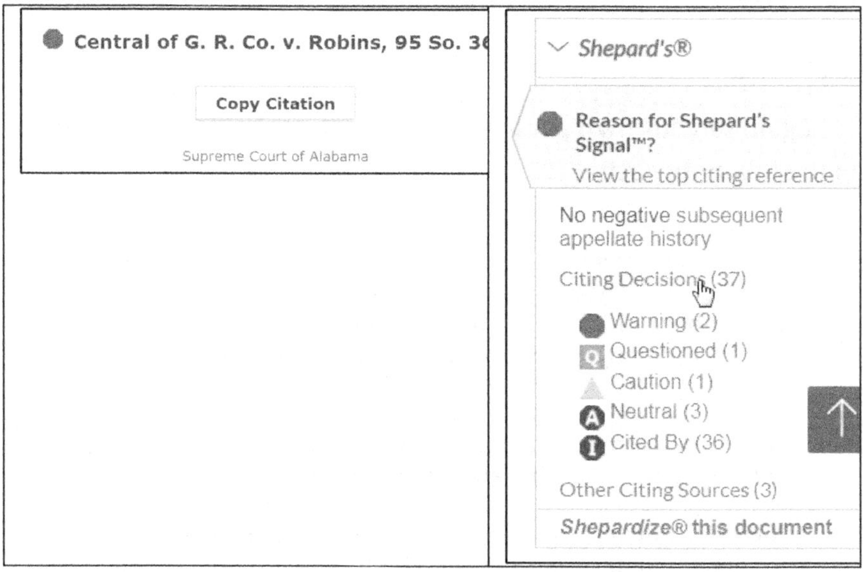

1. **First, Read the *Central of G. R. Co.* case. Briefly explain why this case might be relevant to your research.**
2. **Review the headnotes at the beginning. What is the rule announced in this case? (Headnote 12)**

Now, click on the red stop sign or the link that says: "Shepardize this document."

By matching citing authorities to interesting Headnotes from our case, we can quickly identify which of the citing authorities might be of interest to us.

In this instance, we see that our case was "overruled" by a case named *Lyle v. Bouler*, especially as to Headnote 12.

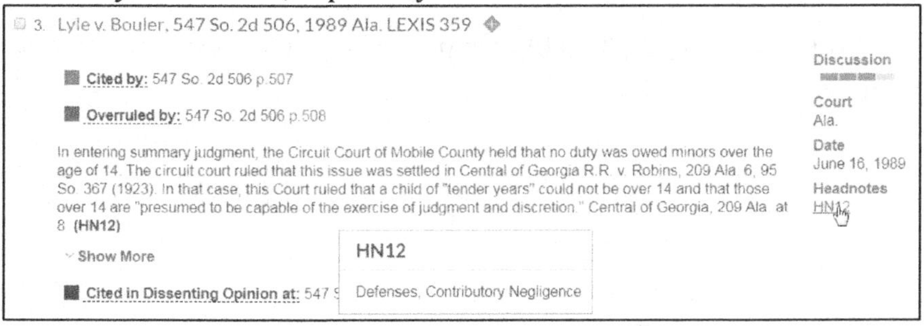

If we look even more closely at the Shepard's guide to the *Lyle v. Bouler*, we see a few other items. First, it tells us that the *Lyle v. Bouler* case overruled the original case. We also learn that the *Lyle* case is a much more recent case (from 1989).

There is a big green "plus mark" next to *Lyle v. Bouler*; hence, we know the *Lyle* case is good law and has "positive" citing references.

There is also a legend that describes the "depth" of the analysis. It also tells us which Headnote from our case is discussed in *Lyle*.

Click on Lyle v. Bouler.

We can use the navigation buttons at the top of the page to find the text in the case relating to our case.

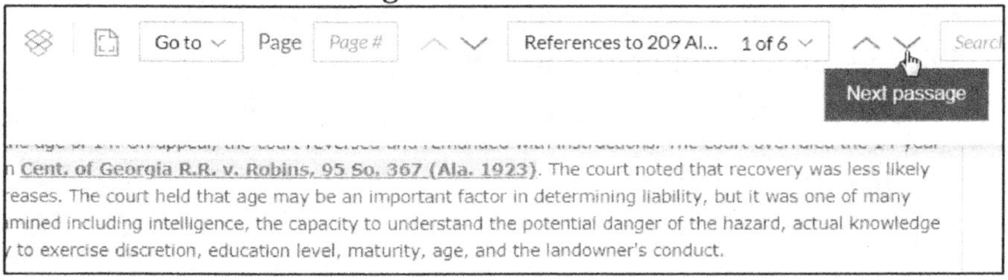

3. **Reading through *Lyle*, how does its discussion of the *Central of G. R. Co.* case affect your answer to Mr. Hwang? Can a lawsuit be brought on behalf of a 15-year-old in Alabama?**

We could use the *Lyle* case as authority for a rule. It might also be a helpful factually analogous cases.

For example, we might Shepardize the *Lyle* case to find more cases or secondary sources.

In the *Lyle* case, click on the Shepards link that says: "Other Citing Sources."

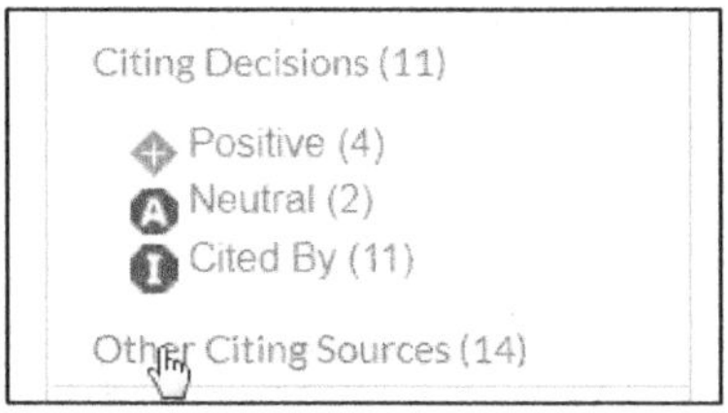

4. **Under the Treatise Citations, give the full citation to the most helpful treatise (@ 2.03).**

Westlaw

Let's use the same problem for our research on Westlaw.

We will use Westlaw's citator service, known as Key Cite.

Please log into your Westlaw account.

Instead of Alabama, **let's pretend Mr. Hwang and Elia are in Texas.**

Say your secondary source research led you to the following case citation: *Texas Utilities Electric Company v. Timmons*, 947 S.W.2d 191 (Tex. 1997).

Please use that citation to locate the case on Westlaw.

We see immediately that the *Timmons* case has a "yellow flag." We also learn that the case has been "distinguished by" the *Colon* case.

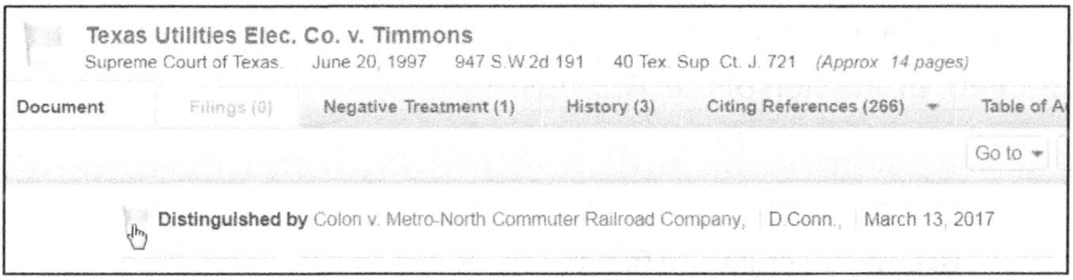

If you want to know what the red flag, yellow flag, and other flags in Westlaw mean, you can click on the "Powered by Key Cite" link.

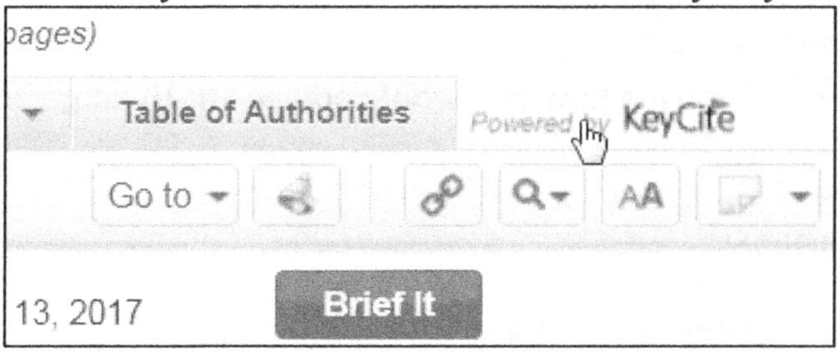

5. **Click on Powered by Key Cite. Does a red flag mean a case is no longer good authority for *all* points of law?**
6. **Browse the *Timmons* case. Briefly explain why this case might be relevant to your research.**
7. **What did the court hold in this case?**

Now, let's click on that Yellow Flag and find out why Westlaw is warning us.

It is telling us that our case has been "distinguished by" the *Colon* case from 2017. We see that the *Colon* case, however, is from a federal district court in Connecticut. We are further told that the *Colon* case has a somewhat in-depth discussion concerning Headnote 7.

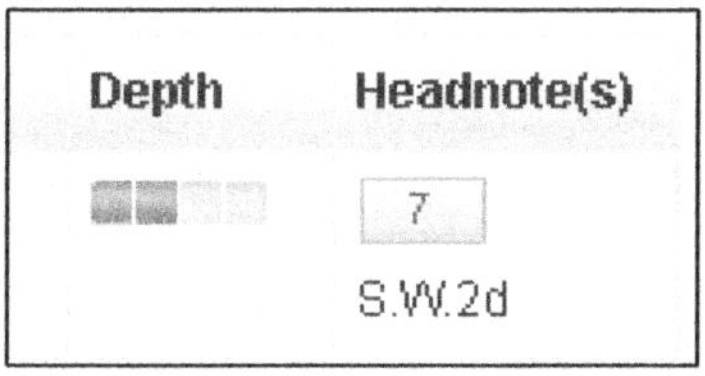

8. **Reading the *Colon* case, is the *Timmons* case still good law for the purposes for which you want to use it (see footnote 2)? Why or why not?**

Let's return to the *Timmons* case.

Let's check the "Citing References" tab of the *Timmons* case.

This brings up a case *Entergy Gulf States, Inc. v. Isom* that has an in-depth discussion of the *Timmons* case.

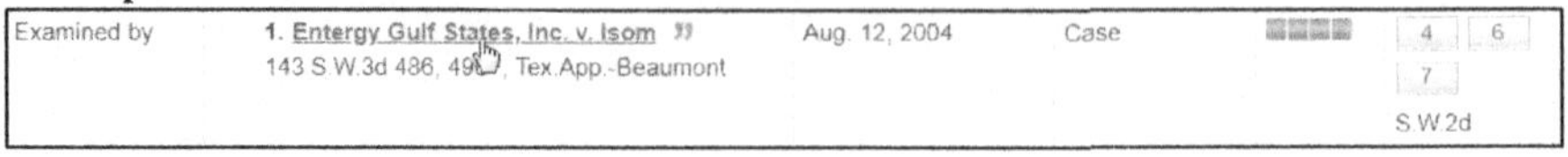

9. **Briefly describe the facts in the *Isom* case.**
10. **What holding did the *Isom* court reach?**
11. **Is that holding similar to or different from the holding in the *Timmons* case?**
12. **Briefly describe how you would advise Mr. Hwang if they lived in Texas.**

Conclusion

I hope you have learned that citators like Shepards and Key Cite can be used to check whether a legal authority is still good law.

They can also be used as powerful research tools to find other, similar authorities!

[27]

Administrative Law Research

Electronic Research Exercise Number 6 (R6)

Introduction

As we learned during orientation, administrative agencies fall under the executive branch of the United States government. They include agencies like the Patent and Trade Office (PTO) as well as the Food and Drug Administration (FDA) and the Department of Agriculture (USDA).

These agencies were created by Congress via "enabling" legislation. Enabling legislation refers to the statute that delimits the mission and power of an agency.

Agencies administer the law. They also make rules. Some agencies even have administrative court systems. For example, if an asylum seeker's petition is denied by the immigration officer, the asylum seeker can appeal to an immigration law judge. If he is denied by the immigration judge, he can appeal to the Board of Immigration Appeals. Only after the BIA denies the petition, can an asylum seeker appeal to a federal circuit court.

Because agencies have executive, legislative, and judicial functions, the U.S. Supreme Court has struggled to fit them into the U.S. Constitution.

Administrative agencies were never part of the original system of checks and balances. They've been "shoe-horned" in by statutes and by court decisions.

For example, the Administrative Procedures Act sets forth the rule-making process.

In order to preserve transparency and a sense of democracy, agencies must follow a "Notice and Comment" procedure. Agencies must provide notice of a proposed change to the rules. They must also allow for public comments. Sometimes they hold hearings or committee meetings. Then the agency must publish any change.

This is all published in the Federal Register.

Federal Register

The Federal Register contains proposed rule changes and all notices as well as interim and final rules. It is updated daily.

Each year, a volume number is assigned. Items are published to the Federal Register in chronological order. Hence a reference to 61 F.R. 20041, would point you to volume 61 of the Federal Register and to page 20041.

The Federal Register also contains presidential documents such as executive orders.

For example, one of President Trump's executive orders on immigration can be found at 82 F.R. 8977. That is, volume 82 and page 8977 of the Federal Register.

Once agency rules are published in the Federal Register, they are then placed by topic into the Code of Federal Regulations. This process is similar to the way laws are published in the Statutes at Large and are then divided by topic into the U.S. Code.

CODE OF FEDERAL REGULATIONS

The Code of Federal Regulations or C.F.R. is a multi-volume set that contains all the rules published by administrative agencies. The C.F.R., like the United States Code, is organized into Titles, Chapters, Parts, and Sections.

The C.F.R. is divided into 50 Titles. The Title numbers for the C.F.R. do not necessarily match the U.S. Code.

Researching the C.F.R. can be a bit confusing at first. For example, the Immigration and Nationality Act section on asylum can be found at 8 U.S.C. § 1101.

However, procedures for processing an asylum claim were developed by the agency and published in the Federal Register at 62 F.R. 10337. Those procedures were then divided by topic and placed in the C.F.R. beginning at 8 C.F.R. § 208.

In addition, an agency might publish its own, internal guidelines. For example, the U.S. Department of State publishes the Field Adjudicator's Manual (FAM), to help its consular workers know how to process immigration claims. The FAM explains the refugee process from the consulate's perspective.

To practice administrative law, you need to be able to work back and forth between the U.S. Code and the Code of Federal Regulations. You also need to be familiar with an agency's internal rules. You also need to be familiar with any administrative court decisions from that agency.

These days, Administrative Law consists of numerous specialized fields including bankruptcy, tax, patents, environmental law, nuclear law, immigration, farm law, and food law. Many of our graduates have successful administrative law practices.

Every state in America also has state agencies. Researching state agencies is similar to researching federal agencies. For this chapter, we are going to focus on federal administrative law research.

Researching Administrative Law

Because administrative regulations are often based on statutes, one tip when researching administrative law is to look for the statute first. You can use the annotated statute to find the relevant regulations.

Agency websites are another good source of information.

Don't forget, as with statutes, regulations must be read in the context of the entire regulatory scheme. Therefore, don't get "tunnel vision."

When you find a regulation, look at the Table of Contents. See if there is a definition section, for instance, or other interrelated regulations.

Also, if you need the "legislative history" to analyze a regulation. You can research the regulation's background, notice and comments, etcetera, in the Federal Register.

Electronic Research Exercise Number 6 (R6)

Instructions

- Please type your answers. Answers should be single-spaced in Courier New Font size 8. Pages should be numbered.
- Your paper must have a header on the first page (not needed on subsequent pages) including the following: a title; your Professor's name; and your student ID number. Do not write your name; use your student ID number.
- Please e-mail your answers prior to class or hand them in at the beginning of class according to your professor's preference.
- If you cut and paste, you must use quotation marks!
- There are 15 total questions in this assignment. Please do not miss any.

PROBLEM 1

You are interning for HILS alumni, Attorney Song Jongme. She asks you to research whether HIV will automatically bar someone's admission to the United States.

AGENCY WEBSITES

Federal administrative law research can be accomplished using government websites. Some government websites, such as the Government Printing Office's GPO Access site (FDsys) and the National Archives, contain the full text of the C.F.R. (eCFR.)

Others, such as agency web sites, limit their coverage to laws, regulations, and other materials in the subject area the agency regulates.

Attorneys who practice regularly in an area of law regulated by a federal agency become familiar with the agency websites and the unique types of information they contain.

However, as with any legal problem, the best place to start may be the internet itself.

Let's run an internet search for the following terms:

HIV immigration Health and Human Services regulation

Several interesting results come back including the one below from the Center for Disease Control which is under the U.S. Department of Health and Human Services:

1. **Browsing that page, what Title and Section of the U.S. Code authorizes the CDC to promulgate regulations concerning Aliens with Diseases of Public Health Significance?**
2. **Next, which Title and which Part of the Code of Federal Regulations concerns the Medical Examination of Aliens?**

3. **Next, on which date was a Final Rule issued that removed HIV infection from U.S. Immigration Screening?**
4. **On what date was the Notice of Proposed Rulemaking (NPRM) issued?**

Please click on the link to the Notice of Proposed Rule Making. We want to read the Notice of Proposed Rule Making. It is a 13-page pdf linked from the GPO Access.gov website. (GPO is the Government Printing Office.)

5. **That NPRM was published in which Volume and starting on which Page of the Federal Register?**
6. **According to the legislative history on the second page of that PDF, third column, HIV was specifically added to the U.S. Code in 1991 by Congress after HHS tried to allow aliens with HIV to enter the U.S. What is the name and citation of the Act[24] that removed HIV/AIDS from the U.S. Code in July 2008?**

As we can see from that page, CDC moved quickly after the election of Democrat President Obama to remove HIV infection from the definition of communicable disease of public health significance—the list that prevents diseased aliens from being admitted into the U.S.

7. **What reason did the CDC give?**

Returning to the CDC website, we can see that the NPRM generated "a high volume of public comments on this rule."

That is how "democracy" works for administrative agencies.

Let's return to our original CDC webpage that we found on our internet search.

Let's click on the link for the "Final Rule Removing HIV Infection from U.S. Immigration Screening."

---

[24] If you are wondering what madness prompted this legislation, you can do your own legislative history research. As can be seen in the comments to the final CFR rule, the reasons given for removing HIV from the language of the statute were similar: that the language had been added to target homosexuals and that specific, singling out of HIV showed animus toward homosexuals. The real reason was that the code prevented faceless bureaucrats from doing what they wanted to do: let people with HIV/AIDS—specifically homosexuals with HIV/AIDS—into America.

Let's open the Final Rule, PDF document, a 16-page document on the GPO access.gov website.

8. **In what Volume and on what Page number of the Federal Register does the final rule appear?**
9. **In the section concerning public comments, approximately how many comments were received? How many of those were form letters supporting the proposed rule?**
10. **In response to negative comments, asking why the U.S. government would put even one person at risk of contracting HIV from an immigrant, what was the government's response?**
11. **According to the section on Conclusion and the Final Rule what changes were made to the CFR?**

Although you found this information on an official U.S. government agency website, you know that a regulation published on an agency web site may not be updated to include changes to the regulation published in the Federal Register since the latest edition of the C.F.R. was published. You need to update your research to make sure it is current.

To do this, you decide to use the e-CFR published by the Government Printing Office (GPO). The e-CFR is an electronic version of the C.F.R. that is updated daily to incorporate changes to regulations published in the Federal Register.

To answer the questions below, please go to www.ecfr.gov.

We are going to browse the Electronic Code of Federal Regulations (e-CFR) which is a regularly updated, unofficial editorial compilation of CFR material and Federal Register amendments.

Although the e-CFR is updated daily, it is NOT a source that you can cite to for a regulation. You need to cite courts to the official version of the CFR. Still, it is a pretty good, and free version of the CFR.

12. **Browse the e-CFR to locate the section you found for Q4 above (Hint: Title 42, Part ##). According to subpart 1, what specific diseases are mentioned by name in the CFR?**

13. **Final answer: In response to Attorney Song Jongme's question, will HIV/AIDS prevent an immigrant from going to the United States?**

WESTLAW & LEXIS

You can also research federal regulations in Westlaw and Lexis Advance. In both services, you can locate federal regulations much the same way you would in print including: get by citation, by keyword search, or by browsing the table of contents.

Using the annotated version of the CFR supplied by Lexis or Westlaw, you can locate cross-references to applicable provisions in the C.F.R.

You can also find a reference to the enabling legislation, or you can locate various cases and secondary sources that have discussed that regulation.

PROBLEM 2

Following the passage of the *Obergefell* decision, legalizing gay marriage across the country, the Internal Revenue Service had to update its definition of "spouse."

Using either Westlaw or Lexis, as you prefer, under the "Federal" or "Federal Materials" tab run a search on the Federal Register for:

"Definition of Terms Relating to Marital Status"

Be sure to include the quotation marks.

14. **In what Volume and on what Page of the Federal Register does the final rule appear?**
15. **According to the "background" section of that document, what was the proposal to amend section 7701 of the Internal Revenue Code? And, reading the document, was that proposal accepted?**

[28]

Research Plan: An Introduction

Introduction

When doing legal research, it is not enough to read a few cases.

This is not undergrad.

In undergrad, when faced with a ten-page paper you may have thought, *okay that means I have to read ten sources.*

At law, you are responsible for knowing everything that has ever been written! If that sounds overwhelming, good. You should feel overwhelmed.

If you miss a case precedent, your client's legal petition could fail. Your client can lose money. They can go to jail.

Thankfully, only a small slice of the legal authorities will be relevant to a given legal topic and to your client's particular facts.

Nevertheless, legal research is difficult and time consuming.

There's an old saying, "If you fail to plan, you're planning to fail."

Before jumping into a research project, do a little planning. In particular, you might consider the following steps (1) obtain preliminary information about your topic; (2) plan your research; and (3) execute your research plan.

1. Obtain preliminary information

Imagine your first internship at a law firm. Your supervising attorney just gave you your first assignment.

First, did you fully understand the assignment?

What kind of work product must you generate: a ten-page memo or a simple e-mail?

How much time do you have?

What research materials are available to you?

Some law firms in Seoul will have Westlaw or Lexis access. Others don't. You *should NOT use your school account to do research for a for-profit entity*!

Hopefully, when you are approached by your supervising attorney, you have a strong attitude like in the *Message to Garcia.* If you remember that story, you won't start pestering your supervising attorney with questions that you could answer on your own.

However, if you have a legitimate question, better to be clear before you proceed.

I want to repeat. Don't ask your supervising attorneys (or your law school professors) questions for which you could easily find the answer. Try to answer your own questions before approaching a busy attorney. That way, even if your answer is wrong, the attorney can see that you put some effort into it.

2. Plan your research

If you go to a grocery store without a meal plan, you may end up buying a lot of ingredients you don't need. Meanwhile, planning your meals while grocery shopping is inefficient—you might forget something and have to return to the store.

In the same way, you need good planning and a good shopping list *before* you begin researching.

A good research plan covers the following items:

a. Preliminary issue statement
b. Jurisdiction
c. Type of law

d. List of authorities to consult (in order)
e. Preliminary search terms
f. List of questions and sub-questions that your research should address?

Let's look at each of these briefly:

a. Preliminary issue statement

Can you articulate in one, simple sentence, the job you've been given? Write that down as a preliminary issue statement.

This is not an issue statement for a case brief. You don't want to get too narrow, too quickly. If you start your research too narrow, you might miss something important.

The preliminary issue statement should describe the scope of your assignment. That's all.

b. Jurisdiction

Do you know which jurisdiction to focus on? Jurisdiction is important because it determines *where* you search. Jurisdiction determines which authorities are primary, mandatory authorities.

Your goal is to find primary, mandatory authority. Therefore, you must determine the proper jurisdiction.

c. Type of law

If jurisdiction determines *where* you search; type of law determines *how* you search.

By type of law, I don't mean tort or property.

By type of law I mean: common law, statutory law, administrative law, or procedural law, and the like.

Type of law determines *how* you search.

You don't research common law the same way you research statutory law. For instance, with statutory law, the first thing you want to do is find the statute. Then read it. Then read any important Notes of Decisions.

When researching common law, meanwhile, you want to find the rule from the case precedent. You might start with secondary sources in order to locate relevant cases; or you might do a keyword search in a case database.

d. List of authorities

If you are unfamiliar with an area of law, for example, you might want to start your research with a secondary source.

Even Westlaw and Lexis Advance consist of a collection of databases (Westlaw) or sources (Lexis Advance).

Don't jump into a keyword search in a case law database. Stop and think about which authority you want to consult, in which order. Think about which source is better for your needs. *Make a list.*

For example, ALR is great at locating cases across multiple jurisdictions; whereas, American Jurisprudence is good at giving a broad overview of a particular legal topic.

Use the right tool for the job.

e. Preliminary search terms

Take some time to craft a word search.

Do you know enough to craft an effective keyword search? For example, do you know the terms of art in that area of law?

If not, you might want to begin by doing some background reading in a secondary source.

f. Shopping list

It helps to create a list of questions that you will need to answer in order to complete your assignment. For example, what are the elements of the cause of action? What cases have interpreted those elements? Who has the burden of proof? What is the statute of limitations on this cause of action?

Some of your questions may be irrelevant. But you won't know until you research them.

Even if your research leads you down a "rabbit trail," it is not a wasted effort. If you had the question, others might have it as well. Having done the research, you can explain why it's irrelevant.

Meanwhile, you are responsible to get that *Message to Garcia*. If you have a question, you must research it. No one else is going to do it for you. It is up to you to become a subject matter expert in that area of law. This means tracking down every lead, doing your due diligence!

You can begin by creating a good shopping list. As you do your research, you might delete items from the list. You might also add items.

You will know your research is complete when all the questions on your shopping list have been fully answered.

3. Execute your research plan

After you plan, you should follow it.

Your plan may evolve as you find additional authorities. Your research might take you in unexpected directions. However, after doing legal research for some time, you will begin to find a path of legal research that feels good and fits your personal style.

For now, follow the research plan provided above.

As you research, take careful notes.

If you copy and paste, be sure to indicate that using quotation marks. Better yet, paraphrase while you are researching. Don't wait till the end.

Make sure you keep citations to the legal authorities, not only to the page number on which the case begins, but also to the page number on which particular material appears.

One way to organize your research is to organize it around the shopping list from your plan. As you answer questions from your shopping list, make a note of the answer and the authorities. If a question is irrelevant, strike it. If another question arises while you are researching, add it to the list.

You will know your research is finished when you've completed your shopping list.

KNOWING WHEN TO STOP

Stop researching when you have completed your shopping list. Or, stop when the same or similar authorities begin popping up over and over again—you can't find new, relevant authorities.

For what it's worth, I always start my research and end my research the same way.

I start by looking for a secondary source that leads to a primary source.

At the very end of my research, at the time when my knowledge of the cases and authorities is at its height, I will do one highly-specific keyword search. I will carefully select a case database. I will then execute a keyword search based on my knowledge of the key legal terms in that area of law. I do this to find any analogous cases I might've missed.

You can see this technique at work in the Chapter on Researching Case Law online.

WHAT IF YOU CAN'T FIND ANYTHING

If you're having trouble getting started on a research project, there may be a few problems.

You might have narrowed your research too much initially. Does your preliminary issue statement properly frame the question you've been asked to address?

Maybe the search you've entered is too narrow. Consider broadening your definition of the "factually relevant" cases.

It also happens that students enter incorrect legal terms or misspell those legal terms. Westlaw and Lexis Advance are not like Google. They may not fix your spelling for you!

The best advice is to start by reading secondary sources. Those will help you understand the area of law. Secondary sources will also clue you in on the key terms of art and how to spell them.

Finally, please read what you find.

Many times, students find the key statute or key cases right away. But they don't read carefully. They skip over it.

Afterward, they may research for hours before finally coming back to the original, correct authority. It's heartbreaking!

Read carefully. The best way to learn to read carefully and quickly is to brief every case in your substantive law courses!

[29]

Research Plan Exercise

Research Plan Exercise (R7)

The goal for this exercise is to demonstrate how to implement a research plan in preparation for your end of semester final project.

Your final project will consist of the following items:

1. **Your research plan (Part I below);**
2. **A description of the implementation of your research plan (Part II below);**
3. **An informal report (Part III below) (NOT REQUIRED FOR THIS PRACTICE EXERCISE); and**
4. **A copy of your Westlaw research history or Lexis Advance research history (see Part IV below).**

This exercise (R7) involves only the creation of Parts I, II, and IV. The final project will involve a different research question and will include the creation of a three-page report (Part III).

Additional Instructions

You may use any resource available in the Library. When you use Westlaw or Lexis Advance, you must use your own personal account and you must include a copy of your Westlaw or Lexis research history.

This is not a group exercise. Prior to turning it in, you should not discuss your research methods or the results of your research with anyone other than your legal writing professor. (Afterward, you may discuss this exercise with your classmates in preparation for the final project.)

Sources must be cited in your report to the best of your ability.

Extensive direct quotation will entail a reduction in points. You should make every effort to paraphrase, summarize, and synthesize – put the legal information in your own words.

Problem Facts

Your client, O.K. Chesterfield, was recently arrested for disorderly conduct. The charge stems from the following facts:

On Saturday, May 13 of this year, Mr. Chesterfield went to the Fishtown Festival at about 10:30 am in order, as he said, "to preach the saving Gospel of the Lord." The Festival is a yearly event held in Fishtown Central Park, is open to the public and there is no charge for admission. When he arrived, he went to the very middle of the park next to Fishtown's WWII memorial and just started reading from the Gospel of John. From those who witnessed this, they characterized his reading more like "shouting at the top of his lungs." As Mr. Chesterfield continued to read, there was a mixed reaction amongst the Festivalgoers. Some started to gather around him, some moved away from him and others shouted for him to "shut up."

About five minutes after he started, Mr. Chesterfield was approached by a Fishtown police officer and was told that he would have to stop. Mr. Chesterfield told the officer that he had a First Amendment right to "preach the Word of the Lord" and that he was not going to stop. The police officer responded that he indeed did have a First Amendment right but that right did not include "incessantly shouting." When Mr. Chesterfield continued to preach the police officer grabbed him, handcuffed him, and told Mr. Chesterfield that he was under arrest for "disorderly conduct." In response to Mr.

Chesterfield's objections, the police officer simply told him "you were warned but you were just being too darned loud."

Fishtown is in the Commonwealth of Pennsylvania. Based upon the above facts, what element (or elements) of the disorderly conduct charge is most at issue? What rules have the courts established for that element (or elements)? How have the courts applied those rules? How would a court likely apply those rules to Mr. Chesterfield's case? What is the likely conclusion to the charge of disorderly conduct?

Research Plan Template

I. Plan your Research

You must do this section before you begin researching. Attempting to recreate a "plan" after you did your research will appear obvious to your professor!

A. Preliminary Issue Statement: [This should be only one or two sentences.]
B. Jurisdiction:
C. Type of law:
D. List of authorities you plan to consult and in what order:
E. Generate preliminary search terms:
F. Shopping list:

II. Execute your Research Plan

A. Research notes.
   1. What order did you actually consult each source? If the order differed from your original plan, explain briefly.
   2. Please provide what you thought was your most useful keyword search for Westlaw or Lexis. Give it exactly as it was entered into the search box.
   3. Give citations for the primary mandatory authorities you plan to use to analyze the legal question. Briefly explain how you located each authority and why you plan to use it.

B. First assessment of your research results.

1. Is the mandatory authority you have found sufficient or do you need to locate persuasive authority in order to answer the question? If so, why?
2. List any persuasive authorities you located and describe why that authority may be helpful.

C. Check your results.

1. Describe your process for validating the sources you have found. (Hint: this likely means using Key Cite or Shepherds)
2. Describe the particular results of your validation process. [Are the authorities you have found good law? Are they regularly cited by other courts? Did you reject any of the authorities?]
3. Did your validation process lead you to any new authorities?

D. Final completion assessment

1. Describe why you determined that your research was full and complete.

III. Informal Report

This part is not required as part of this practice exercise.

For your final project, once you have completed your research, you would then draft an answer to your client's legal question. This informal report will consist of a brief analysis (3 pages maximum, 1" margins, 12-point Courier new font) answering a legal question.

IV. Research History

Attach your research histories from Lexis Advance or Westlaw.

If you used additional sources other than Lexis Advance or Westlaw (i.e. websites, books, etc.) then also list those sources.

Please cut and paste in *chronological order*! Also, make sure your name is not on the history.

APPENDIX A

McBOYLE CASE BRIEF

McBoyle v. United States

283 U.S. 25 (1931)

Justice Holmes

FACTS: McBoyle transported an airplane across state lines that he knew to have been stolen.

PROCEDURAL HISTORY: McBoyle (criminal defendant) convicted at trial. Was sentenced to 3 years prison and fine of $2,000. Lost appeal to 10th Circuit.

JUDGMENT: Reversed!

ISSUE: Whether an aircraft is a motor vehicle for the purposes of the NMVTA

RULE: *General Rule*—"The term 'motor vehicle' shall include an automobile, automobile truck, automobile wagon, motor cycle, or any other self-propelled vehicle not designed for running on rails."

Specific Rule—The word "vehicle" includes those vehicles that commonly run on land

HOLDING: NO an aircraft is NOT a vehicle for the purposes of the NMVTA

RATIONALE:

Everyday use of "vehicle . . . running" calls to mind something "running on land" (plain language)

The US Code doesn't use term that way (Judge reads statute in light of the entire statutory scheme)

Airplane doesn't match other items in the list

Airplane not mentioned in Congress legislative history

Other state statutes don't list airplanes

Criminal statutes must to give fair warning in language common people understand and should be read narrowly not broadly

DICTA: None

CONCURRING/DISSENTING: None

APPENDIX B

"A MESSAGE TO GARCIA"

FOREWORD

This literary trifle, A Message To Garcia, was written one evening after supper, in a single hour. It was on the 22nd of February, 1899, Washington's Birthday: we were just going to press with the March Philistine.

The thing leaped hot from my heart, written after a trying day, when I had been endeavoring to train some rather delinquent villagers to abjure the comatose state and get radioactive.

The immediate suggestion, though, came from a little argument over the teacups, when my boy Bert suggested that Rowan was the real hero of the Cuban War. Rowan had gone alone and done the thing - carried the message to Garcia.

It came to me like a flash! Yes, the boy is right, the hero is the man who does his work - who carries the message to Garcia. I got up from the table, and wrote A Message To Garcia. I thought so little of it that we ran it in the Magazine without a heading. The edition went out, and soon orders began to come for extra copies of the March Philistine, a dozen, fifty, a hundred, and when the American News Company ordered a thousand, I asked one of my helpers which article it was that stirred up the cosmic dust. "It's the stuff about Garcia," he said.

The next day a telegram came from George H. Daniels, of the New York Central Railroad thus, "Give price on one hundred thousand Rowan article in pamphlet form - Empire State Express advertisement on back - also how soon can ship."

I replied giving price, and stated we could supply the pamphlets in two years. Our facilities were small and a hundred thousand booklets looked like an awful undertaking.

The result was that I gave Mr. Daniels permission to reprint the article in his own way. He issued it in booklet form in editions of half a million. Two or three of these half-million lots were sent out by Mr. Daniels, and in addition the article was reprinted in over two hundred magazines and newspapers. It has been translated into all written languages.

At the time Mr. Daniels was distributing A Message To Garcia, Prince Hilakoff, Director of Russian Railways, was in this country. He was the guest of the New York Central, and made a tour of the country under the personal direction of Mr. Daniels. The Prince saw the little book and was interested in it, more because Mr. Daniels was putting it out in big numbers, probably, than otherwise. In any event, when he got home he had the matter translated into Russian, and a copy of the booklet given to every railroad employee in Russia.

Other countries then took it up, and from Russia it passed into Germany, France, Spain, Turkey, Hindustan and China. During the war between Russia and Japan, every Russian soldier who went to the front was given a copy of A Message To Garcia. The Japanese, finding the booklets in possession of the Russian prisoners, concluded it must be a good thing, and accordingly translated it into Japanese.

And on an order of the Mikado, a copy was given to every man in the employ of the Japanese Government, soldier or civilian. Over forty million copies of A Message To Garcia have been printed. This is said to be a larger circulation than any other literary venture has ever attained during the lifetime of an author, in all history - thanks to a series of lucky accidents.

Elbert Hubbard

- December 1, 1913

A MESSAGE TO GARCIA BY ELBERT HUBBARD

In all this Cuban business there is one man stands out on the horizon of my memory like Mars at perihelion.

When war broke out between Spain and the United States it was very necessary to communicate quickly with the leader of the Insurgents. Garcia was somewhere in the mountain vastness of Cuba - no one knew where. No mail nor telegraph message could reach him. The President must secure his cooperation, and quickly. What to do!

Some one said to the President, "There's a fellow by the name of Rowan will find Garcia for you, if anybody can."

Rowan was sent for and given a letter to be delivered to Garcia. How "the fellow by the name of Rowan" took the letter, sealed it up in an oil-skin pouch, strapped it over his heart, in four days landed by night off the coast of Cuba from an open boat, disappeared into the jungle, and in three weeks came out on the other side of the Island, having traversed a hostile country on foot, and delivered his letter to Garcia - are things I have no special desire now to tell in detail. The point that I wish to make is this: McKinley gave Rowan a letter to be delivered to Garcia; Rowan took the letter and did not ask, "Where is he at?"

By the Eternal! there is a man whose form should be cast in deathless bronze and the statue placed in every college of the land. It is not book-learning young men need, nor instruction about this and that, but a stiffening of the vertebrae which will cause them to be loyal to a trust, to act promptly, concentrate their energies: do the thing - "Carry a message to Garcia!"

General Garcia is dead now, but there are other Garcia's. No man who has endeavored to carry out an enterprise where many hands were needed, but has been well-nigh appalled at times by the imbecility of the average man - the inability or unwillingness to concentrate on a thing and do it.

Slipshod assistance, foolish inattention, dowdy indifference, and half-hearted work seem the rule; and no man succeeds, unless by hook or crook or threat he forces or bribes other men to assist him; or mayhap, God in His goodness performs a miracle, and sends him an Angel of Light for an assistant.

You, reader, put this matter to a test: You are sitting now in your office - six clerks are within call. Summon any one and make this request: "Please look in the encyclopedia and make a brief memorandum for me concerning the life of Correggio." Will the clerk quietly say, "Yes, sir," and go do the task?

On your life, he will not. He will look at you out of a fishy eye and ask one or more of the following questions:

Who was he?

Which encyclopedia?

Where is the encyclopedia?

Was I hired for that?

Don't you mean Bismarck?

What's the matter with Charlie doing it?

Is he dead?

Is there any hurry?

Sha'n't I bring you the book and let you look it up yourself?

What do you want to know for?

And I will lay you ten to one that after you have answered the questions, and explained how to find the information, and why you want it, the clerk will go off and get one of the other clerks to help him try to find Garcia - and then come back and tell you there is no such man. Of course I may lose my bet, but according to the Law of Average, I will not.

Now, if you are wise, you will not bother to explain to your "assistant" that Correggio is indexed under the C's, not in the K's, but you will smile very sweetly and say, "Never mind," and go look it up yourself. And this incapacity for independent action, this moral stupidity, this infirmity of the will, this unwillingness to cheerfully catch hold and lift -these are the things that put pure Socialism so far into the future. If men will not act for themselves, what will they do when the benefit of their effort is for all?

A first-mate with knotted club seems necessary; and the dread of getting "the bounce" Saturday night holds many a worker to his place. Advertise for a stenographer, and nine out of ten who apply can neither spell nor punctuate - and do not think it necessary to.

Can such a one write a letter to Garcia?

"You see that bookkeeper," said the foreman to me in a large factory. "Yes, what about him?" "Well he's a fine accountant, but if I'd send him up town on an errand, he might accomplish the errand all right, and on the other hand, might stop at four saloons on the way, and when he got to Main Street would forget what he had been sent for." Can such a man be entrusted to carry a message to Garcia?

We have recently been hearing much maudlin sympathy expressed for the "downtrodden denizens of the sweat-shop" and the "homeless wanderer searching for honest employment," and with it all often go many hard words for the men in power.

Nothing is said about the employer who grows old before his time in a vain attempt to get frowsy ne'er-do-wells to do intelligent work; and his long, patient striving after "help" that does nothing but loaf when his back is turned.

In every store and factory there is a constant weeding-out process going on. The employer is constantly sending away "help" that have shown their incapacity to further the interests of the business, and others are being taken on. No matter how good times are, this sorting continues: only, if times are hard and work is scarce, the sorting is done finer - but out and forever out the incompetent and unworthy go. It is the survival of the fittest. Self-interest prompts every employer to keep the best - those who can carry a message to Garcia.

I know one man of really brilliant parts who has not the ability to manage a business of his own, and yet who is absolutely worthless to any one else, because he carries with him constantly the insane suspicion that his employer is oppressing, or intending to oppress, him. He cannot give orders; and he will not receive them. Should a message be given him to take to Garcia, his answer would probably be, "Take it yourself!"

Tonight this man walks the streets looking for work, the wind whistling through his threadbare coat. No one who knows him dare employ him, for he is a regular firebrand of discontent. He is impervious to reason, and the only thing that can impress him is the toe of a thick-soled Number Nine boot.

Of course I know that one so morally deformed is no less to be pitied than a physical cripple; but in our pitying, let us drop a tear, too, for the men who are striving to carry on a great enterprise, whose working hours are not limited by the whistle, and whose hair is fast turning white through the struggle to hold in line dowdy indifference, slipshod imbecility, and the heartless ingratitude which, but for their enterprise, would be both hungry and homeless.

Have I put the matter too strongly? Possibly I have; but when all the world has gone a-slumming I wish to speak a word of sympathy for the man who succeeds - the man who, against great odds, has directed the efforts of others, and having succeeded, finds there's nothing in it: nothing but bare board and clothes. I have carried a dinner pail and worked for day's wages, and I have also been an employer of labor, and I know there is something to be said on both sides.

There is no excellence, per se, in poverty; rags are no recommendation; and all employers are not rapacious and high-handed, any more than all poor men are virtuous. My heart goes out to the man who does his work when the "boss" is away, as well as when he is at home. And the man who, when given a letter for Garcia, quietly takes the missive, without asking any idiotic questions, and with no lurking intention of chucking it into the nearest sewer, or of doing aught else but deliver it, never gets "laid off" nor has to go on a strike for higher wages.

Civilization is one long anxious search for just such individuals. Anything such a man asks shall be granted. He is wanted in every city, town and village - in every office, shop, store and factory. The world cries out for such: he is needed and needed badly - the man who can "Carry a Message to Garcia." *Elbert Hubbard – 1899*

APPENDIX C

RESEARCH PLAN EXAMPLE

INTRODUCTION

The following student example was taken from a *common law* research problem.

Your Research Plan Exercise (R7) may be common law, statutory law, or administrative law. If so, a different plan might develop!

Not every answer is perfect. Please don't cut and paste from this one. Write your answers in your own, honest words. The professors want to see your plan and how you execute it. We are not grading for eloquence and style.

The format for this example is from an *older version* of the Research Plan assignment. Please follow the instructions and format you are given for your final research assignment.

In addition, we have omitted Part IV, the attachment of the Westlaw and Lexis Advance research history.

STUDENT EXAMPLE

I. Plan your Research

A. Preliminary Issue Statement: Whether a freelance professional with 6 years of experience can bring an action in quantum meruit and testify on her own behalf as an expert witness as to the reasonable value of her work.

B. Jurisdiction: State of Missouri

C. Type of law: State Common Law (contract law)

D. List of sources: I will consult Google to find a Case citation then look it up in in Westlaw or Lexis and look for Secondary sources (such as A.L.R.). Then I will try to locate more relevant cases through secondary sources. Finally, I will Shepardize the primary sources

E. Search Terms: Missouri quantum meruit, reasonable value of services, expert testimony, freelance compensation, expert qualification

F. Shopping list

1. What is quantum meruit?

2. What is the rule?

3. Elements of quantum meruit?

4. What constitutes reasonable value of services?

5. Who can qualify as an expert?

II. Execute your Research Plan

A. Research notes.

1. The general order I ended up following did not differ from my original plan. However, I had go back and forth among all the relevant sources I found many more times than I expected.

2. I did not use the keyword search function until the end, because I searched a specific phrase on google and found a relevant case that led me to many other cases. At the end, I entered "quantum meruit" & expert & qualifi!.

3. The primary mandatory authority I used was *Donovan v. Roth*, 700 S.W.2d 140 (Mo. Ct. App. E.D. 1985). I located this case through the cases listed in A.L.R. and I plan to use this case because this case is not only from the same jurisdiction but it also has some factual similarities to our case.

B. First assessment of your research results.

1. Yes. I may need to search for primary persuasive authority in order to analyze my research issue more thoroughly and fill in some

blanks. Looking through the cases in Missouri, I can find some relevant cases. However, I am not able to find the specific factual situation within the controlling jurisdiction. I also located cases that are more specific than the primary mandatory authority I found in terms of extracting rules. Therefore, it may be necessary for me to locate factually analogous cases from other jurisdictions.

I plan to look for case are more factually similar to our case in different jurisdictions by going through the list of cases in the relevant sections of A.L.R. or Amjur.

The facts in the case do not tell us in which jurisdiction our client would be filing. Assuming that the defendant is in the same city (St. Louis) as the plaintiff and that the plaintiff files in the trial court of Eastern district in Missouri, cases from states and cases at trial court level within the same controlling jurisdiction (Eastern District) would be primary persuasive authorities.

2. Koppe v. Campbell, 318 S.W.3d 233 (Mo. Ct. App. W.D. 2010); Moran v. Hubbartt, 178 S.W.3d 604 (Mo. Ct. App. W.D. 2005); Richard B. Curnow, M.D., Inc. v. Sloan, 625 S.W.2d 605 (Mo. 1981)

3. Yes. I did not find enough primary mandatory authorities that are helpful so I searched for primary persuasive authorities to analyze my research issue more completely. From other jurisdictions, I located some factually similar cases and some cases that supplied specific legal rules. I located them by viewing the secondary sources, such as A.L.R and Amjur.

C. Check your results.

1. I used "keycite" function to make sure the laws in each case that are relevant to our case are still valid.

2. All of the authorities were good. Some had yellow flags but that was okay.

3. Yes, I found some more authorities as I Key Cite the cases.

D. Final completion assessment

1. When I answered all the questions in my shopping list and I keep encountering the same cases as I continue on with my research. Then I knew I was done.

III. Informal Report

The issue here is whether a freelance professional with 6 years of experience in the field of graphic design can file a claim under quantum meruit and testify on her own behalf as an expert witness as to the reasonable value of her work.

The rule is that quantum meruit is a contract implied by the law that a person will pay a reasonable amount of compensation for valuable services provided "at his request or with his approval" and its principal function is to prevent unjust enrichment. *Moran v. Hubbartt*, 178 S.W.3d 604 (Mo. Ct. App. W.D. 2005). According to *Koppe v. Campell*, a service provider who brings a quantum meruit claim against the recipient of the services is required to show that the plaintiff provided the defendant services "at the defendant's request or with his acquiescence," that "the services provided were of a certain and reasonable value," and that the defendant refused to pay for such services after the plaintiff's demand.

Generally, the amount one can seek for services performed in quantum meruit is "limited to the reasonable value of the services." To prove the reasonable value of the services the plaintiff provided to the defendant, the plaintiff is required to demonstrate that "the rate charged was objectively reasonable in the marketplace." *Moran v. Hubbartt*, 178 S.W.3d 604 (Mo. Ct. App. W.D. 2005). In the state of Missouri, a plaintiff who wants to seek compensation for services under quantum meruit can testify as an expert for himself as to reasonable value of the services he provided. *Koppe v. Campbell*, 318 S.W.3d 233 (Mo. Ct. App. W.D. 2010).

Many plaintiffs have been able to show sufficient evidence of their qualifications as an expert by proving that they worked a certain number of years in the relevant field or dealt with many similar cases. *Koppe* (attorney with 25 years of experience dealing with 1,500 cases); *Moran* (construction worker with 15 years experience); *Donovan* (self-employed carpenter with 12 years of experience); *St. Luke's* (office worker with 7 years of experience dealing with patient bills).

However, in *Minor v. Lillard*, a nurse who was from a different area was held not qualified to testify as an expert in the new city. In our case, a freelance graphic designer working in the profession for the last 6 years part time wants to seek compensation for her service in quantum meruit.

Here, applying the *Donovan* case to our case, it seems that working a self-employed professional does not bar our client from qualifying as an expert. In terms of length of experience, however, the factually similar cases show that the plaintiffs who were allowed to testify as an expert generally had more experience than our client. However, there was a case of the hospital clerk who had only 7 years of experience who was allowed to testify as an expert. And there was a case of a nurse who had only 5 years of experience. In both of those cases, however, they were working full time handling many instances. It is not clear from our facts how many similar jobs our client, a part time freelancer graphic designer, has completed. Therefore, while she might qualify as an expert, it seems that a court would more than likely disallow our client to testify as an expert on her behalf.

In case where our client is not allowed to testify as an expert, a possible alternative may be to assert that one does not necessarily have to be an expert to testify and she is still competent enough to testify on her behalf as to the reasonable value of her services. *Nesbit v. Shisler*, 175 Mo.App. 565, 158 S.W. 419 (Mo.App. 1913)

IV. Research History

[Omitted]

Made in the USA
Las Vegas, NV
19 September 2026

54907025R00203